Neighbor Law:

fences, trees, boundaries and noise

BY ATTORNEY CORA JORDAN

EDITED BY MARY RANDOLPH

ILLUSTRATIONS BY LINDA ALLISON

WITH A FOREWORD BY ERNEST CALLENBACH,
AUTHOR OF *ECOTOPIA*

please
read
this

NOLO PRESS   BERKELEY, CALIFORNIA

printing
history

Nolo Press is committed to keeping its books up-to-date. Each new printing, whether or not it is called a new edition, has been revised to reflect the latest law changes. This book was printed and updated on the last date indicated below. You might wish to call Nolo Press (415) 549-1976 to check whether there has been a more recent printing or edition.

New printing means there have been some minor changes, but usually not enough so that people will need to trade in or discard an earlier printing of the same edition. Obviously, this is a judgment call and any change, no matter how minor, might affect you. New edition means one or more major, or a number of minor, law changes since the previous edition.

FIRST EDITION	June 1991
BOOK DESIGN	Amy Ihara
COVER DESIGN	Toni Ihara
PROOFREADING	Ely Newman
INDEX	Sayre van Young
PRINTING	Delta Lithograph

■ Nolo books are available at special discounts for bulk purchases for sales promotions, premiums and fund-raising. For details contact: Special Sales Director, Nolo Press, 950 Parker Street, Berkeley, California 94710

Jordan, Cora. 1941-
    Neighbor law : fences, trees, boundaries & noise / by Cora Jordan.
        p.   cm.
    Includes index.
    ISBN 0-87337-158-5   : $14.95
    1. Adjoining landowners--United States--Popular works.
2. Boundaries (Estates)--United States--Popular works. 3. Fences-
-Law and legislaton--United States--Popular works. I. Title.
KF639.Z9J67   1991
34607304'32--dc20
[347.306432]   91-21036
                                                          CIP

dedication

To Win, Michael, Steven and Mary Beth;
May they have and be good neighbors

RECYCLE YOUR OUT-OF-DATE BOOKS
AND GET 25% OFF YOUR NEXT PURCHASE

OUT-OF-DATE = DANGEROUS

Using an old edition can be dangerous if information in it is wrong. Unfortunately, laws and legal procedures change often. Generally speaking, any book more than two years old is of questionable value. Books more than four or five years old are a menace.

To help you keep up-to-date, we extend this offer:

If you cut out and deliver to us the title portion of the cover of any old Nolo book, we'll give you a 25% discount off the retail price of any new Nolo book. For example, if you have a copy of *Tenant's Rights,* 4th edition, and want to trade it for the latest *California Marriage and Divorce Law,* send us the *Tenant's Rights* cover and a check for the current price of *California Marriage and Divorce,* less a 25% discount.

Information on current prices and editions is listed in the back of this book and in the catalog in the *Nolo News* (see offer at the back of this book).

This offer is to individuals only.

NL 6/91

thank you

Thank you to the talented staff at Nolo Press for assistance with this book: Mary Randolph, for editorial skill and kindness; Jake Warner, for the proposal that I write the book and his editorial aid; Steve Elias and Dave Middleton, for valuable suggestions and information; Linda Allison, for imaginative illustrations; Amy Ihara and Jackie Mancuso, for format design; Toni Ihara, for the terrific book cover; and Kate Thill, for hiring me in the first place.

All of the people at Nolo have given me tremendous support and something even more important—their friendships.

My research was greatly aided by law librarians Herbert Cihak, Molly McCluer, Robert Podlech, Susanne Pierce Dyer and the late Dr. Ellis Tucker. Al LeFebvre contributed thorough research on adverse possession.

For cheerfully educating me on various topics in this book, I am indebted to Tom Davis, Sondra Kennedy, Natalie Richmond, Buford Bryant, Hamp Dobbins, Mary Helen Russell, Andrew Reynolds, Professor Jim Clark, Dr. Lester Estes and Justin Wennerstrom.

Those who taught me the meaning of the word "neighbor" include Leslie Priester, Amna Mathis, Merle Miller, Dot Parsons, Klara and Ro Yee, Ann Martin, Ann and Frank Gilmore, Gwen and Neil Coleman, Alice Powers, Jan and Bill Reynolds, Diane and Bob Guyton and the late Anis Acree.

Family members offered much appreciated encouragement. My husband, Win, supplied constant support and good humor, plus a full course in computer training.

I extend special thanks to Dr. Roy Swank and Dr. Robert Cooper for managing my multiple sclerosis, and Dr. Richard Drewry for his determined success in restoring my eyesight.

Like it or not, we're all neighbors—and we ought to get better at it. With good neighborly relations, you can live more safely, comfortably, sociably and happily. Human beings, after all, are not solitary creatures like cats; we're a sociable species, made for each other's company. And in a period of our history when many of us live alone, or are single parents, a lack of good neighborly relations is likely to make life lonely, dangerous and expensive. The best periods of my own life have been when I lived on small streets where everybody knew everybody. We looked after each other's kids; we sometimes shared potluck suppers; we picked up each other's papers and mail; we loaned each other tools—and returned them immediately, knowing the ill will generated by irresponsible borrowing habits.

Good neighbors share other things too: wisdom, time, vegetables, old car parts, you name it. They also share surveillance of their neighborhood. Neighborhood Watch programs are wonderful not only because they deter criminals, but because they get people together in the process of drawing up a neighborhood map and picking a block captain. Often they go on to have block parties and clean-up days, and work together to get the attention of city hall. But even citizens who know each other just informally and therefore tend to keep an eye on the street and on each other's yards and houses are an enormously more effective force against crime than the police can ever be. They make it possible for small children's lives to be freer of constant parental supervision; they can keep some rein on obstreperous teenagers.

Being neighborly doesn't mean poking your nose into your neighbor's life or business (unless you're asked, of course, and even then you should be cautious). There's a fine practical line about privacy and noninterference that people have to learn to recognize. One of the best neighbors I ever had put this in a wonderfully wise way. We were confronting at the time a neighbor who had serious mental difficulties; she had in fact just come out of the mental hospital. She began tossing bottles off her porch to smash on the street at 2 a.m., while playing loud music through her open door, and one day she threatened some children with a hammer. For my neighbor George, that crossed the line. "What people do in their houses is their own business," he said, "but when they come down on the street, it's everybody's business." (We organized a sizable neighborhood delegation to call on the woman's psychiatrist and discuss the problem, and got it resolved.)

The magnificent positive potential of good neighborly relations, of course, is too seldom uppermost in our minds. We all tend to concentrate on the plentiful horror stories about neighbor conflicts. But it seems to be wiser to expect decent relationships with your neighbors; there is something about the very expectation that makes it more likely to happen. To be sure, there are in this world people so antagonistic, spiteful, bothersome, irresponsible or otherwise impossible to live near that no amount of rational foresight, flexible negotiation or even outright capitulation can bring their neighbors peace. Faced with such a situation, you have only the two alternatives of moving (which I would recommend) or trying to make their lives even more intolerable than yours, so that they move; this will not improve your character, and it probably won't work either. Luckily, such extremes are rare. The ordinary run of neighbors presents an ordinary range of human delightfulness and orneriness; and most people share a quite natural desire to live in a state of reasonable peace with their neighbors.

This desire is far more likely to prove effective if you know not only the commonsense human rules of treating other people decently, but also the specific laws that govern how neighbors (when pinch comes to legal shove) must treat each other. In neighborly relations, as in any other area of life, only an idiot goes to the law when friendly—or even not so friendly—negotiation and compromise are likely to solve a problem. Indeed, applying the law may "settle" a question between neighbors but in the process permanently embitter not only the contestants but other people who live nearby as well. It is also, of course, costly and chancy and likely to bring out the worst in everyone.

But knowing the law can help all concerned to arrange reasonable solutions to neighborly problems in informal channels, either personally or through mediation. People sometimes behave with great certainty that the law is on their side and are surprised to find the situation is more complicated. What, for example, do you think you can legally do to a neighbor's tree branch that overhangs your property, or with the fruit hanging on it? As I was astounded to learn, different legal rules apply; you had better know them before you get out your saw—or, more wisely still, discuss the situation with the neighbor before even thinking about the saw. Or suppose a neighbor's teenager is using a garage for rock band rehearsals; what exactly can you do about it, short of cutting the electrical wires?

This book lays out calmly and sensibly what everybody needs to know about such legalities of neighborhood life. If you tend to be a little hotheaded, it will cool you off. If you tend to give in on things too easily, it will strengthen your resolve. Read it and use it, remembering that what we all really need in our dealings with neighbors is not legal triumph or revenge but sanity, fairness and peace of mind.

Ernest Callenbach
Berkeley, California

contents

4

ENCROACHMENT: INVASION OF BRANCHES AND ROOTS

5

UNSOUND LIMBS AND TREES

6

BOUNDARY TREES

7

FRUIT AND NUTS: WHO OWNS WHAT?

8

OBSTRUCTION OF VIEW

9

BOUNDARY LINES

10

USING ANOTHER'S LAND: TRESPASS AND EASEMENTS

11

FENCES

12

SPITE FENCES

13

LEGAL RESEARCH

14

MEDIATION

15

SMALL CLAIMS COURT

APPENDIX

Neighbors and Legal Questions

Lost is our old simplicity of times,
The world abounds with laws, and teems with crimes.

—Pennsylvania Gazette
February 8, 1775

For most of us, the word "neighbor" carries almost as much baggage as the term "Mom," and considerably more than "apple pie." We give to it a nostalgic quality, similar to a Norman Rockwell painting. We long for the good old days, for simpler times, for safe streets and porch swings, for a setting when people were really neighborly. We watch old reruns of Lucy, Desi, Fred and Ethel. On Sunday mornings we escape to the comic strips and check up on our old friends Dagwood and Herb, and Loweezy and Elviney at the gossip fence. Many of us believe that if we could just turn back the clock our problems with neighbors would disappear.

When we think this way, we are overlooking an important factor—human nature. Disputes between neighbors are older than any laws ever passed. They concern space, property, money and human personalities. When we remember the pleasant past of riding bicycles on shady streets, we often forget that there was usually one spot on the block that our mothers warned us away from, the home of the neighborhood grouch.

The shrinking space of today's world exacerbates our problems, as does the transiency of the society. Often we simply don't know our neighbors and are too busy and too tired to make the effort. Congestion and fear of crime tend to make us isolate ourselves. The basic problems, however, are far from new. The Hatfields and McCoys were not products of the 1990s.

Much of the law—statutes and court decisions—addressing neighbor disputes is quite old. Courts were faced with these dilemmas and published decisions as far back as the 13th century. In the United States, most state statutes on the subject were in place in the 1800s. Laws providing protection for tree owners, for example, were adopted by the state legislatures as the country was expanding.

Consider the times and the importance of having neighbor questions resolved. A settler who went out to string boundary fences had at least two major concerns: water and timber. If he put his fence in the wrong place, taking a few acres of his neighbor's trees, the stage was set for a legal battle.

These were not just wild problems of the wild west. They had to be resolved in every region for property owners, whether they were farmers, ranchers, merchants or small homesteaders. The tree and fence laws in Vermont, for example, are similar to those in the southern and western states.

Relatively few neighbor disputes reach the courts today. There are several reasons for this. Many of the laws are long settled and disputes are resolved early on. And today when a subdivision springs up, the boundary lines are usually set by licensed surveyors. When property changes hands, a title company insures the buyer and his title. If a difficulty arises, the new owner can usually go to the insurance company rather than to court.

One obvious reason that neighbors don't take quarrels to court (except small claims court) is the enormous cost. An argument over a tree is often simply not worth the high fees charged by lawyers. It is one thing to hate the leaves from your neighbor's tree that clutter your yard, and quite another to put out $5,000 and several years in court to try to change the situation.

Lawyers and judges don't like neighbor quarrels because they are destructive, ongoing and congest already over-loaded court dockets. Experience has shown that even after a court rules in favor of one party, the neighbors continue will find something else to fight about.

What we do see today is neighbors taking their disagreements instead to the increasingly popular forum of small claims court. The proceedings are much less expensive and are accessible to almost anybody. No lawyers are necessary, and disputes are settled quickly after the judge listens to each side of the story. There is a limit on the amount of money a person can request in this court, usually between $2,000 and $5,000.

Even small claims court judges, however, dread fighting neighbors. Do not be surprised if you take your neighbor to small claims court and find yourself directed to mediation. This is a process in which you and your neighbor work out your own problems and reach an agreeable settlement, aided by a trained, impartial mediator. Mediation, with or without court involvement, is an extremely effective method of resolving arguments between neighbors. We discuss it in detail later in this book.

Then there are the majority of today's squabbles—the ones neighbors work out between themselves and the ones they don't. Some neighbors simply don't speak to each other, and some occasionally just grumble.

Most of us go along day-to-day being cordial, never mentioning that a problem exists, except behind the neighbor's back. Sometimes, only to ourselves, do we admit that we despise the dadburned tree or ugly fence or barking dog. Often the offending person is never even aware of a problem. We don't dislike the neighbor, we don't want to cause a hassle, and we are unsure of where we stand with the law. We don't know what to do about the situation so we do nothing.

For those neighbors who rush to call the police or think that court is the only answer, this book offers some alternatives. And for those silent neighbors with problems, we hope it will help them assert their legal rights.

Help for Common Complaints

Nothing so needs reforming as other people's habits.

—Mark Twain

The most frequent grounds for serious neighbor disputes—trees, fences, boundaries, easements and noise—are covered in separate chapters in this book. This chapter outlines a strategy for dealing with almost any other kind of neighbor problem, starting with friendly negotiation and, if truly necessary, going all the way to court.

We don't have the pleasure of choosing our neighbors—they simply come with the territory. What a great joy it is to move into a strange city or new area and be warmly welcomed by a courteous and thoughtful person who lives next door. And what a terrible disappointment when instead, the next-door neighbor is thoughtless or given to some activity that is a constant annoyance.

In today's society, the limited space of properties magnifies even a small annoyance. Especially if it occurs every day, what starts out as a bother can turn into a nightmare for a neighbor. And sadly, neighbors (even those who are the cause of the problem) sometimes retaliate when they feel threatened or disturbed, fueling what can escalate into open warfare.

But the law offers protection from a neighbor's disturbing activities. Local laws and subdivision rules prohibit almost anything one neighbor can do that would seriously annoy another. And when there isn't a relevant law, a person can sue a neighbor who interferes with the use and enjoyment of his property.

LOCAL LAWS

If your neighbor is doing something that is terribly annoying to you, the activity is probably against the law. Most everyday activity that could disturb a neighbor is regulated by city or county ordinances. When citizen involvement is high in a community, what bothers residents the most finds its way into a local ordinance. Uncut weeds, dogs roaming at large, even old cars up on blocks may all be against the law.

Whatever your particular concern, always check your local ordinances thoroughly. The best way to find out what your city or county ordinances cover is to go to the public library or the county law library (usually located in or next to the courthouse) and read them yourself. Then you can make copies of anything that you think is pertinent. (Chapter 13, *Legal Research*, has more on looking up local laws.)

Once you have a copy of an ordinance that addresses the problem, your troubles may be almost over. The neighbor probably has no idea that what he is doing is actually against the law. In most circumstances, just presenting a copy to him will resolve the problem.

If the neighbor does not respond, you can report the violation to the appropriate city department. The clerk at city hall will know which department to call, and many departments are in the phone book under the city government listing. For example, offices of the Health Department, Animal Control and Zoning Board will be listed separately, especially in larger cities.

When someone complains about the violation of an ordinance, the city or county can warn the person, issue a fine or take measures to correct the problem. Sometimes, if the person is uncooperative, the city will fix the problem (for instance, cleaning up rubbish) and bill the person responsible. In serious situations, the city or county attorney can sue the person to force compliance with the law. Someone who wants to fight a citation for a violation

CHANGING LOCAL LAWS

If the problem is not covered by the law, you could set about garnering support from your neighbors and try to get one passed. Talk to a member of the city council or county board of supervisors about the possibility of enacting a needed ordinance.

can go to court. If the judge orders the person to comply, violation of the order can result in another fine and, in some circumstances, a jail sentence.

Here are some of the topics most commonly covered in local laws.

Blighted Property

Blighted property is property that has been allowed to fall into a state of disrepair. Ordinances prohibit the maintenance of such property when it creates a danger to others or is such an eyesore that it reduces the value of surrounding property. Some blighted property ordinances prohibit accumulations of weeds, garbage or rubbish.

For example, the blighted property ordinance in Oakland, California mentions weeds and rubbish, and also has a long list of other items not allowed on property. The list includes structures (including fences), windows, driveways, sidewalks and retaining walls that are broken, deteriorated or defaced with graffiti.[1] An uncaring neighbor can be forced to repair the unsightly mess or face a fine.

Weeds, Rubbish and Garbage

Most towns prohibit high weeds, rubbish and garbage on property, and often lump them together in one ordinance. Communities may consider these health problems because they encourage the breeding of insects and rodents, or because they are fire hazards. The city can fine a person for a violation, clean up the property and bill the owner. When necessary, it can also get a judge's order for the owner to keep the premises clean from then on.[2]

Some laws address weeds alone. They prohibit the kinds that bother neighbors the most, such as weeds that are downy, wingy, poisonous or noxious to the community.[3]

Instead of prohibiting garbage and rubbish in yards, an ordinance may instead require a property owner to keep the premises clean and sanitary and the yard neat and orderly.[4] In Emeryville, California, a person violating this law is entitled to a hearing, and the city council makes a decision on the matter. If the violation stands, the property owner is given five days to clean up the premises before the city does it and sends a bill.[5]

Most towns also require property owners to keep the sidewalks in front of their property clean.[6]

Loud and Offensive Language

Loud and boisterous conduct is often prohibited in noise ordinances. (See Chapter 2, *Noise.*) If a neighbor is fighting and screaming, she is probably also violating state or local disorderly conduct laws, which means she can be arrested, fined and jailed. A neighbor can call the police, who will usually warn the person first and then may write a citation or make an arrest. Some local ordinances also prohibit profane and vulgar language that could create a breach of the peace.[7]

Drug Dealers

When someone sells illegal drugs, it is ordinarily a matter for the police and the district attorney's office. But many police departments and prosecutors' offices are overburdened and unresponsive to citizens complaints about neighborhood drug dealing.

Some frustrated neighbors have recently banded together. They have brought individual small claims court lawsuits against owners of properties where drug dealing and associated other crimes flourish—and they have won. Because the small claims court limit in most states is $2,000 to $5,000, clusters of such claims quickly add up to big bucks.

In 1989, 19 neighbors plagued by the crime, noise and fear generated by a crack house in Berkeley, California won $2,000 each (the California small claims maximum has since risen to $5,000) in small claims court against an absentee owner who had ignored their complaints for years. In San Francisco, a similar rash of small claims suits cost a landlord $35,000. Soon after the verdicts, both landlords evicted the troublesome tenants.

Many cities are also passing new laws aimed at getting drug dealing tenants evicted. The laws both make it easier for landlords to evict and punish landlords who sit by while drug dealing goes on on their property. In Los Angeles, for example, the police department can notify landlords when tenants are arrested or convicted of drug-related offenses. In Pasadena, a landlord who refuses to evict the tenants after a request from the city can be fined up to $5,000.

Local governments are also rigorously enforcing laws that allow them to sue landlords to have premises declared a public hazard or nuisance. In New York City and other places, owners have been fined and buildings have been closed down.[8]

Landlords can even lose their property altogether. Federal or local law enforcement authorities can take legal action to have housing used by drug dealers seized and turned over to the government, even if the owner's part in the crime is merely to ignore it. In 1988, the San Mateo County, California district attorney brought just such a suit against the owner of a 60-unit drug haven in the city of East Palo Alto. The owner was fined $35,000 in civil penalties and had to shut the building down and pay tenants' relocation expenses.

Animal Problems

Most towns have several ordinances designed to deal with problems created by animals—or more accurately, by irresponsible animal owners.

Noise. Noise ordinances often single out barking dogs, but dogs are sometimes regulated in separate ordinances indexed under "Dogs" or "Animal Control." Wherever the laws are found, they usually limit the length of time a dog may bark, or the frequency of the barking allowed. The watchdog down the street that barks at intruders, or even occasionally at passersby, is within the law. But the owner of the pooch next door left out to howl at the moon all night is not. (See Chapter 12, *Noise.*)

Leash laws. Almost all towns have leash laws, requiring dogs to be under restraint when they are off the owner's property. Sometimes these are called "running at large" laws. A neighbor can report the dog, and the city will pick up and impound the animal and fine the owner.

As for the nightly cat fight under the bedroom window, some areas—Peoria County in Illinois, for example—also have leash laws for cats.[9]

Pooper scooper laws. Most people are familiar with pooper scooper laws. These require the owner of an animal to immediately remove and dispose of an animal's defecation when the animal is away from the owner's premises. When a town doesn't have such a law to handle this annoying problem, the neighbor whose yard is the target could still sue the owner.[10] (See "Suing the Neighbor," below).

Number of animals. Local ordinances often limit the number of certain animals allowed per household to two or three adult animals. Minneapolis, for example, limits households to three dogs or cats over four months old.[11] These laws are designed to cut down on noise, odors and health problems. Someone who is determined to keep more animals may have to buy a special kennel license from the city.

Although dog and cat owners are the animal owners most likely to be affected by these laws, they are not the only ones. An Albany, California, law restricts the number of geese per household.[12] While such an ordinance may seem out of date, it is far from it. Some people in that city use geese as a substitute for watch dogs. The honking of too many faithful watch-geese can create a neighborhood disturbance for several blocks.

Ordinances also limit the number of ducks, pigeons and chickens on property within the city limits. Raising pigeons is a common hobby in some urban areas, and the laws regulate not only how many pigeons a person can keep, but also how close the coop can be placed to a neighbor's property.

Other farm animals, such as pigs, hogs, goats and horses, are usually not allowed within the city limits. But again in Albany, California, a property owner is allowed to keep one goat—but for only a sixty-day period—for weed control.[13]

Licenses and Special Permits. Dogs and cats must usually be licensed, and special permits are often required for exotic or dangerous animals. Vicious dogs—usually defined as dogs that have injured someone—are outlawed in some areas. In others, the owner must get a special city permit and buy liability insurance.

Regulations may also cover the keeping of bees, both by requiring a permit and limiting the location of hives.

Residential-Only Zoning

In most residential areas, zoning laws allow only single-family dwellings. This means that the investor who purchases property down the street and then turns it into an apartment house for partying college students may be violating the zoning laws.

Zoning laws also prohibit running a business at home that attracts customers and creates traffic in a residential area. These can prohibit, among others, home-based beauty parlors, typing services, tax preparers and car mechanics. The neighbor who has a yard sale once a year is not really in business (although some towns require a permit), but the one who opens the garage door every Saturday morning for a sale is probably violating the law.

Before you complain about a possible zoning violation, always check the zoning map at city hall. The neighbor creating a problem might be located just over the zoning line, and be in an acceptable district for what she is doing. Also be aware that in some circumstances, cities have the power to zone land that lies just beyond their boundaries. In Illinois, for example, towns may zone land that lies up to one-and-a-half miles outside their boundaries.

Vehicles

Old broken-down cars in the yard are an unwelcome sight to neighbors and are usually a violation of local law. A typical ordinance requires any disabled car to either be enclosed or be placed behind a fence. Some limit the parking of RVs and disabled cars to 72 hours, unless they are enclosed or out of sight.[14] Almost all cities prohibit leaving any vehicle parked on a city street too long—often, over 72 hours.

When someone in the neighborhood brings it to their attention, some towns will tow away a vehicle that has been parked for too long. And the relatives in their RV, who have been visiting across the street for the past year, could pay their next visit to a judge.

Outdoor Lights

Some cities where houses are located fairly close together have enacted laws protecting people from a neighbor's glaring lights. These laws prohibit directing an outdoor light in a neighbor's direction.[15]

SUBDIVISION RULES

If you live in a subdivision or planned unit development, you are likely to be subject to property regulations called Covenants, Conditions and Restrictions (CC&Rs). These CC&RS are normally contained in a separate document that is referred to in each property owner's deed.

Although you can still use a local ordinance to help you in most of these communities and subdivisions, the CC&Rs are often much stricter and more detailed than local laws. They restrict all types of activity on the property—for instance, some don't allow the use of outdoor clotheslines, and others prevent installing a basketball hoop on the garage. When the property is subject to these extensive restrictions, just about anything one person could do to annoy another will probably be addressed.

In areas that have these regulations, a disturbed neighbor can inform the homeowners association of a violation of the rules. Depending on the particular structure of the association, complaining can be done quite informally or an official complaint may have to be in writing. The association will notify the person responsible for the violation and demand conformity to the regulations. It may sanction the person by suspending privileges, for instance the use of a tennis court or a swimming pool.

Some associations have the power to sue a member of the group to conform. One neighbor can also sue another to enforce the restrictions, but the lawsuit must be in regular court (not small claims court) and will be expensive.

APPROACHING YOUR NEIGHBOR

Although it is sometimes hard to believe, many neighbors are unaware that their behavior could possibly bother anyone else. The dog owner who lets Rover roam at night doesn't look at the next-door neighbor's yard in the morning and see the recently dug hole where the petunias had been. The car buff who spends every Saturday on his restoration project never even thinks about what his junk looks like from his neighbor's living room window.

These neighbors need to be told that there is a problem. It is never easy to complain to a neighbor, but simply telling your neighbor will resolve a significant number of problems. And it beats the alternative—spending your life irritable and resentful.

The best approach is to assume that the neighbor is unaware he is making your life miserable. Coupling a complaint with a suggested solution can be particularly effective. For example, you could try something like this:

"I'm sure you would want to know that Rover is digging up my yard, so you can keep him in at night."

Or: "That '55 Chevy is going to be a real beauty. If fixing it is going to take much longer, would you be willing to move it into the garage or out back, away from my living room window?"

If the neighbor is hostile to you, have a copy of the law in your pocket.

Don't be surprised if the neighbor answers with a complaint of his own—in fact, be ready for one. If you have ever done anything that bothers her, this is when it will come out. You may have a half-dead tree leaning over her garage, or your outdoor light could be keeping her awake. If you are open and flexible, you could have a great opportunity to listen to your neighbor's concerns and suggest a compromise solution.

USING MEDIATION

If your neighbor thinks your complaints are unreasonable and does nothing to remedy the situation, you have a choice: go to court or suggest mediation. Because most legal mechanisms will cost time, money and any future good relationship, trying mediation first is a worthwhile effort to keep the dispute just between you and your neighbor, and to arrive at your own solution.

In mediation, you work out your own agreement with the help of a trained, neutral third party (mediator). One reason mediation between neighbors is so successful is because sometimes both neighbors simply need to have their say. Often, both have complaints about other issues. Once they are aired, a compromise involving everything in dispute is possible.

You can find a good mediator in just about any urban area. Many communities have free neighborhood mediation centers, designed to handle serious and not-so-serious neighbor disputes. (Chapter 14, *Mediation*, has all the details.)

SUING YOUR NEIGHBOR

If you can't work things out with a neighbor or get help from the city, don't give up. You can sue the neighbor directly for money and for a judge's order making the neighbor remedy the problem. If you sue just for money, you can handle the lawsuit by yourself in small claims court. To get the neighbor ordered to do something, you'll probably need to hire a lawyer.

When someone does something that is unreasonable or unlawful that interferes with the use and enjoyment of property you own or rent, you can sue the person for creating what is called a private nuisance

Some states describe what constitutes a private nuisance in their state statutes. The statutes in California, Indiana and Nevada, for example, make someone who does anything at all to interfere with the use or enjoyment of a neighbor's property legally liable to the neighbor for a nuisance.

The laws in a few states require conduct to be unlawful (in violation of an ordinance, for example) or unreasonable to create a nuisance to the neighbor. In these states, it can be a little harder for a neighbor to win a nuisance lawsuit, but most activities that seriously disturb a neighbor would be considered unreasonable.

Most states don't have a general nuisance statute; instead, they list certain activities that are legally considered nuisances—for example, having garbage on property or keeping anything that's a health hazard. An activity that's not on the list can still be a nuisance under the common law (case-by-case decisions made by courts) if it interferes with someone else's use of property.

Appendix 2 contains a chart that shows each state's definition of a nuisance. In states that require unreasonable conduct, ask yourself if what the person is doing would be considered by most people as an unreasonable use of property. If you are not sure that what the neighbor is doing is unreasonable, you probably have very weak grounds for a legal complaint.

A DELICATE DILEMMA

Ruth lives in a small apartment in San Francisco, where people keep windows open for air. Her neighbors downstairs are chain smokers, and the smoke drifts straight up and into Ruth's apartment, making her sick. The neighbors obey laws banning smoking in many public places, but they aren't about to stop smoking in their homes. The fact that she cannot open her windows without subjecting herself to cigarette smoke shows a definite interference with her use and enjoyment of property.

But even in California, where any activity that interferes with her use of property is a nuisance, Ruth feels on shaky legal ground about bringing a lawsuit against these neighbors. (In a state requiring unreasonable conduct, her chance of a successful lawsuit would be very slim. Smoking cigarettes in one's home has not been ruled to be unreasonable conduct anywhere.)

In California, Ruth might be able to get a money award from a sympathetic judge. But she really doesn't want to sue her neighbors; she just wishes there was already a law to help her. Sooner or later, she'll have to do something about her problem or move somewhere else. Ruth may even find herself trying to break new legal ground.

What You Can Sue For

You can ask the court to give you money to compensate you for your annoyance and also to order the neighbor to stop the nuisance. For a court order to stop the problem, you will need to hire a lawyer and use regular (not small claims) court.

But for money alone, you can use small claims court, which is fast, and where you don't need a lawyer. You must ask for an amount that is within your state's small claims court limit—between $2,000 and $5,000 in most states. A typical annoyance award would be within the limit.

How much money to ask for is always subjective. Approaching the problem on a daily basis is the easiest method. If you had to clean up your yard after your neighbor's dog once a day for ten days, $5 to $10 a day would be considered reasonable by most people. When the dog's mess harmed the lawn, you would include the cost of fixing it. If the problem is more serious, such as something that makes you ill, keeps you awake, or decreases your property value, you could easily ask for as much as $50 a day.

After you sue a neighbor successfully for creating a nuisance, if the neighbor doesn't remedy the situation, the nuisance continues. You can sue again and again until something is done. (Chapter 15, *Small Claims Court*, discusses how to use small claims court and lists each state's small claims limit.)

Suing a Landlord

In many situations, the person causing a problem for a neighbor is a tenant, rather than the owner of the property. The neighbor can sue the tenant in this case, but can also sue the landlord for maintaining a nuisance on the property—allowing the tenant's activities. If a landlord is allowing noisy all-night parties or worse—drug dealing, for example—on the property, suing the landlord can result in the tenant's being evicted.

Neighbors Banding Together

One of the most effective approaches to stopping a nuisance in a neighborhood is for all neighbors who are affected by the activity to sue at the same time. What may seem like a small sum of money multiplied by ten or twenty small claims awards gets the attention of the person responsible (including a landlord) and usually stops the activity.

Neighbors have organized and successfully brought these multiple lawsuits when faced with everything from teenagers squealing tires to noise at a major airport.[16] Increasingly, they are getting together and using this method to aim at drug dealing in the neighborhood.

What You Must Prove

When you sue for a nuisance, you must prove the following:

- The neighbor is doing something that seriously annoys you.

- Your ability to use and enjoy your property is diminished by the neighbor's acts.

- The person you are suing is responsible (and, in some states, the conduct is unreasonable or unlawful).

- How much money you need to compensate you for the annoyance.

You must be prepared to show the judge what the harmful activity is, and exactly how it affects you. In a case of illegal activity such as drug-dealing, a person may rightfully fear being sued himself for making such an accusation. When neighbors know illegal activity is going on but can't really prove it, they can instead, and just as successfully, complain to a court just about the noise, traffic and disturbance created.

If the neighbor is violating any ordinance, take a copy of the law with you to hand to the judge. If your state has a general nuisance statute, have a copy of the statute. And although it is not usually necessary in small claims court, you can do a little legal research and find a similar court case from your state to bolster your complaint. (See Chapter 13, *Legal Research*.)

[1]Oakland, Cal. Mun. Ord. 15-1.01 and following.

[2]A city obtained such a permanent order in *City of Union v. Julius*, 706 S.W.2d 513 (Mo. App. 1986), based on the Union, Missouri ordinance, after the owner continued to ignore the violations.

[3]For example, see Emeryville, Cal. Mun. Ord. 6-10.02.

[4]For example, see Emeryville, Cal. Mun. Ord. 6-2.04 and following.

[5]Emeryville, Cal. Mun. Ord. 6-2.08.

[6] For example, see Hayward, Cal. Mun. Ord. 4-1.62.

[7]For example, see Oakland, Cal. Mun. Ord. § 3-4.01, and Code of Ords., Oxford, Miss. 19-16.

[8]For example, see Berkeley, Cal. Mun. Ord. 13.56.030.

[9]Peoria, Ill. County Code § 5-19.

[10]You can find answers to many dog problems in the book *Dog Law,* by Mary Randolph (Nolo Press).

[11]Minneapolis, Minn. Code § 64.100.

[12]Albany Cal. Mun. Ord. 10-3.6.

[13]Albany, Cal. Mun. Ord. 10-6.1.

[14]For example, see Oakland, Cal. Mun. Ord. 15-1.01, and following. In Oakland, disabled vehicles are covered in the blighted property ordinance.

[15]For example, Albany, Cal. Mun. Ord. 20-3.

[16]A group of neighbors actually forced a policy change at the San Francisco airport by collectively and repeatedly suing in small claims court about the noise.

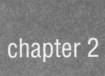

chapter 2

Noise

He is happiest, be he king or peasant, who finds peace in his home.

—Goethe

A LOOK AT THE LAW

If you are a reasonable person and your neighbor is driving you wiggy with noise, the neighbor is probably violating a noise law.

It is 7:00 a.m.. on a Saturday morning. After a long and hard week, you are enjoying one of the great pleasures in life—not setting the alarm clock. Then the noise starts. Your next door neighbor fires up the chain saw. Or the neighbor across the street gets an early start with her power mower. Or the teenager upstairs turns on the boom box. And the dog down the street barks at any and all of it.

Whatever the intrusion, your plans for peace are shot. You cover your head with the pillow for a while and then give up. Not wanting to cause trouble, you begin the weekend irritable, tired, maybe even physically ill.

In case you think you are just being too sensitive, think again. Noise is a very serious matter, and the time may come when you realize that you should have acted long ago to curb the situation. In California, if you sell your house, you must fill out a disclosure form for the new buyer, pointing out any problems. There on Line 10 is a blank to mark "yes" or "no" to the question: Neighbor Noise Problems.[1] Then what do you do?

LAWS AGAINST NOISE

You are protected from a noisy neighbor by the law—mostly local, occasionally, state law. Additionally, rules in rental agreements and planned communities further restrict allowable noise. Noise regulations are enforced by the police, landlords, neighborhood associations and the courts. And when you are affected by your neighbor's excessive noise, you can sue her for creating a private nuisance. You can ask a court for money damages and to have the noise stopped.

Local Noise Laws

The most effective weapon you have to maintain your peace and quiet is your local ordinance. Almost every community has a noise ordinance prohibiting excessive, unnecessary and unreasonable noise. And most laws designate certain times as quiet times, such as nights and some hours on weekends. Some noise may be allowed at some times, and the same noise not at other times.

Certain necessary noises occur all of the time and we simply have to put up with them—for instance, noise from a heavy industry or from traffic on the freeway. But when we can control the noise, the ordinances apply. Running a power mower may be perfectly acceptable at 10:00 a.m. on Saturday, but not at 7:00 a.m., and watching a ball game on T.V. or playing a stereo may be okay at five in the afternoon but not at two in the morning when the neighbor is trying to sleep.

Many towns also have decibel level noise limits and electronic equipment for measuring the noise when a neighbor complains. A few cities have special noise units to enforce the laws and to free the police for other calls.

A typical noise ordinance, this one from Oxford, Mississippi, begins like this: "Creation of any unreasonably loud, disturbing and unnecessary noises in the city is hereby prohibited."[2] Some cities use the language "loud, raucous or nerve-wracking noise."

Some sounds that bother us the most are placed in special categories that are either not allowed or have special rules. These noises are assumed to disturb people. For instance, most cities prohibit either in their noise laws or vehicle laws the honking of auto horns unless there is danger. This means that the daily early morning tooting across the street for the carpool is a violation.

Dogs are usually singled out; sometimes they are allowed to bark for very short periods, say under ten minutes. The dog that barks only at intruders or a passing fire engine is probably within legal limits. But the neighbors down the block who allow their dog to howl all night are violating the ordinance.[3]

Motorcycles may be mentioned by name in an ordinance. Unnecessary running of the engine, for example, may be presumed to disturb a neighbor.[4]

In addition to actual lists of troublesome noises, certain types of noise are sometimes included in the special categories. Examples are sounds of annoying pitch, such as a screech, and persistent or repetitive sounds, like the hum of a motor of the pounding of a hammer.

When is Noise Unreasonable?

Most ordinances prohibit unreasonable noise, but they don't define it. The police may have to make the decision, or later, a judge. But to be unreasonable, the noise should be—in the mind of an average person—too loud, prolonged or disturbing for that time of day. It usually boils down to common sense and to what most people consider unacceptable. For example, the child who practices the piano for an hour each day is certainly not a matter for the law. A roaring piano at 11 o'clock every night is. A rollicking party several times a year—probably acceptable. Every three days? No way.

Music can present special problems. Sometimes it is a matter of taste. What is pleasant to some ears quickly hits the discomfort level of others.

Example: In a case in Illinois, a teenage rock band was practicing at two o'clock in the afternoon. It disturbed a neighbor who was on night shift and trying to get some sleep. It also woke up his young son from a nap. The police came out and stopped the noise, but there was an interesting twist. One of the police officers who responded to the call immediately called the noise unreasonable. The other one liked the music and had more difficulty. He had to overcome his own preference to admit that the noise was unreasonable to others.[5]

These unreasonable noise laws are enforced by the police and the courts according to the effect of the noise on a normal, reasonable person. If you jump out of your skin at the slightest peep of a puppy, you may find no help from the law. Sometimes cities try to have the noise affect two or more persons before it can be stopped, to prevent complaints from excessively sensitive people.

If you are the only neighbor on the block who is being bothered by a noise everyone hears at the same level, you may be too picky. People usually know deep down whether they are being reasonable, and most people actually allow more noise in their lives than the law does.

TODAY'S REASONABLE PERSON

The reasonable person in today's society is a strange mixture of adaptation and resistance. Consider for a moment your everyday life in the city. You slip your car into rush hour traffic in the morning with several thousand noisy, honking others. Huge trucks fill the lane beside you. Stereos blast the air. Road crews pound with heavy equipment.

On your lunch break, you zip over to the diner, waving at the fellow with the jackhammer, stopping to let a screaming police car go by. You don't talk at lunch because the din of voices and clatter is so loud that you can't be heard. On the way back to the office, you pause to allow the garbage truck in the alley to lift and dump a bin into the back of the truck.

You step into the elevator filled with music, get off on your floor and return to work in a room with 200 typewriters or a steam press, or the drum of machinery.

After work, back into the thundering traffic, and then finally home. Thirty minutes later a lone dog starts to bark. You tense, then bristle with the invasion. What's going on here?

The human brain is an incredibly flexible machine. Sometimes it seems that it imposes its own limits. We all know people who live next to train tracks and freeways and who don't notice that particular noise after a while. In a time of relentless noise, we also see ourselves tuning it out at certain times. It just doesn't register.

Several hundred years ago, this kind of constant noise would have been unthinkable. Now you and I, today's reasonable people, have created an amazing compromise. Some noises are tolerable and some are not. Noise in some places at some times is okay and not in others—definitely not at home.

We may not realize it, but we have set very strict limits and cannot bend at all under certain circumstances. Fifty years ago, if music from your neighbor's house drifted into your window, you might have not only tolerated it but tapped your toe to the rhythm. Today you react with resentment and can't allow it. An argument can be made that the reasonable person today is much more sensitive to noise at certain times and in certain places than in years past. As the tolerance for noise increases on one end, it decreases on the other to prevent an overload. We are looking at a method of survival. The Saturday morning lawn mower is not just a bother to some people; it is a nightmare.

It is no wonder that our police can hardly keep up with noise complaints, that neighbor to neighbor fuses are so short. What's the answer? Who knows? Awareness of the situation is a beginning.

Decibel Level Laws

Many towns prohibit sustained noise that exceeds a certain decibel level. The decibel limits are set according to the time of day and the neighborhood zoning. For example, higher levels are allowed anytime in industrial areas. In residential areas, the limit is lower than the industrial limit during the daytime, and much lower at night. There are exceptions for emergency situations, such as road repair. Also, some cities allow people to apply for a variance to the noise law—a permit to exceed the noise level for a certain period of time, for instance during major construction. You may also be able to get a permit for a one time event.

Unless you are a sound engineer, the language of these statutes may mean nothing to you. It does mean something to the police, or the special noise unit. They have a machine and they know how to read the noise level.

What happens under a decibel level ordinance is that a neighbor complains and the noise unit comes out. If the noise is still going on, the noise officer places the machine on an estimated property line and takes a reading. If the noise level coming into the other property is above a certain number, it violates the noise ordinance. However, the offending noise has to be measured against what is called the ambient level—the background noise level without that particular disturbance.

Finding the ambient level with a live band playing can be difficult. The noise units have become experts at finding comparison levels, and many people insist that this method is the fairest one of all in controlling noise. For apartment living, the decibel level is measured inside, and it is common for the levels allowed to be much lower and more protective.[6]

Once the machine shows that the particular noise is above the allowed level, the person responsible will usually be warned. If the noise continues or is repeated, he will be cited and fined. Fines are often levied according to how many violations there have been—for in-

MEASURING THE NOISE LEVEL YOURSELF

If you are curious about the noise level where you live, you can purchase a decibel level machine at an electronics store. Some models run around $35. Taking your own reading may give you an indication of how severe a problem is, even though if you complain the police will want to take their own measurements.

stance, $100 for the first time, $200 the second, $300 the third.

When a town adopts the decibel level method, it usually keeps the unreasonable noise law too. When a town has both kinds of laws, either one may be used. In a New Mexico case where a group of neighbors complained about music from a car wash, the decibel level was measured and found to be within the allowed limits. But the neighbors were obviously disturbed (some were contemplating moving), and the court relied on the broader ordinance prohibiting all unreasonable noise. The car wash was found to be in violation.[7]

Times of Day

Most local ordinances include what could be called "quiet times." The noise level allowed is lower during these times, the hours when most of us try to sleep. An average ordinance prohibits loud noises between the hours of 11:00 p.m. and 7:00 or 8:00 a.m. on weekdays and 11:00 p.m. or midnight until 8:00 to 10:00 p.m. on Sundays and holidays. Some cities set the evening hour as early as 9:00 p.m.[8] or even 6:00 p.m.[9]

What this really means is that if any noise is loud enough to keep a reasonable person awake during these hours, it is above the limit allowed. Towns that use a decibel system also lower the limit during these hours.

These quiet hours can vary from one residential area to another within the same city depending on the zoning for the particular spot. In a residential only zone, for example, the morning hour may be 8:00 a.m. and in an industrial area 7:00 a.m.

Having quiet times listed does not mean that there are no noise restrictions at other times. A blasting boom box can be a violation at any time. What it does mean is that you have the right to expect not to be disturbed during the quiet hours. If your neighbor starts up his chain saw at

6:00 a.m. on a Sunday, he is breaking the law. In suburban areas, the lines between different towns may meander around and different restrictions may apply from one block to the next. It's a good idea to not only know your own ordinance but those in areas that can affect you.

Example: Bill and Barbara liked to stay out late and party every Saturday night and sleep in on Sunday mornings. Every Sunday morning the church down the street pealed its large bell at 9:00 a.m. It was the only noise for the whole morning, but it meant waking up at nine.Bill read his local ordinance and saw that the quiet time lasted until 10:00 a.m. on Sundays. He was extremely un-comfortable complaining about a church, but he finally called the pastor. He then learned what real discomfort was when the pastor politely informed him that the church was located just two lots inside the next suburban town. Their quiet hours? 11:00 p.m. to 9:00 a.m. on Sunday.

Other Local Laws

Once in a while, a neighbor noise problem can be solved by using another local ordinance. For example, the neighbor who is running a little machine shop business in his back yard at night and on weekends may be violating a zoning ordinance. Any business conducted at home which creates customers and traffic probably doesn't fit residential-only zoning.

Other miscellaneous laws also have an effect on noise. Discharging firearms and shooting off firecrackers are forbidden by separate laws. Having too many animals on one property can violate another law. Even working on a broken car for too long of a period may be prohibited.

Noises in some of these situations can be very annoying, yet don't quite fit the noise ordinance. To find out what other local laws might be applicable, read your particular ordinances. (See Chapter 13.)

State Laws

If a neighbor's noise is excessive and deliberate, it may be a violation of state laws against disturbing the peace or disorderly conduct. For example, New Mexico law says that anyone whose conduct is boisterous or unreasonably loud and tends to disturb the peace is guilty of a misdemeanor.[10] This means that the police can arrest anyone who is being unreasonably loud. Misdemeanors are minor criminal offenses usually punishable by fines and less than a year of jail time. And California has a criminal law that provides for a fine or jail or both for any person who willfully and maliciously disturbs another person by loud and unreasonable noise.[11] You can find out what state laws a neighbor may be violating by asking the police or checking the law library.(See Chapter 13 on legal research.)

Also many states have noise control laws that address problems affecting us as a public, such as airport, heavy industry and transportation noises. Some states have an office to receive complaints, and a staff that works with the federal government in its efforts to curb unnecessary noise. If a "big neighbor" is making your life miserable, you can find out from your city attorney's office how to proceed under these state provisions or look up your state's law in the library. (See Chapter 13).

Rental Agreements and Restrictive Covenants

If you live in a planned community or rent an apartment, you can use not only the town noise ordinances when you have a problem, but you have extra remedies that may be available. You may not even need to ask for help from the city.

Renting: An Additional Weapon Against Noise

When your residence is a rented apartment in a large complex, you can be more vulnerable to noise. Problems arise not just because the walls can be a little thin, but also because you simply have more neighbors with which you must contend. Sometimes the neighbor creating a problem is a complete stranger.

Many apartment dwellers seem to think they have given up a right to quiet, and they tolerate too much noise. They are afraid to be labeled as troublemakers and don't insist on their rights.

People who live next door to apartment complexes also sometimes take too much noise for granted.

If you are in either of these groups, you have a lot of avenues open to you to regain your quiet. Laws that prohibit unreasonable noise apply to apartments, as do decibel level laws (usually a lower level of noise allowed within buildings than would be permissible outdoors). You can also sue the noisy neighbor for a private nuisance. But there is more. The person making the noise can be evicted, and you can sue the landlord.

Standard rental and lease agreements contain a clause entitled "Quiet Enjoyment." In this clause you will find wording somewhat like this:

"Tenant(s) shall be entitled to quiet enjoyment of the premises. Tenant(s) shall not use the premises in such a way as to violate any law or ordinance, commit waste or nuisance, or annoy, disturb, inconvenience, or interfere with the quiet enjoyment of any other tenant or nearby resident."

If the neighbor's stereo is keeping you up every night, the tenants are probably violating the rental agreement. They can be evicted for the violation. Informing the neighbor of the lease restrictions may be all that is necessary. If that doesn't help, complaining to the landlord can be very effective.

Most apartment owners don't want problems among their tenants, and they won't put up with somebody who ignores the signed agreement and causes trouble. Especially if several tenants complain at the same time, the landlord will probably order the tenant to comply with the lease or face eviction.

The landlord also may know that he can be sued for his tenant's activity. By allowing the situation on his property, he is maintaining a private nuisance. If you have the same landlord, you may not want to sue him, but you have the right to do so. If you are just a neighbor, going after the landlord can often solve the problem.

Planned Communities and Condos

When you buy a condominium or a house in a planned community, the deed often contains restrictions called restrictive covenants. These can range all the way from what color you can paint your fence to what activities are allowed on your property. You agree to the restrictions when you buy the residence.

Restrictions against excessive noise are quite common. The restrictions apply to you, your neighbors and any tenants who are renting. What's more, they place responsibility for the tenant's actions on the owner. The owner is the one who agreed to the restrictions, and when a tenant breaks the rules, the owner can be disciplined and even sued to conform.

In planned communities and condos, the right to enforce the rules is usually placed in the hands of a residents committee. Someone who violates the rules is sanctioned, for example, by having privileges to common areas revoked (such as a swimming pool). These remedies are above and beyond the regular noise laws, which are also applicable to people in these locales. They provide another possible step to take before calling in the law. Some owners associations have the power to sue members of the group to enforce the restriction. One neighbor can also sue another neighbor for violation of a restrictive covenant, but the time and expense probably won't be worthwhile unless the problem is very serious.

WHAT TO DO

There are two common reactions to noise coming from a neighbor. The first is a sense of helplessness and resignation. You hate the noise, but you do nothing. The second is anger. You lose your temper and call the cops. There are better ways to handle the situation.

Approaching the Neighbor

Discussing the problem with a neighbor is not easy. In fact, it can be very painful. But it is always the first step and if done with respect and sensitivity, will hopefully be the last.

Often the neighbor is unaware of a problem (for instance, the dog barks only when nobody is home). Or he may just not realize that his noise is bothering someone else. An effective approach is to assume that the neighbor doesn't know and would like to be told. Before you complain about it behind the neighbor's back, and certainly before you think of calling the police, tell the neighbor. Step over there or pick up the phone and give communication a chance.

Example: When I began writing this chapter, the puppy belonging to my lovely new next door neighbors decided, as if on cue, to serenade me. I had only met the neighbors once, and I could not believe what was happening. It was as if the puppy knew when I sat down to write. Every word was punctuated with a yelp. He barked until he became exhausted, slept for a while and then started again. He barked only when the neighbors were not at home.

Several days of this went by, much to the amusement of my family. It was not the least bit funny to me. I began to make mistakes in the text and had to rewrite whole paragraphs. For several nights, I looked at the telephone and cringed, wanting to call the neighbor but not wanting to call more strongly.

I knew the dog's name and discovered if I yelled loud enough at him, he would be quiet for a few minutes. My family became more amused. Now the neighborhood had turned into "bark, bark, yell; bark, bark, yell." I was becoming part of the problem.

Finally, I had to call. How could I tell my readers to do something I couldn't do myself? The neighbors were horrified to learn that there was a problem, and very apologetic. They shut him up and now I write this in silence.

This example is typical. Most of us really hate to complain. Yet look what happened. The dog isn't barking, the owners were grateful to be told, and the lines of communication are open. Once all of the apologies settle, these neighbors will probably be friends for years. All it took was one phone call.

Warning the Neighbor

When complaining doesn't work, the next step is to go get a copy of your local noise ordinance at city hall or the public library. Send a copy of the law to the neighbor accompanied with a letter like this:

                              September 2, 19__

Dear Mr. Thoughtless,

    I have enclosed our local noise laws so that
you may read them. You will see that the
playing of your stereo so loudly is against
the law. It is very disturbing to me. Please
turn down the volume as I have asked you to do
in the past. Otherwise, I will be forced to
notify the authorities.

Sincerely yours,

Bob Bothered

Keep a copy of the letter because you may want it later if you sue the neighbor. (See Section 15 below.) Then see what happens. The neighbor may not know the law and finding out about it may put an end to the problem. She also knows you mean business when she sees your complaint in writing.

Bringing in the Landlord

If you live in a rental unit or restricted housing area, send a copy of the lease agreement or special rules to the neighbor. This can result in prompt action, especially if you suggest that your next complaint will be to the landlord or the neighborhood association. In an area with a homeowners association, if a neighbor does not respond, notify the association.

If a tenant refuses to comply with your requests, report it to the landlord in writing. You are not a troublemaker. In fact, you are assisting the landlord in protecting his interests. A sample letter is below.

May 14, 19___

Dear Mr. Wilson:

I live in Unit 5 of your Ridgeland Apartments complex. Mr. Jones in Unit 7 plays his stereo at such a loud volume that it is a serious disturbance to me. I have asked him several times to please turn it down and he has not responded. Last week, I sent him the enclosed letter pointing out to him that he was violating his lease.

I regret having to bother you, but I know that you would want to be alerted to this situation so it can be corrected. Thank you for your cooperation.

Sincerely yours,

Teri Tenant

Strength in Numbers

In dealing with a landlord or a hostile neighbor, one of the most effective things you can do is to get someone else to complain also. This is not nearly as hard as you might think. If you are being bothered, someone else probably is too. What is likely is that they are just waiting and hoping somebody will do something. They don't want to act alone either. The greater the number of people complaining, the faster the relief should be.

Suggesting Mediation

When a neighbor is uncooperative, before you call the cops or rush to court, consider using mediation. You and the neighbor can sit down together with an impartial mediator and resolve your own problems. Mediation services are available in most cities and often they are free.

In a noise dispute, you could not only try to settle the current problem but work out an agreement that would avoid problems in the future. This is a much better solution than simply calling a police cruiser to the door, which will guarantee hard feelings from then on. And especially when there are more problems than just the noise, the neighbor may be delighted at a chance to be heard. If you value the neighbor relationship at all, or just want peace in the future, give mediation a try. (See Chapter 14 for more on how this works.)

Calling the Police

No response from the neighbor? Stereo turned up another notch? Now is the time to bring in the police.(If the problem is a barking dog, this may be the Animal Control officer in your town. And some cities have special noise units that respond to complaints. You can find out by calling the police office.) You are in a very different position than you were originally. You have tried to solve the problem yourself. You have done what you could on your own and even have a copy of a letter to prove it.

Of course you don't have to take all these steps before calling the law. But look at the difference between you, standing there with the written ordinance and the letter in your hand, and the thousands of people who call the cops over the slightest (and often frivolous) matter. The police know the difference. They will know your complaint is serious and that you need help.

Try to notify the police while the noise is continuing. If they are using a decibel meter, they need to be able to measure the noise level to see if it is above the allowed limit.

Suing for Nuisance

Whenever someone else's unreasonable action interferes with your enjoyment of your property, that action creates what is called a private nuisance. If you are the one affected by the nuisance, by your neighbor's blasting stereo or howling dog, you can sue the neighbor directly. You can ask the court for money damages or to make the neighbor stop the noise (have the nuisance abated). For money damage alone, you can use small claims court; for a court order making somebody stop doing something, you have to sue in regular court.

What you really want is for the noise to disappear. However, having the neighbor ordered to pay you money can be amazingly effective in regaining your quiet. If the noise continues, you have a "continuing nuisance" and can sue again and again.

A lot of neighbors are using small claims court for noise situations. It's is easy, inexpensive and you don't need a lawyer.

To sue for private nuisance, this is what you need to show:

- There is excessive and disturbing noise.
- The person you are suing is either creating it or is the landlord and therefore responsible.
- Your enjoyment of your property is affected. (You don't have to own the property—you can be a tenant.)
- You have asked the person to stop the noise (a letter should be enough).

This can be shown by police reports, other witnesses, your own testimony or even a recording.

The effect on you is called your damages. This may include loss of sleep, annoyance or the inability to carry on normal activity without interference. You can ask for a reasonable dollar amount per day for damages. The amount you can sue for in small claims court is limited, usually between $2,000 and $5,000. (Appendix 2 lists each state's limit.) If you have been bothered for twenty days and want $20 a day for it, this would usually be considered reasonable and would be well within the limit. If the noise problem is really severe—keeping you from sleeping or working and making you completely frazzled—$100 a day.

Once you have sued in small claims court, if the noise continue, you can sue again. Also, if other people are affected, get together with your neighbors. If ten people sue for $2000 each, that's $20,000. Do it again—another $20,000. Sooner or later, the noise should stop. (For more on small claims court, see Chapter 15.)

If you choose to sue in regular court and hire a lawyer, get her to write a threatening letter before you sue; that may be all that it takes. Sadly, some neighbors can be pretty rotten, and nothing short of a judge's order or high money damages will change the situation.

For example, consider one nasty neighbor and an owner attempting to rent his house next door. Every time a prospective tenant looks at the property, the neighbor revs up his huge motorcycle. When the police come out, all is quiet. Damages can mount up quickly for the owner of the house. For extreme situations like this, you will need an attorney.

Most noise problems between neighbors (and most neighbor disputes in general) can be solved by following a few simple guidelines:

- Know the law and stay within it.
- Be reasonably tolerant of your neighbors.
- Be assertive of your rights.
- Communicate with your neighbors—both the neighbor causing the problem and others affected by it.
- Ask the police for help when it is appropriate.
- Use the courts when necessary.

---

[1]Cal. Civ. Code § 1102.

[2]Oxford, Miss. Mun. Ord. 18-1.

[3]If you are having problems with a dog, or are a dog owner, Nolo publishes an entire book on this subject called *Dog Law* by Mary Randolph.

[4]*City of Everett ex rel. Cattle v. Everett Dist. Ct.,* 31 Wash. App. 319, 641 P.2d 714 (1982).

[5]*Town of Normal v. Stelzel,* 109 Ill. App.3d 836, 65 Ill. D. 378, 441 N.E. 2d 170 (1982).

[6]Berkeley, Cal. Mun. Ord. 13.40-2.

[7]*City of Farmington v. Wilkins,* 106 N.M. 188, 740 P.2d 1172 (1987).

[8]Oakland, Cal. Mun. Code 3 - 1.02.

[9]Piedmont, Cal. Local Ord. 12.8.

[10]N.M. Stat. Ann. 30-20-1.

[11]Cal. Pen. Code § 415.

When a Tree Is Injured or Destroyed

Woodman, spare that tree!
Touch not a single bough!
In youth it sheltered me,
And I'll protect it now.

—George Pope Morris

We human beings exhibit some complicated, often conflicting, emotions over our trees. In the abstract we understand our dependence on timber for shelter, comfort,
even the daily newspaper, yet we are slowly compre-
hending the critical importance of standing forests to the
environment. In our daily language we have adopted the
tree as a symbol—the tree of liberty, the tree of knowledge and the old favorite, the family tree. We also seem
to have a personal craving for trees. We bring them into
our office buildings and shopping malls, tend little forests
along city streets, and many of us fondly remember the
excitement of childhood tree-planting ceremonies on
Arbor Day.

But by far, the most powerful feelings emerge over the
trees in our own yards—the trees we own. We plant, water, trim, even decorate them. We build treehouses and
hang swings and birdfeeders in them. And we relax under
them, relishing the shade and beauty. Most tree owners
expect everybody else to love their trees. This, of course,
is not always the case. The neighbor who lives downwind
and has to rake up somebody else's leaves may despise
the tree. And large trees can cause enormous problems—
blocking views, producing invasive roots and, especially
if ill, threatening to fall on houses, cars or people.

But one thing is certain: we take ownership of our trees
and their protection very seriously in this country, and
this is reflected in the law. An annoyed neighbor who
decides simply to get rid of someone else's tree and gets
out a chainsaw can be in for some very nasty legal consequences.

WE DIDN'T THINK YOU WOULD MIND.

Ascertaining ownership by looking at the trunk appears to reflect good plain common sense, but it has not always been the law. Years ago there was a very different rule. It said that if the roots of a tree took nourishment from a neighboring land, sapping the strength of that land, then the neighbor also had part ownership of the tree.

As one might expect, judges began to have trouble with this. In 1836, a court in Connecticut discarded the rule, stating that it was impossible to apply because tree roots move around.[2] Other courts ruled the same way, and the law shifted to what we have today. Can you imagine the problems in our urban society if the nourishment test were still enforced?

WHO OWNS A TREE?

It is accepted law in all states that a tree whose trunk stands wholly on the land of one person belongs to that person. If the trunk stands partly on the land of two or more people, it usually belongs to all the property owners. (Special rules apply to such trees. See Chapter 9, *Boundary Trees.*)

Some states—California, for example—place this definition of ownership in their state statutes (laws passed by the state legislature).[1] But even in states where the legislature has not done this, the rule is still the same under what we call the common law, case-by-case decisions made by the courts.

AN OWNER'S RIGHTS WHEN A TREE IS DAMAGED

The basic rule is this: Someone who cuts down, removes or hurts a tree without permission owes the tree's owner money to compensate for the harm done. The owner can sue to enforce that right.

To run afoul of the law, you do not have to chop down a tree. You can also get in trouble by damaging the health of someone else's tree. For example, you have the legal right to trim branches of a neighbor's tree that hang over your property. (See Chapter 4, *Encroachment: Invasion of Branches and Roots.*) But seriously injuring the tree while doing the trimming can make you liable to the owner for the harm done. Or if you use a chemical in your own yard to destroy unwanted roots, and it seeps under to the neighbor's property and kills his tree, you can be liable.

An owner can also recover damages for harm to shrubs, flowers, vines and growing crops as well as trees. This means there is legal protection for a straggly little box-wood as well as a favorite old lilac bush.

For a tree owner to have a legal right to compensation for a damaged tree, there are two requirements:

- The owner's own property must be damaged. For instance, if a neighbor trims the part of your tree that is over his property, making it look terrible, you have no right to recovery unless the portion on your property is damaged.

- The tree in question must not create an immediate danger to others. Unsound trees that threaten a neighboring property are not under the same legal protection as healthy trees. In some circumstances, for example, if a dead tree is about to fall, a neighbor can even enter an owner's property to prevent the harm. (See Chapter 5, *Unsound Limbs and Trees.*)

WHAT THE TREE OWNER CAN SUE FOR

Someone who has lost a favorite tree by the actions of a neighbor can't get what he or she really wants—to have the tree back. But if the person responsible for injuring or removing a tree won't make good the loss, and it isn't covered by insurance, the owner has the right to sue the tree chopper for money to compensate for the loss. Often the owner can sue in small claims court, with no need to hire an attorney.

A general principle is applied again and again in tree damage cases: If the hacker of the tree did not do the harm intentionally, or made an honest mistake, she will have to pay the owner only the amount of the owner's actual loss. If she didn't care or willfully entered the neighbor's property, penalties will be triggered. Often the penalty is two or three times the amount of the actual loss.

Let's take a moment to look at the three kinds of monetary awards (called damages) that may be available, depending on the circumstances and state law:

1. Compensatory (Actual) Damages: The amount of the actual loss of the owner due to the destruction of the tree.

2. Statutory Damages: An extra amount of money, determined by state statute, that the person responsible pays to the owner. When damage to a tree was intentional, it is often three times the compensatory damages.

3. Punitive Damages: A sum awarded by a judge or jury when the conduct of the person who damaged a tree was especially outrageous or malicious.

We discuss each of these kinds of damages below.

CRIMINAL PENALTIES

A neighbor whose intent was to do harm and whose conduct was outrageous can be in for an enormously expensive lesson in neighbor law. Penalties for willful, malicious destruction of someone else's tree can include a fine and in very extreme cases even a jail term. See "Criminal Penalties," below.

Compensatory (Actual) Damages

Compensatory damages are intended to reimburse the owner for what he has actually lost. Although it can be difficult to put a dollar value on the loss, this sum can be quite large when a mature tree is destroyed.

Here are the kinds of losses for which an owner can be compensated in a lawsuit over a damaged or destroyed tree.

Cost of Replacing the Tree

Some trees are small enough—usually, less than twelve inches in diameter—to be replaced at a nursery. In that case, the amount of actual damages would be the cost of having a new tree of similar size planted to replace the dead or damaged one. The cost of removing debris and clean-up would also be included.

The homeowner's insurance policy of the tree owner will commonly pay up to $500 to replace a tree, plus up to another $500 for clean-up. (See "What to Do If a Neighbor Damages Your Tree," below.)

Example: Boris is putting an addition on his house. He rents a bulldozer and begins clearing the area. Accidentally, he flattens a young maple tree belonging to Fran next door. Embarrassed over his lack of bulldozing skill and genuinely sorry about the tree, he goes to Fran and offers to reimburse her for her damage. Fran orders a new tree of the same kind and size, has the old stump and debris removed and the new one planted. Boris pays the bill. Fran has been compensated for her actual damages by having the tree replaced.

Had Boris not been so cooperative and had Fran sued him in small claims court, the judge would probably have ordered him to pay Fran the same cost for replacement.

A landscaping business can help an owner replace much larger trees—even a fifty-year-old oak. At a tree farm, a tree is carefully removed, roots and all, and shipped on a flat-bed truck to its destination. There are some possible problems; some states prohibit the importation of live plants, and if the tree is too big, it may not be allowed on the highway. The cost is another barrier—it can be as much as $10,000 to $20,000.

Diminished Property Value

For various reasons, replacing a tree may be impossible. Then the most significant consequence of the loss is the lowering in the value of the owner's property as a whole. The tree owner is entitled to compensation for the decrease in property value caused by the loss of the trees.

For a reliable estimate of the drop in property value, an owner generally needs an expert opinion. The best opinion to obtain is that of a licensed arborist. For several hundred dollars, an arborist will consider many factors, including the size of the tree, its type, its age, its condition and the benefit it provided to the property. Special benefits the tree provided, such as lowering utility bills and serving as a windbreak, will also be taken into account.

And if you are replacing the tree with a smaller one, an arborist can tell you what the loss is when considering the time it will take before the new tree reaches full size. Arborists use an elaborate formula for assessing tree value that has been accepted in court.

Landscape architects, real estate appraisers, developers, consultants and horticulturists can also estimate diminished property value. These experts assess the property's market value before and after the loss of the tree. A good real estate agent (not an appraiser) can also give you an accurate estimate of property value loss, but in many areas, real estate agents do not give official appraisals.

If you use any expert other than an arborist, be aware that you may have to figure out on your own any special losses you have, such as a loss of shelter that affected utility bills. Always ask an expert exactly what factors are being considered in an appraisal. If a tree lowered utility bills substantially, or its loss renders a patio unusable in summer heat, and these losses are not included, you need to take them into account. The same would be true when the tree served as a windbreak, blocked an unsightly view, produced fruit or nuts—anything that would be considered if an arborist had done the appraisal.

The cost of any expert opinion will probably run several hundred dollars. If you go to court, include this fee as an expense of the incident, and ask the judge to order it paid back to you by the neighbor who caused the damage.

Some judges simply accept expert opinions as adequate proof of a loss. Occasionally, the property is actually viewed by a judge or jury.

Aesthetic Loss and Mental Anguish

Some trees are simply more valuable to us emotionally than others. Courts in one state, Louisiana, have now compensated a tree owner for aesthetic loss and mental anguish.

In Louisiana, in 1984, a judge considered the aesthetic loss of a man whose row of trees was mistakenly cut down by a neighbor. Actual damages to the property were put at $1,487.50. The judge obviously did not feel that this amount fully compensated the neighbor. Commenting that the beauty would not be restored for many years, the judge ordered an extra $2,500 paid to him for his "loss of aesthetic value."[3]

Another case, again in Louisiana, resulted in an award for the mental anguish of the damaged tree owner. A house mover, needing more space to accomplish his task, proceeded to remove limbs from six pecan trees on the property of an extremely upset woman. The court found actual property damages of $117.36. Again, unhappy with the measly sum, the judge considered the agitation of the injured owner. He took into account that the pecan trees had been planted by her grandfather sixty years earlier and tended by her father, who had just died. She was awarded an extra $1,250 for mental anguish.[4]

It is too soon to tell how courts in other states will respond when asked for to compensate tree owners for aesthetic loss and mental anguish. If the tree that has been lost was a huge spreading oak, housed by wildlife, climbed by the children or planted by a loved and departed spouse, courts may be receptive to the idea.

Out-of-Pocket Expenses

Any money reasonably spent to try to save an injured tree or remove a dead one, or to cover the loss, can often be recovered as part of actual damages. This includes the cost of appraisals, cleaning up debris and repairing the yard. If you missed time from work to cope with—or try to stop—the injury, or incurred medical bills because the incident made you ill, you can also sue for these costs, but you will have to convince the judge they really resulted from the tree problem. Some states also allow court costs and attorneys' fees to be awarded if a neighbor must sue over the loss.

Adjustments to the Actual Loss

If an insurance company compensated the tree owner for part of the loss, the amount paid must be subtracted from the damages claimed (unless the company must be repaid; see "What To Do If a Neighbor Damages Your Tree," below). Once this adjustment is made, the amount is the real amount of the loss.

THE IMPORTANCE OF COURT PRECEDENTS

Decisions made by courts are called the common law. It exists alongside statutes and ordinances as an interpretation of them, and it can stand alone in areas of the law that legislatures haven't addressed. Whenever a judge writes an opinion deciding a case, the opinion becomes part of the common law. This court-made law becomes a "precedent," which serves as a guide to future courts faced with a similar situation.

If the decision was made by the highest court in a state (usually the state supreme court), that ruling binds the other courts in that state until time, custom and social change lead the court to change the doctrine, or the law is changed by the legislature. If it was rendered by a lower state court, it is typically implemented, but not necessarily binding on courts in that state. Similarly, courts are not obligated to follow other state courts' decisions, but judges are often influenced by them.

Double or Triple Damages (Statutory Damages)

YOUR STATE'S LAW

Appendix 1 lists citations to every state's tree laws. To read your state law, go to your public library or county law library. Chapter 13, *Legal Research*, explains how to find a particular statute.

Almost every state has a statute that makes people who deliberately injure someone else's tree liable to the owner for two or three times the amount of actual monetary loss. These civil penalties, which protect the owners of trees by providing harsh deterrents to would-be trespassers or tree pirates, have been described by one judge as a punishment for stealing.[5] Although many of these laws were originally designed to protect the large timber grower, they are just as applicable to you and your next-door neighbor.

In California, for example, if you wrongfully injure or remove timber, trees or underwood, you are liable for triple the amount of actual damages to the owner. If you did not do the damage intentionally or you made a mistake, then the amount owed is twice the compensatory sum.[6] In Maine, unless the damage was done by mistake, the law provides for triple damages to the owner plus attorney fees and court costs.[7]

A few states, such as Alabama, make the wrongdoer liable for a specific dollar amount for damage to a tree, depending on its size and sometimes its kind.[8] An example would be $50 for an oak tree with a diameter of two feet, money owed to the owner by the cutter.

A very few states do not have statutes that protect injured tree owners. In those states, normally the owner can only be compensated for actual damages.

Whether or not someone who damages a tree is liable for double or triple damages under one of these statutes depends on the person's intent.

Someone who makes an honest mistake and injures another's trees is responsible at the least for reimbursing the owner for the actual damage. But in most states, she probably won't have to pay the double or triple damages many statutes allow if the destruction was unintentional.

Example: While thinning out trees on his property, an Alabama man relied on a map that he honestly believed reflected his boundary lines. The map, however, was hopelessly out of date, and he removed trees that were actually on his neighbor's land. When the neighbor sued, the local court slapped him with actual damages of $2,500 for the trees, plus a penalty of $2,590. The penalty was authorized by the statute that penalized willful conduct that harmed another's trees. He appealed to the state supreme court, and the justices ruled that his honest mistake should not have triggered the second sum. The penalty portion was removed.[9]

On the other hand, a person who intentionally injures a neighbor's tree and is sued will probably end up paying double or triple the amount of actual damages to the owner.

Example: A determined tree cutter in California waited until the owner was out of town, and then sneaked a tree service in and removed her offensive trees. The judge found that his action was willful and malicious, and that the unsuspecting woman was deprived of beauty, shade and shelter. Verdict: triple the amount of actual damages, as allowed by California statute.[10] Did the misguided man think that she wouldn't notice or just wouldn't care?

Punitive Damages

Punitive damages are an extra sum of money tacked on to an award in a civil lawsuit as a way of punishing the wrongdoer. As discussed above, many state statutes allow actual damages to be doubled or tripled if the court finds that a tree was intentionally damaged or removed; essentially, this allows for punitive damages.

Occasionally, however, extra punitive damages are added even above the statutory doubling or tripling of actual loss. This happens when the conduct of the person responsible for the harm is especially outrageous, reckless or malicious.

Although most judges have the authority to award punitive damages, in a few states small claims court judges cannot award them. Normally, you must request punitive damages separately from all other damages. If your neighbor acted maliciously, they may well be appropriate.

Example: This case from Maine gives us a real understanding of the legal term "maliciously." We can use our imaginations as to what the relationship was between these neighbors, and we can wonder how in the world it all started. A man was sued for going next door, moving his neighbor's fence, cutting down her ash tree, mowing over her rhubarb and peony beds, digging up her pole beans and pulling up the boundary stakes. He also threw her animal house over a wall. When this mess finally came before the court, the woman was awarded double damages (this was in 1981; Maine later changed its statute to allow triple damages). She was also given an extra $3,000 in punitive damages.[11] Surely this was a high price to pay for what sounds like a temper tantrum.

CRIMINAL PENALTIES

In many states, intentionally harming someone else's trees is a criminal act. The person responsible for the damage can be arrested, fined and jailed. For example, in California it is a misdemeanor punishable by a fine of not more than $1,000 or a sentence of not more than six months in the county jail or both.[12]

Michigan also makes the intentional act a crime, a misdemeanor that carries a punishment of imprisonment for not more than 90 days, a fine of not more than $100 or both, plus restitution to the owner.[13] And in the District of Columbia, someone who maliciously cuts down or destroys a tree or shrub or sapling valued at more than $50 faces imprisonment for not less than one year or more than three years.[14]

These criminal penalties can be important in the timber industry and Christmas tree business, where tree loss can affect a person's livelihood. They are rarely used in residential situations, but if one neighbor deliberately inflicts great harm on another, criminal punishment may be warranted. And if your hostile neighbor storms onto your property with an ax and begins hacking away at a favorite tree, your first reaction would probably be to call the police. The criminal laws are also effective as a threat to a nasty neighbor who is eyeing the sacred oak in your yard that rains debris on his.

WHAT TO DO IF A NEIGHBOR DAMAGES YOUR TREE

Okay, enough legal theory. Let's ground this discussion in the rich, thick dirt of real life. You come home from work one evening and find an empty spot in your yard (and in your heart). Your neighbor has taken his ax (and the law) into his own hands and killed your favorite maple. After the moaning, weeping and wringing of hands, what do you do?

Talk to the Neighbor

If you know who did the deed and you are still on speaking terms, step over and ask what in the heck happened. There may have been an awful mistake or accident, and the neighbor could be waiting with tail between legs, ready to reach for his wallet or call his insurance company (which may cover your loss).

Even if you don't know or like the neighbor, a short conversation probably won't make things worse. You really do want to know what happened—was it outright murder or the mistake of a new gardener? If the loss is small and a good relationship important, the problem may be solved over a cup of coffee.

Talk to Your Insurance Company

But what if the loss is large and your neighbor unrepentant, or you don't even know who's responsible? Promptly call your insurance company.

Most homeowners policies cover the destruction of your property when caused by someone else, and a lot of policies specifically cover damage to trees. If your own company pays you, it may then turn around and sue the neighbor. If that tactic is successful, you might even have your deductible portion returned to you.

Many policies, however, only pay up to a certain dollar amount per tree, often $500. They may pay an additional sum up to $500 for cleaning up debris or removing the dead tree. Because most trees are worth more than $500, you can still demand or sue for, if necessary, your actual loss from the neighbor.

If you sue successfully after your company has paid, you may have to reimburse the insurance company for what it paid. For instance, if the company pays you $500 and you are later awarded $2,000 from the neighbor, unless you deducted the $500 from your damages, you have been paid twice, and $500 may have to go back to the company.

Some companies provide a release form that will allow you to go ahead and sue without refunding any of what you win to them. When you have a large loss, be sure to find out from your insurance agent what the company does in this situation, and try to obtain a release before you sue the neighbor.[15]

If the neighbor responsible for the harm is also insured, his insurance company might pay you when he notifies it. This method of recovery is preferable because the limit on amount in a homeowner's own policy doesn't apply. Under the liability portion of some policies, when the insured person damages someone else's property, unless the damage was done intentionally, the company will pay for all of the damage—anything the neighbor could be found legally liable for.

An insurance company may require a police report before it will pay for the damage. When the damage appears to have been intentional, promptly call your local police station, which may send an officer over or ask you to come down to the station. The officer will ask you questions, possibly look at the damage, and fill out a form. In those states that make tree cutting a crime, you will be asked if you want to press charges, and the procedure explained to you. The police report itself will provide an official record of what happened, when and what you have lost. If the police officer doesn't give you a copy, ask for one.

Document Your Loss

Get your camera and take photographs. Hopefully, you have "before" pictures of your house and yard, taken for insurance purposes; now you can compare them to the "after" snapshots. You can use the pictures to show your insurance company or, if necessary, a court what you have lost. They will help to show the diminished market value of the property.

If your tree can be replaced, obtain a written estimate of the cost. If it cannot, refer to the kinds of losses for which you're entitled to compensation ("What the Owner Can Sue For," above). Convert what you think you have lost to a money amount. Keep all receipts and a detailed list of any costs you incur.

Get Copies of the Law

Presenting the neighbor with a copy of the relevant state statute might result in prompt action and prevent a lawsuit.

Look at the chart in Appendix 1 and see if your state has a statute on tree damage. If so, write down the citation number. Many public libraries have copies of the state statutes. Your local law library, usually located inside or next to the county courthouse, will have them. Make several copies of your statutes on damage to trees.

If your state doesn't have a statute, you can use a court opinion as a guide if you like. To find one that applies to your situation, you will have to do some research in a law library. (See Chapter 13, *Legal Research*.)

Ask for What Is Due You

The next step is to write a letter to the person at fault. This may sound like a waste of time if you have already had a fruitless conversation, but often it is not. It is amazing how many people never get what is owed to them simply because they don't make a formal demand for it. Later, if you do end up in court, you will find that in some states you can't win without proving you sent a demand letter. The letter also tells the judge that you attempted to settle the problem before coming to court. If your loss can be replaced, write a letter like the one shown below.

26 Elm Drive
Happy Hollow, CA 94260

May 4, 19__

Mr. Tom Turner
28 Elm Drive
Happy Hollow, CA 94260

Dear Mr. Turner,

On April 30, you were responsible for the destruction of my fifteen-foot maple tree. I have consulted Nona's Nursery and enclose their estimate of $600 for them to replace it with a similar tree. Please send a check to me for this amount.

I am sure that you will wish to attend to this matter as soon as possible. I expect to hear from you within the next two weeks.

Sincerely yours,

Wilma Ward

Enclose a copy of the statute if you think it will help, even though you are not requesting the double or triple damages that may be allowed by your state's statute. Since you are asking only for replacement value, seeing the law may scare the neighbor so badly that you receive a check the next day. Remember that it is a waste of time to sling insults, even if they are deserved. Be polite, be firm and keep a copy of the letter. And give the person a reasonable amount of time to respond before you go running to the courthouse.

Consider Mediation

If your efforts with the neighbor are not producing results, you may want to suggest mediation—the process of sitting down with the neighbor and a neutral third party to work out an agreement. This is inexpensive and keeps the neighbors in control of their own decisions. Many communities even have free neighborhood mediation services.

Mediation can be extremely effective when one neighbor owes money to another. Fear of the enormous expense in a tree damage case could be the reason for the neighbor cutting off communication with you. If you are willing to be flexible, for instance simply arranging several partial payments instead of one big sum, a mediated agreement is ideal. And if salvaging a good neighbor relationship for the future is important, even lowering your demands could be far preferable to a hostile and expensive lawsuit. (See Chapter 14 for more on the mediation process.)

Suing the Neighbor

If the loss is large, the act was intentional and the neighbor is nasty, you may have no choice but to sue the neighbor for your loss. First, try a stiffer letter, like the one below, that lets the neighbor know your intentions.

14 Oak Lane
Neighborly, CA 95327

May 3, 19__

Mrs. Alice Adams
16 Oak Lane
Neighborly, CA 95327

Dear Mrs. Adams,

On April 30, you were responsible for the wrongful and intentional destruction of my large redwood tree. I have researched the law and found that you are liable to me for three times the amount of my loss. You will see that this is correct by reading the enclosed state statute.

The tree is irreplaceable, and the market value of my property has been diminished because of your action. I have enclosed two separate appraisals of the property. They both estimate the diminished value at $3,000. Your legal liability to me under state law is therefore $9,000.

Please contact me immediately so that we may settle this matter. Otherwise, I will be forced to take legal action against you.

Sincerely yours,

Paul Palmer

The letter shows that you know the law and you mean business. You may well hear from the neighbor or her insurance company.

If your requests elicit no response, or the neighbor calls you and tells you where to go in an unfriendly manner, sit down and do some serious thinking. What do you really want: Another tree? Compensation? Revenge? How much time, energy and money are you willing to commit to this dispute? Before you pick up the phone and call a lawyer, think again. Attorney's fees can eat up a good part of any amount you win unless you are in a state which allows you to recover attorney's fees in the lawsuit. And if you do hire a lawyer and file a formal lawsuit, you may be dealing with the tree drama for several years.

Fortunately, if you must sue, there is an easier, cheaper and faster alternative to hiring a lawyer. You can use small claims court, without an attorney. The amount of money you can ask for is limited—usually from $2,000 to $5,000. It is sometimes wiser to just ask for this limit even if your loss is much larger. You won't have to pay attorney's fees, and the case will be resolved much more quickly—you can get a new tree, plant it and get on with your life. (See Chapter 15, *Small Claims Court*.)

PREVENTING DAMAGE

A neighbor sometimes gives warning to a tree owner that harm is on its way. If your tree is dropping huge amounts of leaves on someone else's property, beginning to shade a treasured vegetable garden or, especially, starting to block an expensive view, be aware of it. The neighbor could be sending signals to you, ranging all the way from nasty looks and remarks about the tree to actual threats to chop it down. If you think the tree is in danger and you want to protect it, don't just sit there until the neighbor gasses up his chainsaw. Do something.

A Neighborly Approach

First, have a chat with the neighbor—and be ready to compromise. You may learn that your beloved tree is driving the neighbor absolutely crazy or actually harming the value of his property. Try to work out some solution you both can live with that will preserve the tree. For example, a good trimming may benefit both the tree and your neighbor's disposition. If you can't agree, this is a good time to suggest mediation. You may find out that the tree is only the most obvious of the problems that need to be talked out. (See Chapter 14 for information on mediation.)

If you still suspect trouble, make sure that the neighbor knows the law. Share your copy of this book with him or give him a copy of the statute. Make sure that he knows what your rights are as an owner, and that you fully intend to enforce them.

A Legal Approach

Even knowing the law, some people may hate an offending tree so much that they still intend to chop it down. If you think that you are in immediate danger of losing a beloved tree to a neighbor, make it clear to the neighbor that you will call the police if the tree is harmed, and that you will sue for all that state law allows.

You may want to hire an attorney to write the neighbor a formal letter and follow up with a phone call. Many lawyers are very good at this type of approach, which normally isn't prohibitively expensive—probably $100 or $200. However, if this approach only seems to confirm that the neighbor is bent on tree mayhem, you may want to hire a lawyer to ask a court for an emergency temporary restraining order (TRO) to prevent the neighbor from going ahead. A judge will consider the request promptly—within a day or so—and rule on it favorably if you can convince the judge that the neighbor really poses an immediate threat to the tree. If the judge issues a TRO and the neighbor violates it, he will be found in contempt of court and may land in jail or be fined.

The TRO is only temporary, however, and just a first legal step. It must later be replaced with a permanent order from the judge. If your neighbor decides to fight, your fairly simple dispute may escalate into legal warfare. You could be getting into a big, expensive mess to save your tree.

If there is a question about whose tree it really is—for instance, a threatened tree is close to the boundary line and your neighbor claims it's on her side—you can file a lawsuit asking the court for "declaratory relief." This means a judge will determine what your rights are. Again, keep in mind that this sort of legal approach will cost a lot of time and money. It is far better to make an earnest effort to work the problem out with the neighbor and avoid the courts.

---

[1] Cal. Civ. Code § 833.

[2] *Lyman v. Hale*, 11 Conn. 177 (1836).

[3] *Howes v. Rocquien*, 457 So. 2d 1220 (La. App. 1984).

[4] *Harkness v. Porter*, 521 So. 2d 832, *writ denied*, 523 So. 2d 1323 (La. App. 1988).

[5] *Hickox v. Vester Morgan, Inc.*, 439 So. 2d 95 (Ala. 1983).

[6] Cal. Civ. Code § 3346.

[7] Me. Rev. Stat. Ann. tit. 14, § 7552.

[8] Ala. Code § 35-14-1.

[9] *Vick v. Tisdale*, 56 Ala. App. 565, 324 So. 2d 279 (1975).

[10] *Butler v. Zeiss*, 63 Cal. App. 73, 218 P. 54 (1923).

[11] *Auburn Harpswell Ass'n. v. Day*, 438 A.2d 234 (Me. 1981).

[12] Cal. Penal Code § 384(a).

[13] Mich. Comp. Laws Ann. § 750.382.

[14] D.C. Code § 22-3108.

[15]Homeowners insurance policies vary on whether they require an insured person to reimburse the company if the person is later awarded money for the same loss. Some write into the conditions of insurance that this is to be done unless the company issues a waiver before a lawsuit. Check with your insurance agent to determine the procedure under your particular policy.

Encroachment:
Invading Branches and Roots

Disputes between neighbors can arise when trees do what they do naturally and predictably: they grow. The tree owner may be blissfully unaware that the mighty oak has crept outward as well as upward, and that it now hangs over a neighbor's property. A tree owner who does notice may assume that the neighbor is delighted by the shade and beauty. This is often the exact situation before an unhappy disagreement and even a lawsuit between neighbors.

Frequently the problem is a matter of degree. A few limbs over the fence present no problem; several years later those same limbs, now huge and pressing against the garage, are indeed quite a problem. The same principle applies to debris raining down from above and roots creeping underneath. A little autumn shedding is acceptable, but not clogged gutters every few days, and definitely not broken pipes from aggressive roots.

The law often reflects these matters of degree. For a simple inconvenience, the neighbor himself is usually expected to trim away any branches or roots on his own property that are a bother. If the injury to the neighbor is more severe, the neighbor may be able to sue the tree owner.

But there are several strategies to deal with encroaching branches or roots that are far simpler (and cheaper) than going to court.

LOOKING FOR HELP

You may not have to lift a finger to trim invading branches or roots. In some cases, notifying the city, a utility company or a homeowners association will bring prompt action.

Local Government

Cities routinely prune trees that are on city property or that might endanger city property. Just bringing the problem to the attention of the correct department may be all it takes to get the tree trimmed.

To see if the tree is on a strip of city property, go to city hall and look at the city map. If it is, notify the city department in charge of tree maintenance. In some cities, this is the public works department; others have a tree service office. The city clerk can point you to the right office.

Even if the tree is on private property, the city may trim it back if it might interfere with city property—for example, by obstructing a sidewalk or blocking the view at an intersection.

The city might also order the owner to trim or even remove a tree that is in violation of a local ordinance. Local rules often govern the following:

Trees that are used as fences. When trees are planted close together and used as a barrier, they are natural fences and may be subject to local laws regulating fences. Fence laws can govern the height allowed and also the location of fences on property. (See Chapter 11, *Fences.*)

Trees that block a neighbor's view. In a few cities, if a tree is blocking a neighbor's view, the neighbor can follow a procedure outlined in a view ordinance to force the owner to trim it back. (See Chapter 8, *Obstruction of View.*)

Trees that are prohibited by law or exceed height limits. Some local ordinances have a list of undesirable trees that are not allowed in the area. If the tree is of a species that is prohibited, the neighbor can be ordered to remove it, or the city may remove it for her. And occasionally, cities restrict tree heights in certain areas—for example, near an airport.

Diseased or unsound trees. Many cities require the owner to remove dead and hazardous trees. And a few cities consider any damaged or diseased tree their responsibility, rather than the owner's. A city crew will simply come in and take care of the problem. (See Chapter 5, *Unsound Limbs and Trees.*)

You can find find out about local laws by calling your the building or planning commission or reading the ordinances yourself at the public library. (See Chapter 13, *Legal Research*).

Utility Companies

Check for utility use around the tree. A utility company, such as the telephone company, will trim a tree that might damage its equipment—for example, if limbs are growing into or hanging menacingly over the lines.

Homeowners Associations

If you live in a subdivision or planned development, residents may be subject to the restrictions in a document called the Covenants, Conditions and Restrictions (CC&Rs). Each property owner's deed will refer to the CC&Rs. CC&Rs sometimes dictate the location, kind and especially height of trees. For example, they may require keeping tree height to roof level, or set an absolute height limit.

When an owner has a tree that is in violation of these regulations, a neighbor can notify the homeowners association. It may formally direct the owner to trim the tree. Some homeowners associations enforce deed restrictions by applying sanctions to a member in violation—for instance, removing swimming pool privileges. Some will even sue a resident who doesn't cooperate. And one neighbor can sue the other for enforcement of deed covenants, although this is complicated and expensive and is appropriate only in extreme cases.

TRIMMING A NEIGHBOR'S TREE: THE RIGHT OF SELF-HELP

Property owners in every state have the right to cut off branches and roots that stray into their property. In most states this is the only help provided by the law, even when damage from a tree is substantial.

This right to cut away at somebody else's property is not written down as a state statute or local ordinance. It is a common law right, created by court decisions. The reasoning behind the rule is that neighbors should sort out their own problems, along with a distaste for lawsuits between neighbors cluttering up the courts. Numerous judges also share the sentiment that a property owner should have the wit and responsibility to prevent harm to his property when he can do so, that "his remedy is in his own hands."[1]

Generally, the neighbor who does the trimming must pay for it himself. In Hawaii, however, a neighbor who faces substantial damage from a tree may have the trimming done and then demand payment for it from the tree's owner.[2]

Limits on Self-Help

A neighbor who cuts back limbs or roots of a tree belonging to someone else must stay within certain guidelines. The neighbor:

- can trim only up to the boundary line

- needs permission to enter the owner's property, unless the limbs threaten to cause imminent and grave harm[3]
- may not cut down the tree itself
- cannot destroy the tree by the trimming.

A permit may be necessary in some cities for any tree trimming or for pruning certain species of trees; check with the city clerk's office.

If a large tree is involved and the tree service must climb it or use ladders to reach some of the branches, permission of the owner must be obtained before the trimming.

It's wise to use a professional tree service whenever possible. Cutting branches and roots stresses a tree at the very least. If a neighbor doesn't know what he is doing, especially when large branches are involved, he could destroy the tree unintentionally.

Destruction of the tree is not measured by aesthetic appearance but by the health of the tree. When a tree is located near the boundary line, heavy pruning can produce a pretty funny looking object. However, if the tree is alive and healthy after the cutting, the neighbor has stayed within his legal rights. On the other hand, if the main trunk system is damaged and the tree withers away, he can be liable to the owner for money damages. (See Chapter 3, *When a Tree Is Injured or Destroyed.*)

An owner who fears trimming will destroy the tree can hire a lawyer, go to court and ask a judge for a court order preventing the trimming.

Before You Cut

If you decide to trim encroaching branches or roots of a neighbor's tree, always warn the tree owner before you hack away at the tree. If you want to do a major job of pruning, the owner may well want to take responsibility

PESKY ROOTS

The risk of causing permanent damage to a tree has always been particularly great when roots, not branches, are removed. In the past, blocking tree roots was not only intimidating but tricky as well, because chemicals used to block invading roots often poisoned the tree itself.

Fortunately, a new method of stopping invasive roots is easier, less expensive and unlikely to harm the tree itself. It consists of cutting the roots and installing a physical barrier (a synthetic shield) to prevent regrowth. A good tree service can provide further information. You can either tackle the job yourself or have the professionals do it.

for the work to assure the health and symmetry of the tree. An effective approach might be to offer to share the cost of trimming the whole tree.

Another practical reason to give the neighbor notice is to prevent a breach of the peace. Tree owners can be extremely protective; the last thing you want to do is create a screaming disturbance that lands you and the neighbor on the evening news.

If the Owner Is Uncooperative

If a tree owner objects to your trimming plans, you should sit down and describe the situation and your intentions in writing. A sample letter is below.

801 Shady Street
Greenacres, CA 96678

Oct. 17, 19__

Dear Edith,

As I told you yesterday, I am concerned about the encroachment of your elm tree over my property. The leaves this fall are so numerous that I have paid someone $80 so far to remove them from my yard. This will have to be done again at least twice within the next few weeks. I am also alarmed by the new crack in my patio and wish to avoid more serious harm from the roots. The branches and roots have become a nuisance to me.

I have engaged Loving Care Tree Service to trim back the limbs over my property and to cut and block the roots near the patio. They have assured me that the health of the tree will not be endangered and that the trimming will be done with skill and care. It is my legal right to take this action, and I hope that you find this arrangement satisfactory.

Sincerely yours,

John

Hopefully, this will end Edith's objection. She's worried about the tree, and John has given her reassurance. Paying a professional service is probably worth the money to maintain a good relationship. John has also made it clear that he means business and gives his reasons. Edith may seek a legal opinion and that will be the end of her objection.

But suppose Edith doesn't bother to learn the law. Instead, she calls John and tells him that she will meet him outside with a shotgun if he so much as touches one twig. Does John wait until she is not at home and then sneak the tree service in? This does happen, but it's a poor choice. Angry neighbors seek revenge, and problems with Edith would escalate.

A better approach is to send another letter, explaining the law in more detail. Unfortunately, because the right to lop off branches and roots is a common law right, there is no specific statute or ordinance waiting in the library to be photocopied and mailed to Edith. John could do a little legal research and present her with a court opinion on the subject. (If you need to do this, read Chapter 13, *Legal Research*.) Under these volatile circumstances, however, it may be easier to pay a visit to a lawyer. Often a letter on a legal letterhead will get prompt attention and cooperation. Some lawyers will write a letter for around $100, and once in a while this can be money well spent.

If the dispute is still not resolved, any good neighbor relationship has probably vanished. John may choose to proceed to trim at his personal peril. But he can also contemplate remedies other than self-help.

One good alternative for neighbors who can't agree on tree trimming may be mediation—that is, working out a solution with help from a neutral third party can help you resolve the problems without resorting to a courtroom. Whether you are dealing with a protective owner who won't allow trimming or one who won't accept responsibility (see "A Tree Owner's Legal Responsibilities," below), mediation can help you resolve your dispute without resorting to a lawsuit.

The underlying problem with encroaching branches and invading roots is usually that of expense. Pruning a large tree can run anywhere from $300 to over $1,000. In mediation, a compromise is possible that considers who is willing and able to pay what. You may also work out a prevention program that could later save time, money and civility. Chapter 14 explains how the mediation process works.

A TREE OWNER'S LEGAL RESPONSIBILITIES

Generally, a neighbor who is bothered or worried by encroaching branches or roots of a healthy tree cannot sue—his only remedy is trimming the tree himself.[4]

Courts in several states, however, allow a neighbor to sue when invading roots or branches cause serious harm to the neighbor's property. And in three states, California, Louisiana and Washington, a neighbor can sue the tree owner over encroaching branches or roots even when the tree is healthy. The court can order the owner to compensate the neighbor for any harm suffered.

States Where Neighbors Can Always Sue

In California, Louisiana and Washington, encroaching branches and roots that interfere with the enjoyment of a neighbor's property are always considered a private nuisance to the neighbor. That means that a neighbor may cut them off, sue the owner for any damage or sue to make the owner cut the branches.[5]

In Washington state, a court once ruled that just having to rake up pine needles was enough of an interference in the neighbor's enjoyment of property to justifying suing the owner of the tree.[6]

Louisiana law places the burden of trimming the tree on the owner when branches or roots interfere with a neighbor's enjoyment of his property.[7]

In any of these states, if you are on the receiving end of unwanted foliage, you don't have to put up with it. The owner is responsible for any injury done by her trees, including the shedding of debris. You may be able to convince a neighbor in these states to resolve the problem and avoid a lawsuit simply by informing her of the law.

If you are the owner of a tree in these states, and in a dispute with a neighbor over the tree, you might as well face your responsibility and work out an agreement with the neighbor. Otherwise you could find a court doing it for you.

Example: In a 1981 Louisiana case, a fifty foot oak was wreaking havoc on a neighbor by raining debris, and the neighbor sued. The judge went out to the property and inspected the tree. He discovered that trimming it back to the property line would destroy it. To save the tree and the neighbor's sanity, he ordered the owner to keep the tree trimmed ten feet away from the neighbor's roof. The tree owner was also responsible for the debris. The owner had to pay to screen and repair the neighbor's gutters and to have the debris removed once a month from then on.[8]

States Where Neighbors Can Sue for Substantial Damage

In Hawaii, Kansas, Minnesota, Oklahoma, New Mexico and Virginia, courts have ruled that encroaching branches or roots are a legal nuisance when they cause or threaten substantial harm to the neighbor.

How much damage is enough to justify a lawsuit? Too much shade, leaves and debris are not enough. The court in Virginia used the term "sensible damage" for a measure.[9] The term has interpreted to mean structural damage to property—damaged roofs or walls, crushed pipes or cracked foundations.[10] A New Mexico court has stated that when there is imminent danger of substantial harm, a neighbor may sue the tree owner to cut back the branches or roots to prevent damage.[11]

And in Hawaii, if a neighbor faces substantial damage from a tree, he may also have the trimming done himself and then demand payment for it from the owner.[12]

States Where an Owner May Be Liable

Other state courts have allowed a neighbor to sue over encroaching branches and roots or indicated that they would do so when the right case came along. In the following states, a lawsuit would be worth a try if the neighbor has suffered serious structural damage to property:[14]

- Arizona
- Idaho
- Indiana
- Michigan
- Mississippi
- New Jersey
- New York
- Ohio
- Texas

In other states, a lawsuit may also be worth a try, but it may require making a different kind of legal argument. Instead of arguing that the encroaching branches or roots are legally a nuisance, a neighbor might have better luck claiming that the tree owner had a duty to prevent severe harm to a neighbor when possible.

For example, in 1986 an Illinois court ordered a land owner whose tree roots had damaged a neighbor's garage to compensate the neighbor for the damage.[15] The tree owner, the court said, had a duty to take "reasonable steps to prevent damage" to the neighbor's property. This case was decided just one year after the same court ruled

THE HEALTHY TREE ITSELF

A neighbor who sues over a roots or branches of a neighbor's tree can ask only that the offending branches and roots be removed. A court won't order a healthy tree removed if the problem can be solved by less drastic measures. A Minnesota court, for example, ordered a tree cut down because to have trimmed it would have killed it, and the tree was creating major problems for the neighbor.[13]

Generally, however, a court will order a whole tree removed only if it is rotten, dangerously unsound or causing grave harm. (See Chapter 5, *Unsound Limbs and Trees.*)

that a tree owner had no responsibility to his neighbor when the neighbor sued, claiming the tree was a nuisance.[16]

Most neighbors who go to court over an encroaching tree use small claims court, where they just tell the judge what happened and don't get bogged down in legal theory. But it can't hurt to be aware of this promising legal argument.

Judges in most states, however, still expect neighbors to protect themselves from damage when possible. For example, if a large limb was breaking its way through your roof, and you sue for the damage, the judge may ask why you didn't just cut off the limb.

If a neighbor admired or helped maintain a tree, she may also have trouble turning around and then claiming it is a nuisance to her. And someone who chooses to pour a patio or build a house fully aware of the growing roots from a neighbor's tree beneath may have no case.

RESEARCHING THE LAW

If you want to sue a tree owner, you can read what judges in your state have actually said about encroaching trees by doing some research in the law library. See Chapter 13, *Legal Research*.

States Where the Law Is Unclear

Some state courts haven't ruled on the question of whether or not a neighbor can sue the owner of healthy tree. For a successful lawsuit, the damage done by the tree will probably have to be substantial. And some states may never budge from requiring neighbors to handle these problems themselves, out of court.

GOING TO COURT

For a court order making the owner cut back the tree, the neighbor will have to use regular trial court (not small claims court), which probably entails hiring a lawyer.

A neighbor who is suing only for compensation should bring suit in small claims court, if the amount requested is within the state's small claims limit. Most states limit small claims to $2,000 to $5,000. (Chapter 15, *Small Claims Court*, lists each state's limit.)

Encroaching trees can cause a lot of harm, especially when concrete foundations are involved. But even if a claim is over the small claims court limit, you may want to stick with small claims court and just ask for the limit. If you have to hire a lawyer and use regular court, between the lawyer fees and the time it takes, you still may come out ahead in small claims court.

Notifying the Owner

Notifying the tree owner of the law actually avoids the courtroom in most cases. Just talking to the owner and asking him to please cut back the tree can be very effective, once the owner understands his responsibility.

If the owner won't cooperate, the neighbor should write a letter. This letter is called a demand letter. Many small claims court judges require proof of the demand before a lawsuit. A sample letter is below.

2345 Shady Avenue
Oakton, CA 95544

July 7, 19__

Dear Mike,

   As I pointed out to you two weeks ago, the
limbs of your oak tree are pressing against my
garage, and the roots are buckling part of my
driveway. I have obtained the enclosed estimate of $500 to repair the broken concrete.

   According to the law, these branches and
roots are a nuisance to me, and you are
responsible for my damages and for cutting
back the tree.

   Please have this tree cut back immediately
before it causes further damage, and contact
me about the repair bill. Otherwise, I will be
forced to take legal action.

Sincerely yours,

Robin

Keep a copy of the letter and give the neighbor time to
respond. Before you head to court, make one last attempt
to avoid the bitterness of a lawsuit and suggest mediation
to the neighbor. (See Chapter 14, *Mediation.*)

What the Neighbor Must Prove

A neighbor who files a nuisance lawsuit against a tree
owner must prove several things to the court:

- The tree belongs to the person being sued

- The branches or roots are over or under the neighbor's property
- The neighbor notified the tree owner in writing
- The tree adversely affects the neighbor, and what the damage is.

Figuring Damages

A neighbor who has suffered harm because of an encroaching tree is entitled to compensation (damages) for all repair costs, including money spent to fix or clean up the property. The Hawaii court awarded a neighbor the cost of having the tree trimmed, and other courts might do the same, especially if the trimming prevented further harm. The court will want to see proof in the form of receipts of amounts spent due to the tree and written estimates for work yet to be done.

If the property is seriously damaged and can't be fixed, the neighbor is entitled to the difference in the property value caused by the damage. A real estate appraiser can estimate the amount.

For more on how to use small claims court, see Chapter 15.

---

[1]*Michelson v. Nutting*, 275 Mass. 232, 175 N.E. 490 (1931).

[2]*Whitesell v. Houlton*, 2 Haw. App. 365, 632 P.2d 1077 (1981).

[3]This legal rule is called the doctrine of private necessity. Restatement (Second) of Torts, § 197 (1977).

[4]Some states, such as Florida, Massachusetts, Maryland and Missouri, have flatly refused to let neighbors sue over healthy encroaching branches and roots. *Gallo v. Heller*, 512 So. 2d 215 (Fla. App. 3 Dist. 1987); *Ponte v. Da Silva*, 388 Mass. 1008, 446 N.E.2d 77 (1983); *Melnick v. C.S.X. Corp.*, 312 Md. 511, 540 A.2d 1133 (1988); *Hasapopoulos v. Murphy*, 689 S.W.2d 118 (Mo. App. 1985).

[5]For example, see *Fick v. Nelson*, 98 Cal. 2d 683, 220 P.2d 752 (1950).

[6]*Gostina v. Ryland*, 199 P. 298 (Wash. 1921).

[7]La. Civ. Code art. 688.

[8]*Scott v. Ramos*, 399 So. 2d 1266, *writ denied*, 404 So. 2d 279 (La. App. 1981).

[9]*Smith v. Holt*, 174 Va. 213, 5 S.E.2d 492 (1939).

[10]For example, see *Pierce v. Cassidy*, 711 P.2d 766 (Kan. App. 1985). In Oklahoma, clogged sewer pipes were enough damage. *Mead v. Vincent*, 187 P.2d 994 (Okla. 1947).

[11]*Abbinett v. Fox*, 703 P.2d 177 (N.M. App. 1985).

[12]*Whitesell v. Houlton*, 2 Haw. App. 365, 632 P.2d 1077 (1981).

[13]*Holmberg v. Bergin*, 285 Minn. 250, 172 N.W.2d 739 (1969).

[14]These are the court cases where a lawsuit in nuisance was allowed or the possibility suggested. The written court opinions can be found in a law library. (See Chapter 13, *Legal Research*.)

Arizona: *Cannon v. Dunn*, 700 P.2d 502 (Ariz. App. 1985).

Idaho: *Lemon v. Curington*, 306 P.2d 1091 (Idaho 1957).

Indiana: *Luke v. Scott*, 187 N.E. 63 (Ind. 1933).

Michigan: *Hickey v. Michigan Cent. R. Co.*, 55 N.E. 989 (Mich. 1893).

Mississippi: *Buckingham v. Elliott*, 62 Miss. 296, 52 Am. Rep. 188 (1884); *Grierfield v. Gibraltar Fire & Marine Ins. Co.*, 199 Miss. 175, 24 So. 2d 356 (1946). Tree must be "noxious."

New Jersey: *D'Andrea v. Guglietta*, 208 N.J. Super. 31, 504 A.2d 1196 (1986).

New York: *Turner v. Coppola*, 102 Misc. 2d 1043, 424 N.Y.S.2d 864 (1980); *Loggia v. Grobe*, 128 Misc. 2d 973, 491 N.Y.S.2d 973 (1985). There must be very substantial harm; the neighbor is expected to reasonably protect the property through self-help before suing.

Ohio: *Rautsaw v. Clark*, 22 Ohio App. 3d 20, 488 N.E.2d 243 (1985).

Texas: *Rossi v. Johnson*, 355 S.W.2d 582 (Tex. App. 1962).

[15]*Chandler v. Larson*, 148 Ill. App. 3d 1032, 102 Ill. Dec. 691, 500 N.E.2d 584 (1986).

[16]*Bandy v. Boise*, 132 Ill. App. 3d 832, 87 Ill. Dec. 714, 477 N.E.2d 840 (1985).

Unsound Limbs and Trees

The tree will wither long before it falls.

—Byron

PREVENTING DAMAGE

If you own large and older trees, it is probably wise to invest in an annual inspection by a tree expert. I f you are a fearful neighbor, you could do the same thing. Getting an expert's opinion could reduce uncertainty and possibly avoid a disaster. Court decisions abound with the testimony of tree experts—sadly, most of them are called in only after the damage is done.

The flip side of the years of shelter provided by trees is that they grow old, become diseased and die. What was a source of great enjoyment can seemingly overnight become an unwelcome object of peril—especially when it hangs menacingly over the property of the next-door neighbor.

Even a cordial relationship between neighbors may be strained by the prospect of a large expense. Trimming or removing large trees is not a nickel and dime matter.

Smart tree owners keep an eye on the health of their trees. They may be liable for injury or property damage caused by an unsound tree, even if they wouldn't be liable for the problems caused by a healthy tree in similar circumstances.

Happily, there are ways to prevent harm from unsound trees, so neighbors don't end up in nasty court battles. This chapter explains them.

GETTING HELP FROM THE CITY GOVERNMENT

City governments often step in to take care of, or make the owner take care of, dangerous or unsound trees. If you are imperiled by someone else's tree, contact your local city or county government. Someone at city hall or a county courthouse can direct you to the appropriate office. (You may also get help from utility companies and homeowners associations; see Chapter 4, *Encroachment: Invasion of Branches and Roots.*)

Trees on Private Property

In many cities and towns, after the appropriate city office is notified of a dangerous or diseased tree it will demand that the owner eliminate the problem. In some cities, if the owner doesn't respond within a brief time—48 hours, for instance—the city will step in and remove the hazard. It then bills the owner for the cost. Some place a lien (legal claim) on the property if the owner doesn't pay.

A few cities remove hazardous trees, even on private property, when requested. They have the equipment and consider eliminating the danger a city responsibility.

Some cities have a general ordinance that prohibits maintaining any dangerous object or condition on private property. A menacing dead tree would violate such a law, and the city could issue a fine and demand that the owner comply with the ordinance.

Unfortunately, most cities do not have ordinances that cover dangerous trees on private property. If the tree menacing your property was damaged by a storm or other natural event, your city may take emergency action to protect you. We have all watched on television, for example, as crews work to clear dangerous situations after a disaster. But if a tree has simply grown old and died, you may not receive any help.

Trees That Threaten Public Property

If a dangerous tree is located on city property, the city is responsible for removing it. And when a large private tree is threatening to fall, city streets or sidewalks—and people using them—may be in the path of potential destruction. The city, in protecting its own interest, can protect you as well.

Sometimes it is unclear where city property begins and private property ends, especially in border areas near the streets. Many people live under the impression that their lots extend all the way to the curb. This is often not the case. The city may be responsible for a wide strip across what appears to be a private yard. To find out who owns the property a tree is located on, go to city hall and look at the official city maps.

TRIMMING A NEIGHBOR'S TREE: THE RIGHT OF SELF-HELP

A property owner always has the right to cut down dangerous limbs of a neighbor's tree that hang over his property. This is the right of self-help, of cutting off the offending branches up to the boundary line.

How a neighbor can legally exercise the right of self-help is explained in Chapter 4, *Encroachment.* The main points to remember are that a neighbor:

- may not go onto the neighbor's property when trimming, unless it's necessary to avert imminent danger
- may trim only up to the boundary line
- may not cut down the tree and
- may not destroy the tree itself.

When the branches are dead and dangerous, the owner would probably welcome having the neighbor trim the tree. Often it's the easiest, most expedient avenue a neighbor can take, especially if immediate action is necessary to avoid harm from branches.

One note of caution if you're considering trimming a neighbor's unsound tree: Although you probably have the legal right to go onto your neighbor's property to trim a tree so you can prevent serious damage to your property, we do not recommend any such deliberate trespass. You would be liable for any harm done, and if the danger is not as serious as you think it is, you could be arrested for trespass or sued. There is almost always another way to deal with the problem.

TALKING TO THE OWNER

If you're worried about the danger posed by a neighbor's unsound tree, and you can't fix the problem by trimming the branches yourself, ask the tree owner to remedy the situation. It may help to explain the owner's legal liability—that if he is warned of the danger and does nothing, he'll probably be liable for any damage that results. (See "After Damage from an Unsound Tree," below.) Prevention is likely to be much less expensive. (And if you decide to sue to try to force the neighbor to remove the dangerous trees or limbs, you'll need to show that the owner refused your requests to solve the problem.)

Expert Opinions

The most effective way to notify a tree owner that his tree is unsound and threatening you is to put it in writing, accompanied by an expert opinion on the tree's condition. Sometimes an expert will come out and give an opinion for free.

Qualified tree experts can be found by looking in the phone book under private tree services, arborists, horticulturists, landscape consultants,the U.S. Forestry Service, local government forestry services or university forestry or landscape architecture departments. If you can't find anything listed in your town, look under state government offices, under Department of Forestry, Division of Plant Industries or Landscape Architects Board.

Once you find an expert who confirms your fears, enclose the opinion when you write to the owner. A sample letter is below.

June 14, 19__

Dear Josh,

As I mentioned to you last week, several limbs of your oak tree that hang over my back yard are dead and in danger of falling. I enclose the opinion of a registered forester that confirms this dangerous situation. The dead limbs create a hazard and are a nuisance to me; I am afraid to go outside.

Please eliminate this risk by having them cut back immediately. Thank you.

Sincerely yours,

Monica

It's also a good idea to take photographs of the tree and keep copies of all correspondence with the neighbor.

Negotiation Procedures in Local Laws

Some cities have ordinances that set out a procedure to follow when a neighbor suspects that a tree is dangerous but the owner disagrees. Oakland, California is adopting such a law, which encourages neighbors to agree on a solution. If the owner refuses to have the tree removed, the law allows the neighbor to sue. And if a court rules in favor of the threatened neighbor, the tree owner can be fined another $1,000.

Neighborhood Mediation Services

When neighbors can't agree on what to do about a tree that at least one of them thinks is dangerous, mediation can help them resolve the problems without going to court. Many communities have free neighborhood mediation services.

The big problem with dead trees or limbs is usually the expense. Pruning or removing a large tree can run anywhere from $300 to over $1,000. In mediation, a compromise is possible that considers who is willing and able to pay what. (See Chapter 14, *Mediation.*)

SUING TO PREVENT DAMAGE

If a tree owner knows harm is likely from an unsound tree and does nothing, maintaining the tree may be considered an unreasonable use of property—which means it is, legally, a private nuisance.

That means a neighbor can sue the tree owner for interfering with the use and enjoyment of his property. He can ask the court to make the owner cut the limbs, remove the tree or pay compensation. He will need proof that the tree poses a real danger.

A neighbor who wants an order requiring the tree owner to eliminate the problem must sue in regular (not small claims) court, which probably involves hiring a lawyer.

But a neighbor who wants only monetary compensation can sue in small claims court, where lawyers are not necessary. A neighbor, for example, could ask for money to compensate him for not being able to enjoy his property. If he can't use his back yard for fear of a dead tree, he could ask for a reasonable sum per day—as much as $50 a day in some circumstances.

For a discussion of small claims court, see Chapter 15.

HOMEOWNERS INSURANCE

Most homeowners insurance policies allow payment for damage done to your own property if a neighbor's tree falls. (The insurance company will compensate you and then probably turn around and sue the neighbor.) If the company won't pay, or won't pay enough, you can sue the tree owner. (See "After Damage From an Unsound Tree," below.)

Homeowners policies also pay, under the liability section, for damage done to property of another by your tree, even if the damage is due to your carelessness.

The only time some policies won't pay is when damage is caused intentionally. So if you intentionally damage someone's property, don't expect your homeowners insurance to pay for it. But if you are warned that your tree presents a danger but do nothing, and the tree does in fact cause damage, your insurance will pay, because you did not intentionally cause the harm.

Surprisingly, a tree owner's liability insurance can create a problem for a neighbor threatened by a dangerous tree: It can sometimes encourage the owner to drag his feet or even ignore the neighbor. The problem arises because insurance pays only after the damage is done. This gives the owner a choice: incur heavy out-of-pocket expense to prevent harm, or do nothing until the tree falls and insurance steps in.

Insurance companies, however, do not enjoy paying large sums of money when a claim could have been avoided. If the company knows about the situation, it may order the policyholder to eliminate the dangerous condition on the property or face cancellation of the policy. And once a company does cancel a person's insurance, it can be quite difficult to get a policy from anybody else. Threatening a tree owner with a lawsuit can sometimes be very helpful because the owner will probably inquire of the insurance company whether or not he is covered. The company may then give the policyholder an ultimatum.

SOME THOUGHTS ABOUT INSURANCE

Liability insurance may even pay for punitive damages—a sum above the cost of actual damage to the injured person, designed to punish the wrongdoer. They are awarded when conduct has been outrageous or wanton. For instance, if a large dead tree—obvious to anyone—is threatening a neighbor's house, the neighbor begs the owner for help, and the owner refuses, the owner has shown reckless disregard for the neighbor's safety, and a court may award punitive damages.

There is much debate over whether or not liability insurance should cover punitive damages. If insurance companies refused to pay them, uncaring, reckless tree owners who know their inaction will cause grave harm would have strong motivation to act.

AFTER DAMAGE FROM AN UNSOUND TREE

There is a strong trend across the country toward making tree owners legally responsible for damage caused by unsound trees, if the owner knew or should have known that the damage was likely.[1]

The legal theory is that the owner, by not acting to prevent the harm, was "negligent." Negligence is conduct that is unreasonably careless under the circumstances. A failure to act can be negligent if a reasonable person would act under the circumstances.

Liability in Urban Areas

In most states, landowners in urban areas are legally liable for damage caused by an obviously unsound tree. That means that if a rotten limb or dead tree itself falls on a neighbor's property, and the owner knew or should have known of the danger, the neighbor can sue the tree owner for compensation for the damage.

When should an urban tree owner know a tree is endangering the neighbor? If the question goes to court, a judge will look at what should have been obvious to the owner: lack of foliage, for example, which signals a dead limb or tree, or a tree that is leaning precariously to one side.

The owner is not expected to be a tree expert. A city slicker could look elm disease in the face and not recognize a problem. And if a rotten tree falls but there was no outward or obvious sign of decay, the tree owner may not be liable, even if severe damage results.[2] A landowner who has a degree in forestry, however, could be alerted to danger from a casual observation of his property.

Because each situation is loaded with variable facts that could present problems in court, if you have questions about liability when an owner "should have known" a tree posed a danger, consult a local lawyer.

A TREE OWNER'S DILEMMA

Several years ago I had the privilege of living in a house sheltered by an enormous oak. The tree's limbs hung over our property and that of two neighbors.

One day in January, following a heavy rain, there was a thunderous crash. A 20-foot limb had fallen across the back yard, but caused no damage. There had been no warning, no sign of decay the previous summer. I called the local county agricultural extension service, whose expert took one look at the tree and refused to go in the yard. He predicted that many more limbs could come down, even though the tree itself was very much alive.

Because it was January (no foliage) and because the tree was watersoaked, a tree service couldn't go in and trim the tree. We would have to wait. Wait? I was terrified.

State law did not make tree owners liable for harm caused by a tree in this situation.[3] But it was simply against my nature to deny responsibility for my tree (keep this in mind when you approach a tree owner). I told the neighbors of the danger and we all huddled inside until the tree, or rather part of it, budded. Several limbs fell during this time, luckily with no damage.

When the tree service finally pruned the tree, I watched closely, pretending that I actually knew what the trimmers should and should not do, attempting in some way to be part of the decision-making process. Like most tree owners, I would have been most unhappy had the neighbors or a court been in charge of the work.

Liability in Rural Areas

In all states, the rule is that in a rural area, a tree owner is liable for harm caused by the tree only if he or she actually knew of the danger and failed to prevent the damage. Even when there is obvious decay, an owner who is unaware of it is not liable. Rural owners are not expected to routinely inspect acres of trees for potential danger.

If you live in a rural area and believe a neighbor's tree is endangering you or your property, notify the neighbor in writing. An expert opinion delivered to the owner is the best possible notice to be sure the owner realizes the danger. (See "Expert Opinions," above, on where to find a tree expert.)

THE CHANGING RESPONSIBILITIES OF TREE OWNERS

Until recently, if a neighbor was damaged by a naturally growing tree (not planted by the owner), the owner was not required to pay. No one was responsible, the theory went, for consequences of nature. Courts felt that imposing a duty to inspect property for dangerous natural objects would have placed an unacceptable burden on the landowner.

Even in horse-and-buggy days, however, some judges ruled that a property owner who actually knew of a dangerous condition had a duty to alleviate the danger. For example, in 1896, a neighbor asked a tree owner on three separate occasions to remove a 75-foot pine tree that was obviously decayed. When a heavy gale deposited the tree on the neighbor's house, the New York judge declared that the landowner had been negligent (unreasonably careless) by failing to do something to avoid the harm.[4]

The New York ruling was far from an overnight success. Other courts remained for many years unwilling to make landowners responsible for preventing tree damage to neighbors. In the 1970's and 1980's, however, one court after another declared that urban landowners were liable for harm from dead or rotten trees. Owners were liable if they knew or should have known of potential harm, whether the tree was one the owner planted or had just grown naturally on the land.

Sometimes it takes a case with very harsh facts or peculiar circumstances to persuade a court to shift its views. The South Carolina court recently chose, without much enthusiasm, to make owners liable when it was faced with very severe injury from a tree's rotten limbs.[5] California jumped on the bandwagon in a case where a nun had informed the tree owner of the danger and the owner denied her story.[6]

Going to Court

Often, claims against tree owners case end up in small claims court, where neither side needs a lawyer. Most states limit small claims cases to $2,000 to $5,000. (Chapter 15 lists each state's limit.) If you're suing a neighbor, you may want to reduce a larger claim to the allowed limit, avoiding legal fees and the delay of going to regular trial court.

Writing a Demand Letter

Before a neighbor can sue, he must demand compensation from the tree owner. Because nobody wants to go to court, just telling the owner about the problem and what the law is usually results in a solution.

A sample letter is shown below.

```
                         1602 Oak St.
                         Oakton, CA 95544

                         May 2, 19__

Dear Steve,

    As I pointed out to you two weeks ago,
several dead limbs from your oak tree have
fallen against my garage, damaging the roof. I
have obtained the enclosed estimate of $500 to
repair the damage.

    According to the law, you are responsible
for my damages.  Please contact me about the
repair bill. Otherwise, I will be forced to
take legal action.

Sincerely yours,


Yvonne
```

Keep a copy of the letter to show the judge; it explains your case in a nutshell.

You may still avoid a lawsuit if you're willing to be flexible—for example, accepting several smaller payments instead of a lump sum. Before you head to court, make one last attempt to suggest mediation to the neighbor. (Mediation is discussed in "Talking to the Owner," above.)

What the Neighbor Must Prove

Someone who files a lawsuit against a tree owner must prove to the court these elements:

- The tree that caused the damage belongs to the person being sued.

- The tree owner knew of the danger the tree posed (or, in an urban area, should have known) but didn't take reasonable steps to prevent it.

- The tree (or its branches) damaged the neighbor's property.

- The money value of the damage.

How Much the Neighbor Is Entitled To

The neighbor is entitled to compensation for all repair costs, including money spent to fix or clean up the property. The court will want to see proof (receipts) of amounts spent due to the tree and written estimates for work yet to be done.

If the property can't be fixed, the neighbor is entitled to the difference in the property value caused by the damage. A real estate appraiser can estimate the amount.

If the neighbor was physically injured, he is entitled to be reimbursed for all medical bills and money lost from missing work. If the incident turned the neighbor into a complete emotional wreck, resulting in loss of sleep, lost work or physical illness, he can request money for mental anguish. How much? Try figuring it on a daily basis. Someone in terrible shape for ten days might ask for at $50 a day—that's $500.

If the tree owner showed reckless disregard for the neighbor's safety, the neighbor can also ask the court to make the owner pay punitive damages. This is an extra amount designed to punish a person for extremely careless behavior. For example, punitive damages might be awarded if an owner knew the tree would fall, could have easily chopped it down or pruned the dangerous branches, but refused to act even after the danger was pointed out. (Small claims courts in some states, however, don't have the authority to award punitive damages.)

---

[1]For example, see *Barker v. Brown*, 340 A.2d 566 (Pa. 1975); *Mahurin v. Lockhart*, 71 Ill. App. 3d 691, 28 Ill. Dec. 356, 390 N.E.2d 523 (1979); *Dudley v. Meadowbrook, Inc.*, 166 A.2d 743 (Mun. Ct. App. D.C. 1961); *Keenan v. Smith*, 149 Cal. App. 3d 576, 197 Cal. Rptr. 32 (1983).

[2]That's what happened in *Ivanic v. Olmstead*, 66 N.Y.2d 349, 497 N.Y.S.2d 326, 488 N.E. 72, *motion denied*, 67 N.Y.2d 754, 500 N.Y.S.2d 103, 490 N.E.2d 1229, *cert. denied*, 476 U.S. 1117, 90 L. Ed. 2658, 106 S. Ct. 1975 (1985).

[3]*Grierfield v. Gibraltar Fire & Marine Ins. Co.*, 199 Miss. 175, 24 So. 2d 356 (1946).

[4]*Gibson v. Denton*, 4 App. Div. 198, 38 N.Y.S. 554 (1896).

[5]*Israel v. Carolina Bar-B-Que, Inc.*, 292 S.C. 282, 356 S.E.2d 123 (1987).

[6]*Keenan v. Smith*, 149 Cal. App. 3d 576, 197 Cal. Rptr. 32 (1983).

INSURANCE PROCEEDS

Some insurance companies demand reimbursement for what they have paid if the insured person is also paid by someone else. If your company has paid you, ask whether you are required to pay the money back if you sue successfully. If you get to keep it, subtract what they paid you from your total. The resulting figure is the amount of your actual damage.

Boundary Trees

When a tree stands on or near a boundary line, sometimes we are not really sure who is supposed to take care of it or who owns it. When the tree is a bother, we want it to be our neighbor's; if it is loaded with fruit, we would just as well it belong to us.

The laws concerning boundary trees are not the same as the general laws on trees (see Chapter 1) because they are based on co-ownership. Co-owners have different legal responsibilities and different legal remedies if a tree is damaged.

Trees that are fences: Rows of boundary trees grown close together and which spread to form a barrier can be considered fences. When they are, they are subject to state and local fence regulations. (See Chapter 11, *Fences.*)

OWNERSHIP

The location of a tree's trunk usually determines who owns the tree.

The Basic Rule: Location of the Trunk

If a tree's trunk is entirely on one person's property, that person owns the tree, even if the roots spread under a neighbor's land or the branches hang over it. When a tree trunk straddles a boundary line, the common rule is that it belongs to all the owners of the properties.

A few states—California, Louisiana, North Dakota and Oklahoma—have written this definition of ownership into their state statutes.[1] California calls trees whose trunks are partly on the land of two or more persons "line trees." Other states have no statutes, but the common law—decisions written by the courts—usually says that a tree whose trunk straddles a boundary belongs to both property owners.

Sometimes, however, neighbors don't know exactly where the boundary between their properties is, so they don't know if a tree truly sits on the line. When the boundary line can't be found from deed descriptions or property records, neighbors may agree on where they believe the boundary is. Any tree whose trunk straddles that line is a boundary tree, co-owned by both neighbors. In fact, in this situation, neighbors often choose a tree or other landmark to mark the boundary line.

This agreement doesn't have to be explicit between the neighbors; it can be implied when both neighbors act as if the tree marks the boundary between their properties. Even mowing the grass on each side up to the tree can reflect a neighbor agreement about the location of the boundary line. Such agreements can sometimes create uncertainty. If you're concerned about a tree that may sit on an agreed boundary line, see Chapter 9, *Boundary Lines*.

There is an exception to the rule that the trunk alone determines ownership of a boundary tree. This is discussed next.

RESEARCHING STATE TREE OWNERSHIP LAWS

In states without statutes, to determine the exact law on boundary tree ownership, you will have to do a little research on court decisions in your state. Chapter 13, *Legal Research*, will show you how to get started.

Conduct of the Neighbors

If a tree trunk is located on two properties, there is a strong legal presumption of joint ownership. But if the boundary line is in dispute at all, a court presented with the question of who owns a tree might look at the conduct of the property owners. In two court opinions, one from Nebraska[2] and the other from Colorado,[3] the judges suggest that for any tree to be a boundary tree, the neighbors must either jointly plant it, jointly tend it or treat it as the boundary between their properties.

Example: In the Nebraska case, a man sued for an order to prevent his neighbor from cutting a large cottonwood.

The neighbor who wanted to remove the tree claimed it was all his; the other argued that it was a boundary tree. The boundary line was unclear. These neighbors had jointly tended the cottonwood for years. It had become diseased and together they had treated it, cabled it, even strengthened it with concrete. The court declared that because the boundary was unclear, their conduct indicated that they both owned the tree. The judge ordered the ax-happy neighbor not to harm it.

Because there is so little written law on this subject, it is difficult to predict what another court might do in a similar situaton. It is doubtful that a judge would allow the presumption of common ownership to be overcome unless there were other circumstances present—for example, when the boundary line has been in dispute, or when the trunk has grown into the boundary line (see below).

When the Trunk Grows Into the Boundary

A tree that starts life wholly on one person's property may, as the trunk grows, spread into the adjoining yard. Does the neighbor become a co-owner? It depends on what state you're in and how the neighbors treat the tree.

In all states, when the trunk grows into the boundary and both neighbors treat the tree as a boundary tree, it is one. In some states, trees growing into the line become common property no matter how the property owners act. Once the trunk starts to straddle the line, the originally treeless neighbor automatically becomes an owner. This is true in the four states that define boundary trees in their state statutes—California, Louisiana, North Dakota and Oklahoma—and others where the courts have ruled this way.

Courts in some other states, however, including Colorado and New Mexico, require the neighbors to agree that a tree which has grown into a boundary line is a boundary tree, or to act as if it were—for example, sharing the cost of maintenance. Otherwise, if the original owner remains in total charge, it still belongs to that owner.[4]

Let's look at two examples with opposite results.

Example 1: Fred plants a small eucalyptus tree on his property near the boundary line. His next-door neighbor Henry thinks Fred is making a big mistake and refers to the tree as Fred's Folly. During the next 15 years, Henry ignores the tree except for periodic complaints about how dirty and ugly it is. Finally, the roots begin to buckle any concrete within their reach, including Henry's patio and Fred's driveway, and the tree becomes a real nightmare to both of them. By now the trunk is huge and firmly straddles the line. They live in California, where the location of the trunk determines the ownership. When they decide to have it removed, who is legally responsible for paying for it? Both of them, half and half. Fred's Folly has become the Co-owners' Common Problem.

Example 2: Ken has an oak tree whose trunk has slowly grown into the property of his neighbor, Suzy. Suzy enjoys the tree but has never acted as an owner—she's never paid for a trimming, for example. One day Ken gets very tired of the leaves and debris and chops the tree down. They live in Colorado, where a tree growing into the boundary line must be affirmatively treated as a boundary tree for both neighbors to become owners. Suzy sues Ken for cutting down a tree that also belonged to her, and she loses. The tree was never treated as a boundary tree, and it still belonged to Ken.[5]

WHO OWNS HOW MUCH OF A BOUNDARY TREE?

Usually, ownership of a tree on a boundary line is shared equally by each co-owner. But how about arguing that if the trunk is mostly on one property, that neighbor owns a proportionately larger share? You could, although the only law supporting that theory is a suggestion to that effect in a court case in 1895.[6]

Nevertheless, if each owner maintains the tree roughly according to the percentage that the trunk occupies, and perhaps also reaps proportionate rewards, this would seem fair. In case of a dispute, say over a large tree service bill, or even over who gets how much fruit, a small claims court might allow proportionate ownership and responsibility.

CO-OWNERS' RESPONSIBILITIES

When a tree is owned in common, both owners are responsible for it. Each owner usually maintains the portion on his property, but when the tree as a whole needs attention, both owners are obligated to pay for the work. And if the tree harms someone else, both owners are liable—for instance, if the tree fell on a third property, both would be responsible for the damage.

Maintenance and Care

Most neighbors have no problem with sharing responsibility for a boundary tree's care and maintenance. In fact, they may never think about it. They go about year after year cleaning up whatever debris falls on their own properties, and trim any limbs on their sides that may bother them.

If the tree demands the attention of both owners—for instance, if it grows higher than a legal limit, becomes diseased or poses a problem to passersby or other neighbors—the co-owners may need to cooperate. Both owners are legally responsible for the cost of necessary maintenance.

But for one owner to demand contribution, the tree as a whole must need work. If a co-owner can solve the problem without help, on her own property, she shouldn't expect the neighbor to share the cost. For example, if one limb of a boundary tree is dropping sap on your car and you can easily lop it off, don't ask the neighbor to pay for trimming the whole tree. You always have the right to cut limbs of any tree over your own property as long as you don't harm the tree. (See Chapter 6, *Boundary Trees.*)

Getting a Co-owner to Cooperate

But one owner may refuse to do his share, or they may disagree about what care is needed. In this situation, the more conscientious owner can have essential maintenance done and then demand half the cost from the neighbor. If the neighbor won't pay, the other can sue for reimbursement. If you co-own a boundary tree with an uncooperative neighbor, or you and the neighbor disagree about how much work the tree needs, here are some guidelines for working out the disagreement. If all your attempts fail, you can try taking the neighbor to small claims court.

Be Sure You Know Who's Responsible for the Tree

If it's not a boundary tree, the neighbor isn't responsible for its care or maintenance, so be sure that both you and your neighbor co-own the tree before demanding contribution from the neighbor. Co-ownership rules are discussed in "Ownership," above.

Be Sure the Problem Requires Joint Contribution

If you determine that a particular tree is a boundary tree, the next question is whether the problem that bothers you is one your neighbor is legally obligated to help put right. These problems usually fall into the following categories:

- legal necessities, such as conformity with a height limit in a local ordinance or mandatory spraying for insects

- care essential for the health of the tree, for instance, treatment if it becomes diseased

- avoidance of serious damage, such as from falling limbs when danger is predictable.

Many other types of problems don't require contribution. Overhanging branches that are cluttering one yard with debris shouldn't be the other owner's responsibility. Even aggressive roots that threaten one driveway are usually considered that owner's problem if he can remedy it himself.

Document the Problem and Obtain Cost Estimates

Take photographs and obtain a written expert opinion if necessary. Get several estimates from tree services so you know you won't be overcharged.

Example: The mighty oak belonging to neighbors Kelly and Arthur has become top-heavy. Arthur, fearing that it may be dangerous, contacts a tree expert who has a degree in forestry for an opinion. The expert confirms that the danger is real and suggests having a number of heavy limbs removed to greatly reduce the danger and save the tree. Arthur knows that Kelly will be reluctant to help with the cost, so he gets this opinion in writing and obtains estimates for the work from three different tree services. He now has written proof of the necessity for the work and of what a reasonable charge is for the job.

Ask the Other Owner to Contribute

If a friendly conversation with the co-owner doesn't solve the problem, you should always follow up in writing. Sometimes people respond better to a written request—they take it more seriously than an over-the-fence chat. And later you may need to document your requests for a judge.

You should keep copies of these requests. Here are examples of the sort of letter you should write.

First Request

```
                        March 1, 19__
Dear Kelly,

   The oak tree growing on the boundary of our
properties has become top-heavy, which is not
only dangerous, but also unhealthy for the
tree. John Edison of Edison Tree Service (a
licensed arborist) confirms that several large
limbs are unsound. In his opinion, removing
the limbs should save the tree and prevent any
damage they could cause if they fell. I am
enclosing Edison's opinion, and three cost
estimates to have the necessary work done.

   Since this tree straddles our boundary line,
we both own it and are mutually responsible
for this expense. Please contact me so that we
may agree on the details of the work. Thank
you.

Sincerely yours,

Arthur
```

Second Request

March 25, 19__

Dear Kelly,

Having received no response from you concerning our dangerous boundary tree, I have arranged to have the necessary work performed on April 20.

Enclosed is the estimate from Edison Tree Service for pruning and treating our tree. As you can see, the tree is extensively damaged and in need of professional care for its survival.

The total bill for the work will be $500, which means your half is $250. Please send me this amount by April 20.

Sincerely yours,

Arthur

Between letter #1 and letter #2, if your neighbor has told you to go jump in a lake, or what you can do with the precious tree, don't waste time and effort with anger. Just include a line about this being a legal responsibility of both of you. At the end of the letter add "or I will take this matter to small claims court." Keep your cool. All the name-calling in the world doesn't change the fact that you and your neighbor are jointly obliged.

And remember, even if your neighbor really is a hopeless idiot, it makes sense to save your sarcasm and write a polite businesslike letter. Demand letters can be presented to a small claims judge and are an excellent way to outline the facts of your case if you end up going to court.

Suggest Mediation

If you still receive no response, suggest to your neighbor that you try to resolve the problem through mediation. Mediation involves meeting with a neutral third party (mediator) whose job it is to help the disputants come up with their own solution. Unlike a lawsuit, mediation lets the owners themselves keep control of decisions about their properties and provides a framework for future discussions if other problems arise. It also has the advantages of being inexpensive and, if it works, avoiding the long-term hostility a lawsuit breeds. For more on mediation, see Chapter 14.

Go to Small Claims Court

If nothing works out with the neighbor, you can file a lawsuit against the neighbor for the money owed to you. In most cases, small claims court is the best place to sue—amounts are almost never enough to justify hiring a lawyer and going to regular trial court. The amount that you ask for must be within the small claims court limit, which is usually $2,000 to $5,000.

When you go to court you must show the following:

- The tree belongs to both you and your neighbor
- The work done was necessary
- The amount charged was reasonable
- You asked the neighbor for his share.

Chapter 15 discusses how to prepare and present a claim in small claims court, and lists each state's small claims court limit.

BOUNDARY TREES
AS OFFICIAL BOUNDARY
MARKERS

If a boundary tree is officially
used as a marker to describe
property in a deed or a
survey, it is protected under
state law. Almost every state
has a statute providing for a
hefty fine or jail for someone
who removes such a tree.
These statutes are easy to
look up in the law library.
See Chapter 13, *Legal
Research*.

DAMAGE TO OR REMOVAL OF A BOUNDARY TREE

One owner of a healthy boundary tree may not remove the tree or harm it without the permission of the other owner.

Co-owners' Rights

Except in rare circumstances—usually necessity for building purposes (see below)—a co-owner may not harm or remove a healthy boundary tree without the other owner's permission. Each owner can trim away at his side, but may not damage the tree. If your neighbor has the major part of the trunk on his property and he cuts away at it, damaging the remainder, you are entitled to compensation for your loss, no matter how small.

If a boundary tree is dead or diseased beyond repair, a co-owner may remove it without the other's permission. The other co-owner can't complain because she really has no loss. In fact, a co-owner may be under a legal duty to remove a dead or diseased tree if it presents an obvious danger to people or property. (See Chapter 5 for a discussion of tree owners' liability.)

If you and a neighbor share a row of boundary trees, each tree is common property, and you can't harm any of them without permission. This may seem like common sense, but apparently it wasn't to one fellow who went along his boundary and cut down every other tree for firewood. He evidently thought that if he and his neighbor owned twenty trees together, then ten could be considered his. Not surprisingly, he found himself in court, with the judge ruling against him.[7]

The only time a co-owner can remove a healthy boundary tree over the neighbor's objections is if destruction of the tree is absolutely necessary for the reasonable use of one neighbor's property. This would be the case if one owner had to remove a tree entirely, or excavate roots or remove a large portion of a boundary tree, in order to build a house, driveway or business building close to the line.[8] If the builder exercises all possible care to protect the tree—cutting as little as necessary—but the tree still dies, under these circumstances, normally he won't be liable. When one co-owner protested in court, however, the judge refused to let a co-owner remove a tree without the other owner's permission, even though one owner needed the space to build a house.[9]

Few uses of land, however, justify destroying a tree that belongs, in part, to someone else. Thus a neighbor who wants to build a 20-foot deck will likely find a judge unsympathetic—17 feet ought to be big enough if it would spare the tree. And someone who wants to kill a boundary tree because its roots interfere with a proposed tennis court will likely learn that the judge considers tennis less necessary than he does.

Even the cultivation of crops does not usually justify destruction of a boundary tree when one of the owners is benefiting from the trees. A good example of this is when a row of boundary trees is used as a windbreak. If you drive down a country highway, you will notice these strands of windbreak trees. Sometimes they stand to the side of a residence; often they form a line to protect growing crops from the elements. The owner who is downwind relies on the trees, and their loss can be disastrous. The upwind owner has a different problem as the roots invade crops, or the foliage blocks the sun.

If the upwind owner threatens or begins to remove the trees, the other owner may go to court. In most cases, a judge will order the neighbor to leave the windbreak standing.[10]

You Want to Remove a Boundary Tree

If you want to remove a boundary tree and your neighbor is reluctant to allow it, try a little negotiation. Perhaps the co-owner would agree to several smaller replacement trees, or a tree in a different place, or be more cooperative if you agree to fix the broken sidewalk in front of your house that has bothered him for years. You could also offer to pay the co-owner for her loss of the tree, as well as paying for the entire cost of removal.

Once you reach an agreement with a co-owner allowing removal, it would be wise to get it in writing before you act. If it's practicable, have all owners, including spouses, sign the agreement. Also, be aware that some cities require a permit to remove any tree at all—even your own.

Never cut a tree if there is any doubt of the ownership. The city may own the strip of land between the sidewalk and the street, for example. If you want to remove a tree from city land, you'll need the city's permission.

Preventing a Co-owner from Removing a Boundary Tree

As a practical matter, what should you do if your neighbor is grumbling about the tree on your boundary and wants to cut it down? If you value the tree and you have reason to believe he may cut it down when your back is turned, inform the neighbor that he may not harm it without your permission. Here is a sample letter.

```
                         14 Shady Lane
                         Pine Hill, CA 98876

                         November 1, 19__
Dear Wayne,

   After our talk about the amount of leaves
this year from the oak on our boundary, I
realize that you're tired of the work the tree
requires and may even be thinking of cutting
down the tree. But please remember that the
trunk of the tree straddles the boundary line
and the tree belongs to both of us. According
to the law, neither of us has the right to
harm it in any way without the other's permis-
sion.

   At this time of year, the tree does require
a lot of work by both of us. But because it
shades my roof and keeps my house cool, it is
also of enormous benefit to me during the
summer and I do not want to lose it. Perhaps,
instead of talking about removal, we can get
together and figure out a pruning schedule
that would reduce the debris that falls on
your yard, and enhance the tree.

Sincerely yours,

David
```

Some people wouldn't be this diplomatic, but it will probably pay off in the long run. At least you are trying to keep lines of communication open. However, if you are sure that a polite approach won't work, add that you will sue him if he cuts the tree.

Should you suspect that despite your letter, the neighbor plans to kill your favorite boundary tree, see an attorney. The lawyer will probably first write a letter and try to get assurances that no action is planned by the neighbor.

If there is a good reason to think your neighbor may soon act illegally, the lawyer can ask the court for an emergency order prohibiting the cutting. You will have to swear in a declaration under penalty of perjury that harm is likely. If the judge issues the order, it is only temporary until a full hearing is held on whether a permanent order is needed. The whole process will be expensive and time-consuming.

When a Co-owner Damages or Removes a Boundary Tree

If one co-owner harms a boundary tree, the other can sue for the value of the tree, and for a court order making her stop the harmful activity. But there are lots of less drastic steps to take first.

Contact Your Insurance Agency

Many homeowners insurance policies will reimburse a policyholder whose tree is destroyed. Some have a dollar limit on tree claims—$500 a tree is common. Sometimes the policy of the person who caused the damage will pay the neighbor for the entire loss, especially if no harm to him was intended. Always check with your insurance agent before you do anything else. The company may handle the whole situation for you.

Most trees are worth more than $500; if your loss is larger than what the company will pay, you can still sue the neighbor for the extra amount to compensate you for your actual loss. If you do, find out from your insurance company whether you will have to give back what the company paid you. Some companies require reimbursement if you collect from someone else; otherwise, you would be paid twice. But sometimes, a company will issue a waiver that frees you from reimbursement obligations; always ask for one.

Calculate Your Loss and Demand Compensation

If your insurance won't pay—or won't pay enough—you can seek compensation for your actual loss from the neighbor.[11] Anyone who ever cuts down a tree belonging to someone else is in legal trouble, and boundary trees can provide an expensive lesson about this rule. You should be entitled to the amount it would cost to replace the tree. If the tree cannot be replaced, the basis for the damages is the diminished value of your property as a whole.[12]

For a full discussion on how to calculate your loss in dollar terms, see Chapter 1, *Help for Common Complaints.*

After putting a dollar figure on your actual losses, make a written demand to your neighbor for that amount. A sample letter is shown below.

---

568 Shady Lane
Forest City, CA 98878

November 1, 19__

Mr. Howard Henson
570 Shady Lane
Forest City, CA 98878

Dear Mr. Henson:

Last Tuesday, October 28, 19__, you removed the large oak, which was a boundary tree between our properties. You had no right to do this as the tree straddled our property line and so was owned by us in common.

The tree's appearance greatly enhanced the value of my property, and it also sheltered my house from the sun in the summer. I have enclosed an estimate of my loss of $3,500. Please submit this amount to me immediately, or if your insurance company will handle it directly, please have it contact me.

Sincerely yours,

Carolyn Smith

You may well hear from the neighbor or his insurance company. The neighbor may have mistakenly thought the tree was his, and his homeowner's policy may cover your damages.[13]

Suggest Mediation

Before you file a lawsuit against the neighbor, try to arrange mediation. You and the neighbor can sit down together with a neutral third party (mediator) and work out an agreement between you. An acceptable payment plan, a replacement tree or even a compromise is far better than a lawsuit between next-door neighbors. (See Chapter 14 on how mediation works.)

Sue in Small Claims Court

If all else fails, go ahead and sue for the money owed you. The loss of a large tree can easily be equal to the small claims court limit ($2,000 to $5,000 in most states) in property devaluation alone. Unless your loss greatly exceeds your state's small claims court limit, you're probably better off to voluntarily scale your claim back to that amount and avoid paying an attorney to take the action to formal trial court.

If there is a serious dispute over the location of the boundary, you may need to get a survey done before you go to court. This can cost between several hundred and several thousand dollars. (See Chapter 9 on what is involved in a survey.) If the neighbor is claiming the land that the tree stands on, you need to see a lawyer. The legal issues can be very complex and may require not only regular court but also an experienced property lawyer.

In small claims court, you will need to prove the following:

THE CASE OF THE DISAPPEARING DAMAGE

A lawsuit over boundary trees in Connecticut gives a great example of why judges are always complaining about neighbor disputes clogging up their courts unnecessarily. The trees at issue were actually a fence, a privet hedge, twelve feet high. One neighbor cut the whole thing down to five feet, and the other neighbor sued for harming the joint property. By the time the case came before a court, the hedge had not only grown back, but was healthier than ever from the pruning. The judge wearily lectured the neighbors on invading each other's rights, and noted that the damage had disappeared.[14]

- The tree belonged to both of you (see "Ownership," above).

- The neighbor removed it without your permission.

- You suffered losses in the amount you're asking for.

Have copies of all documents ready to let the judge see them. This includes the letter to the neighbor requesting payment and written receipts or estimates showing all of your losses.

For pointers on preparing and presenting a small claims court case, see Chapter 15, *Small Claims Court.*

---

[1]Cal. Civ. Code § 834; N.D. Cent. Code Ann. 47-01-17; 60 Okla. Stat. Ann. 67, 68. Louisiana's statute, La. Civil Code 687, creates a presumption of common ownership when trees are located on the line. This presumption means that the tree is commonly owned unless one neighbor proves otherwise—for instance, that one owner planted it and only one always tended it.

[2]*Weisel v. Hobbs,* 138 Neb. 656, 294 N.W. 448 (1948).

[3]*Rhodig v. Keck,* 161 Colo. 337, 421 P.2d 729 (1966).

[4]For example, in New Mexico, the court ruled in *Garcia v. Sanchez,* 108 N.M. 388, 772 P.2d 1311 (1989), that either an oral or written agreement was necessary to establish common ownership when a tree's trunk grows into the boundary line.

[5]See *Rhodig v. Keck,* 161 Colo. 337, 421 P.2d 729 (1966).

[6]*Robinson v. Clapp,* 65 Conn. 365, 32 A. 939, *app.,* 67 Conn. 538, A. 504 (1895).

[7]*Scarborough v. Woodill,* 7 Cal. 39, 93 P. 383 (1907).

[8]In *Higdon v. Henderson,* 304 P.2d. 1001 (Okla. 1956), one owner was allowed to remove a boundary tree to build a residence.

[9]*Robinson v. Clapp,* 65 Conn. 365, 32 A. 939, *app.,* 67 Conn. 538, 35 A. 504 (1895).

[10]For example, see *Musch v. Burkhart,* 83 Iowa 301, 48 N.W. 1025 (1891); *Anderson v. Weiland,* 12 Cal. 730, 55 P.2d 1242 (1936).

[11]Many state laws provide stiff penalties, above the amount of the actual loss, for the destruction of someone else's trees. (See Chapter 1.) However, the courts do not appear to apply any of these when the damage is done by one co-owner to a boundary tree.

[12]For example, see *Blalock v. Atwood,* 154 Ky. 394, 157 S.W. 694 (1913), and *Cathcart v. Malone,* 33 Tenn. App. 93, 229 S.W.2d 157 (1950).

[13]The insurance company was forced to pay in the case of *York Indus. Center, Inc. v. Michigan Mut. Liab. Co.,* 271 N.C. 158, 155 S.E.2d 501 (1963).

[14]*Cooke v. McShane,* 108 Conn. 97, 142 A. 460 (1928).

Fruit and Nuts: Who Owns What?

Where the apple reddens
Never pry—
Lest we lose our Eden,
Eve and I.

—Robert Browning

In this scenario, your neighbor's branches are intruding over the property line into your yard. But you don't mind a bit. They are hanging heavy, loaded with ripe succulent peaches. Whose peaches are they?

WHO OWNS THE TREE?

The location of a tree's trunk determines who owns the tree. If the trunk stands next door, the tree, branches, leaves and peaches belong to your neighbor. You may not legally help yourself to the fruit. If you do, you are, in theory, converting someone else's property to your own use, and your neighbor could sue you.[1]

Most people don't actually run to the courthouse over a few pieces of fruit. When there is almost no value attached to the items, there simply are no lawsuits. Nevertheless, this doesn't change the principle of ownership— the fruit still belongs to your neighbor.

There is a certain logic to this rule—since a tree owner is sometimes liable for damage to his neighbor caused by overhanging branches, it makes sense that if those same branches are full of fruit, they also belong to the owner of the tree.

Rights of the Fruit Tree Owner

This rule of ownership may seem pretty nit-picking when we are talking about one peach, plum or walnut. But think for a moment about living next door to an orchard, with thousands of peaches involved rather than two or three. The owner of the orchard is not in the business of giving truckloads of fruit to an adjoining landowner. The owner of the lone fruit tree has the same legal rights as the orchard owner.

Given that the tree owner owns the fruit that hangs over a neighbor's property, a practical question instantly arises: Can he go get it? It is easy to picture a situation where the grower claims the fruit and wants to collect it, but the neighbor orders him not to set foot on the adjoining property.

The law in the United States is very unclear on the question. People don't take a lawsuit over a few apples all the way to a court where written opinions are given, and the legislatures have not considered this issue worthy of attention.

Some legal scholars say that an owner has the right to enter another's land and retrieve her possessions under certain circumstances.[4] An example would be when a boat breaks loose from a dock in a storm and lands on somebody else's beach. But these occasions are instances of unexpectedly losing valuable property, not wanting to collect a few peaches.

A court faced with a dispute over access to fruit would probably weigh the conflicting legal rights of the people involved. You have a right to keep intruders off your property, to have them arrested for trespass if you forbid them from coming on your yard. This right will be protected by the law unless there is a good reason for an exception. When compared to the right to possess a few pieces of fruit, a strong argument could be made that the neighbor's right to keep people out outweighs that of the owner of the tree who demands entry.

ARGUMENTS THAT WON'T WORK

When fruit tree owners have sued neighbors for stealing fruit, the neighbors have used several unsuccessful arguments to try to establish rights to the forbidden fruit. For example, one man who took twenty bushels of pears claimed that he was a part owner because the roots of the tree extended into his property and were nourished by his soil. The court disagreed, informing him that the location of the trunk alone established ownership.[2]

Another case came before a court after the attempted picking of a handful of cherries resulted in a physical fight and injury. The cherry collector insisted that she possessed everything above as well as below her land. "Not so," said the judge. She could use the space over her land, but she couldn't have the cherries.[3] Although these cases are quite old, they are still cited and followed by contemporary courts.

What about just leaning over the fence and picking what belongs to you? People do this all the time with no complaint from their neighbors. But should you be the unfortunate one who lives next to a truly nasty neighbor, even this could put you in danger of trespassing.

There is another factor to consider here besides legal rights. The ripening of fruit is a predictable event. A tree owner not only knows it will happen, but probably can be fairly certain when it will happen. If he wants the fruit, he should have the wit to make an arrangement in advance.

The Right to Trim the Neighbor's Fruit Tree

A landowner has the right to trim overhanging branches of a neighbor's tree up to the property line (within certain guidelines—see Chapter 4, *Encroachment: Invasion of Branches and Roots*). Does this mean that someone can get around the fruit picking prohibition by finding a legal reason to cut off a fruit laden branch? It's not so easy.

When overhanging branches, fruit and all, are creating problems on someone's property, that person is allowed to eliminate the problem—that is, to cut back the branch. This is not the same thing as taking the branches and fruit for his own use. Or more directly, a neighbor gets to remedy your annoyance; the tree's owner gets to make the pie.

Extending this logic, a tree owner probably also has the right to request possession of limbs that have been legally removed from his tree. Because the limbs are often worthless, however, there is almost no law on the subject.[5]

The safest rule to follow is very simple: Anything growing from a tree or a bush, whether it is fruit, nuts, vegetables or flowers, even if it extends into another person's yard, belongs to the owner of the tree's or bush's trunk. If you cut branches that the neighbor may want, ask the neighbor if he wants them. If you suspect a misunderstanding may arise, do it in writing. And of course it is always a wise idea to notify the owner any time you are planning to prune his tree (see Chapter 5, *Unsound Limbs and Trees*).

Just in case this whole concept of ownership appears blatantly unfair to anyone, let's take an example that would seem absurdly picky in any other legal area, but is all too ordinary when it comes to neighbor spats.

Example: Oscar and his neighbor, Mildred, both grow kumquats as a serious hobby. The annual local kumquat festival approaches, complete with prize money of several hundred dollars. Oscar is deeply disappointed with his own puny fruit, and Mildred is unexpectedly called out of town. There on Mildred's tree, growing over Oscar's property, hangs the most splendid kumquat he has ever seen. He plucks it, enters it in the show and wins first place. Mildred returns the next day, sues Oscar and recovers the prize money. Oscar is stripped of his award and banned from the kumquat festival for life.

FRUIT THAT HAS FALLEN

But what about the apple that has fallen to the ground? Who does that belong to? Common sense and common practice would seem to favor a neighbor's claim to fruit and nuts that fall on her land.

In the autumn, when the tree next door drops its leaves into your yard, the leaves usually become your problem. Can you imagine a tree owner rushing over and saying "Oh, I'm so sorry. Those are my leaves; let me rake them up for you." If the same tree also deposits apples or pecans in your yard, you may have a right to them. There is precious little, if anything, written on the subject.[6]

If one looks at what is called "finder's law," the finder of a lost object is under an obligation to its true owner. But the apple in question is not really lost, so this doesn't seem to fit the situation. If an object is abandoned by its owner, it belongs to whomever picks it up. But to determine if something really was abandoned means struggling with questions of the owner's intent and how long to leave it, while the apple is rotting on the ground.

In the frustrating attempt to answer this overwhelmingly important question, we finally took an informal poll of several lawyers.

The question posed was "Would you take the fruit and eat it if it fell on your property?" Some of the answers:

"Of course, it's on my property."

"Of course not, it doesn't belong to me."

"Only at night."

"No; if the tree isn't mine, neither is the fruit."

"If the neighbor isn't home."

You get the general idea; nobody really knows. We asked the lawyers who assumed the fruit was theirs what they would do if the neighbor's coconut fell and cracked them on the head. Suddenly the tree owner still owned the coconut and was liable for every injury they could dream up.

We did find it most interesting when we took the survey that not a single lawyer suggested a very simple answer: Why not ask the neighbor's permission?

And now for our view. Practically speaking, we believe it's safe to pick up and eat small quantities of fruit that a neighbor's tree or bush has shed on your land. In the rare situation where your neighbor becomes upset, the fact is that fruit that has fallen to the ground has little or no value. So even if a small claims judge ruled that it was your neighbor's fruit and not yours, you would have to pay the neighbor only a nominal amount to compensate for the loss.

AVOIDING PROBLEMS

Fruit trees along the borders of property create a potential for friendly and comfortable neighbor relationships. Whether you are the owner of the tree or the neighbor, consider this example.

Example: Eliot and Kathe moved into a new house. The yard next door boasted lovely fruit trees, some of them hanging over the fence with fruit exactly at picking height. Art, the next door neighbor, stepped over to introduce himself and to welcome them. They walked together along the division fence and Art asked permission to enter the yard once a year and trim his trees. At the same time, he suggested that they help themselves to any fruit hanging over their property or on their ground. Within five minutes the foundation of a cordial and responsible good neighbor relationship was in place.

We are not all as lucky as Art's neighbors. Sometimes we are too timid, don't have time, never meet the neighbors or there is an absent landlord. Under these circumstances, perhaps the easiest solution is to simply follow a rule of custom. If the tree owner says nothing about the fruit year after year, she probably does not consider it her property or doesn't want it. If she races over to grab it, the neighbor knows from her action that she claims it.

Either way, a little courtesy and common sense can actually avoid any problems. This is one time when their use could result in freshly baked apple pie for everybody involved.

---

[1] *Skinner v. Wilder*, 38 Vt. 115 (1865).

[2] *Lyman v. Hale*, 11 Conn. 177 (1836).

[3] *Hoffman v. Armstrong*, 48 N.Y. 201 (1872).

[4] *Restatement (Second) of Torts* § 198 (1977).

[5] One case does discuss the value of the wood itself and gives a guideline. In that instance, 800 pounds of oak limbs had been legally cut by the neighbor over his property because the limbs were an annoyance to him. The oak had value as firewood. The court did inquire whether the tree owner wanted access to the wood. *Beals v. Griswold*, 468 So. 2d 641 (La. 1985).

[6] One state, Mississippi, has statutes that address the matter of fallen pecans, a major business in the state (Miss. Code Ann. § 69-33-3 and following.) The statutes make it a misdemeanor to gather someone's pecans when they have fallen onto public property during harvest season. One can be fined up to $100 and jailed for 30 days. Only after the harvest season are the pecans considered abandoned by the owner and available to anyone. These statutes talk only about public property. Silence about private property lets us assume that the pecans falling on your own yard are your pecans.

chapter 8

Obstruction of View

From the plains, seas and sparkling city lights, to the purple majesty of mountains, Americans want to look at this beautiful country. The privilege of sitting in one's own residence and gazing out over desirable scenery is a highly prized commodity. And especially in and near our cities, it can be a very expensive one.

In many areas, especially where there are oceans, bays, lakes or mountains, buyers and sellers put a price tag on views. If you pick up a newspaper and read the classified ads for houses for sale, you will find such terminology as "view," "partial view," and the ultimate, "panoramic view." Houses that are quite similar in size, construction and other amenities can be priced many thousands of dollars apart depending upon what the occupant sees from the breakfast table. Potential buyers, sometimes overwhelmed by the stunning landscape, commit their life savings to properties, assuming that the view is permanent. Sometimes it is not.

Suppose a neighbor builds on the property down the hill. A second story addition can suddenly stand in place of city lights, the Hudson River or San Francisco Bay. Similarly, apartment buildings can spring up, ten stories high, to block the mighty Mississippi or a panorama of the Blue Ridge mountains.

And it's not just new construction that can cause a problem. As nature runs its usual course, the sapling on the property several blocks away may slowly become a huge and untamed tree, at first an annoyance, and finally a maddeningly unwelcome obstruction to the precious view.

Whether near the lakes of Washington state or the hills of Tennessee, when a view is threatened, the property owner often looks to the law for help. But help will be forthcoming only if:

- a local law protects views, or

- the obstruction exceeds local or subdivision height limits, or

- the obstruction violates some other specific law.

THE BASIC RULE: NO RIGHT TO A VIEW

In our country there is no right to light, air or view, unless it has been granted in writing by a law (usually local) or subdivision rule. The exception to this general rule is that someone may not deliberately and maliciously block another's view. If a structure has no reasonable use to the owner and serves a purely malicious function, the affected neighbor can sue and ask a court to order it removed.

Almost any structure, however, is useful to the builder, whether it's a high-rise office building, fence or tool shed. It's uncommon that a structure is built maliciously solely to annoy or inconvenience a neighbor. (Spite fences are the exception; see Chapter 12, *Spite Fences*). Since trees are considered to have reasonable use to the owner, they may legally block another's view unless a specific local law or subdivision rule is violated.

This legal rule that a property owner has no right to light, air or view has been favored in this country because it encourages building and expansion. But the consequences can be harsh in individual cases. A typical court case from the late 19th century, before widespread access to electricity, involved a photographer. When a bank was built only eighteen inches from his windows, he lost not only air and view, but the light necessary for his livelihood.[1] He had no legal recourse because the building that blocked the light had a reasonable purpose.

SOLAR ENERGY ACCESS

A person who is using solar collectors to provide residential energy can sometimes purchase a right to sunlight from a neighbor. The neighbor agrees never to block access to the sun for the collectors.[2] (See "Easements," in Chapter 10.)

Berkeley, California, has a local ordinance that provides protection for solar access from a neighbor's growing trees. The same law protects views and sunlight.[3] (See "View Ordinances," below.)

The Wisconsin Supreme Court recently talked at length about possible rights to sunlight for any user of solar energy. In this case, the owner of a home that used solar energy sued a neighbor who had built a house that blocked sunlight. The argument was that blocking sunlight might be an unreasonable use of property that the solar user could complain about in court. The neighbor who later built his residence evidently had plenty of room to build without obstructing the neighbor's sun. This court ruled that the solar user had a right to sue the neighbor, even when there was no local ordinance.[4]

Is the homeowner who lost sunlight necessary to operate his solar collectors more harmed than our poor photographer? Hardly. But society is shifting its priorities, and the law is beginning to reflect the changes.

VIEW ORDINANCES

Despite the general common law rule that a property owner has no legal right to a view, a few cities have adopted view ordinances, which specifically protect an owner from having his view obstructed by growing trees. Not surprisingly, these ordinances are most common in cities that overlook the ocean or other desirable vistas.

Even if your city has a view ordinance, however, don't expect the city to step in and solve the problem of a lost view for you. The ordinances simply allow someone who has lost a view because of a growing tree to sue the tree owner for a court order requiring him to restore the view.

And a neighbor who wants to sue must first approach the tree owner and request that the offending tree be cut back.

You can find out whether you have a view ordinances addressing trees by calling your city clerk or checking your local ordinances in the public library. (See Chapter 13, *Legal Research*.) Local view ordinances don't cover buildings or other structures that block neighbors' views. If you're concerned about construction of something that threatens to ruin your view, see "Subdivision Rules" and "Other Laws That May Protect Views," below.

What the Ordinances Provide

The view that is protected under a view ordinance is usually the view that you had when you bought the property or moved in. Sometimes the ordinance specifies the date at which the view became protected. If you complain, you must have proof, such as photographs or reliable testimony from others, that your view has become blocked by a tree that has grown into it.

Just because there is a view ordinance, doesn't mean you can sue an uncooperative neighbor and force him to cut down his tree. A judge presented with such a lawsuit will consider more than just the lost view. The health of the tree is also important, and the tree's benefits to the owner. Some ordinances list the remedies available in an order of preference to try to preserve the tree. Thinning is preferred by most experts, and you may find yourself with a filtered view. In some cities, windowing—cutting out part of a tree to allow a view through it—may be suggested. If the tree can bear it, topping may be ordered. In the extreme case of court-ordered removal of a tree, the judge may also order the complaining neighbor to buy small replacement trees for the owner.

The complaining person usually bears the cost of trimming, unless the tree was planted after the law became effective, or the owner refuses to cooperate. Then, depending on the ordinance, costs may be divided. If the complaining neighbor wins in court, some towns place all costs of restoring the view on the tree owner.

While some view ordinances are fairly tough, others contain extensive limitations which, in effect, take most of the teeth out of them. Some examples:

- Some cities exempt certain kinds of trees from view ordinance lawsuits, especially if they grew naturally. In Oakland, California, the list includes redwoods, live oaks, box elders, bigleaf maples and others.[5] If an exempt tree is blocking the view, a neighbor has no case.

- Other cities allow a neighbor to complain only about a tree that is within a certain distance from the property of the complaining person. In Berkeley, California, the base of the tree must be no more than 300 feet from your property.[6] This may seem like a great distance, but it is minimal when a 175-foot Monterey cypress or redwood is involved.

- An offending tree on city property may be exempt from a view ordinance. But even though you can't sue the city, there may be a complaint procedure. In Oakland, California, for example, you complain in writing to the city, and a city office will make a decision. Sometimes a hearing will be held where any citizen can argue to protect the tree. If you disagree with the decision, you may be able to appeal it to a higher level within the city, such as the city council, and the decision made at that level is final.

View ordinances are usually long and complicated. If you hope to use one, the first step is to get a copy of it. (See Chapter 13, *Legal Research*.) Be prepared to spend plenty of time with the language, figuring out exactly what it means. Some, such as those in Oakland and Berkeley, California, lecture us extensively about not just the glory

of nature, but also the responsibility of neighbor cooperation. Once you wade through the discourse on how we
should all behave, you'll find a step-by-step guide for the
owner who wishes to regain a lost view.

How To Proceed

Once you've spent some time reading a local view ordinance, you'll see that it is designed to keep people out of
court. These ordinances encourage efforts at solving view
problems informally, and sometimes penalize tree owners
who don't cooperate. Before you can sue a neighbor for a
lost view, you must take specific steps, which will be set
out in your local view ordinance, to work things out.
These steps usually include:

- Notifying the tree owner of the problem. This will often include documenting how big the tree was on the date you moved in (or when the ordinance was adopted).

- If you and the neighbor can't agree, suggesting the use of a mediator—someone to help you work out a solution yourselves without going to court. (See Chapter 14, *Mediation.*)

- If mediation fails, agreeing to abide by the decision of an arbitrator after a hearing at which you and the neighbor make your arguments and present evidence. In some towns, the arbitrator may be any person the people involved agree on; others require a licensed arbitrator. There may be a fee for arbitration, but nothing like the cost of a lawsuit.

- In a few cities, going before the city tree commission, which holds formal hearings on view claims and issue orders for any trimmings. If the owner does not comply with the city's order, the neighbor can sue the tree owner.

- Documenting refusals of the tree owner to cooperate with you or a lack of response. Most towns require proof that you sent the neighbor letters by certified mail before you can file a lawsuit.

- Filing an official complaint with the city, furnishing proof of the view loss and the previous steps taken. In some cities, you go to city hall and fill out a form between the attempts at mediation and arbitration. In others, you just furnish the city a copy of the actual lawsuit papers when you file the suit with the court.

If none of this solves the problem, you can sue the neighbor and ask for a court order making the neighbor trim the tree. If you win the lawsuit, the neighbor may also have to pay a fine to the city for not cooperating under the ordinance, which can be as much as $1,000.

If your view does becomes obstructed by a neighbor's tree, and the situation fits the ordinance, try to keep the whole situation a private one between you and the neighbor. It will avoid costs of arbitrators and attorneys and keep the city out of your business.

Go down and introduce yourself to the neighbor with the tree. Invite him over to your house for a cup of tea; you want him to see his tree from your property and how it obstructs your view. He may not even know there is a problem unless you tell him. When you offer to pay for having the tree trimmed, he may be delighted.

Have a copy of the ordinance in your back pocket in case you need it; you may want to go over the provisions together. If the neighbor is uncooperative, leave the ordinance with him, and give him a little time to digest it. Try again in about a week. If you still get nowhere, then it's time for the written requests that most ordinances require. Below is a sample letter to a neighbor.

Keep a copy of all correspondence. If you get no response, send another copy to the neighbor, this time by certified mail. Include a copy of the ordinance. All correspondence from then on should be registered or certified so you will have proof of your efforts, if you must later file a complaint. If the neighbor still doesn't respond, write again, suggesting mediation, and then again, to suggest arbitration.

Carefully follow each step of the ordinance, but keep the letters pleasant. You want the neighbor to cooperate, and she probably will before a dispute reaches the lawsuit stage. It is to your advantage to stay on the best terms possible because this problem is going to happen again; you will likely be dealing with the same neighbor over it for many years.

If all efforts fail, you are entitled to sue for a court order making the neighbor allow the trimming. Remember to file a complaint with the city as well as with the court. You must use regular court, not small claims court, which means you will probably need to hire a lawyer. This will be expensive and time-consuming, but if you have proof of your lost view (photographs or the testimony of neighbors) and have carefully followed the required steps, you are likely to regain at least a portion of the view.

WHEN PROPERTY IS SOLD

When property protected by a view ordinance changes hands, usually the buyer only gets a right to any view on the date of purchase. If the seller has allowed the view already in existence to become diminished by neighboring trees, a wise buyer will negotiate to have the seller claim and restore any lost view before purchasing the property.

2411 Skyline Avenue
Ocean View, CA 97765

June 25, 19___

Ms. Doris Dawson
2411 Hill Avenue
Ocean View, CA 97765

Dear Ms. Dawson:

As you know, I live one block directly east of your property. This year your pine trees have grown so large that they obstruct my view of the ocean.

Having them trimmed by a skilled professional would be good for the health of the trees and would restore my view. Our local view ordinance provides that I have a right to the view that I had as of June 11, 19___. I have enclosed a picture of the view from my property that is dated about that time.

Under that ordinance, I am responsible for paying to have the trimming done, and I will be happy to do so.

May we arrange to consult with a licensed tree service of your choice, and at a time that will be convenient for you? Please contact me at 555-6888. Thank you for your cooperation.

Sincerely yours,

Juan Cuevez

SUBDIVISION RULES THAT PROTECT VIEWS

If you live in a subdivision or planned unit development. Another method to protect a view may be found in a property deed. Often, the deeds to subdivision lots contain restrictions on the use the owner may make of the property. Called "restrictive deed covenants" in legalese, these written regulations can protect views.

Usually, the same set of restrictions binds all the lots in a subdivision. The deed itself may contain the regulations if there are very few, but usually it refers to a separate document called the Covenants, Conditions, and Restrictions —or CC&Rs. The CC&Rs regulate most matters that could be a concern to a neighbor—for instance, what can be built on the property and what activities are allowed. If your neighbor is bound by a deed covenant that forbids blocking the view of others in the subdivision, you may be able to force him to comply with the terms of the deed—and get your view back.

Typical Subdivision Rules

You'll have to read your CC&Rs carefully to determine if a neighbor who is obstructing your view with a tree or a new garage is violating them. First look for rules specifically about views. For example, a rule may state: "nor shall any tree be planted that may in the future obstruct the view from any other lot." That means, according to a California court, that tree height is limited to roof level.[7]

Look at other sections, too. A rule may simply limit tree height to twelve or fifteen feet. Most CC&Rs also restrict the height of buildings and fences, and require structures to be placed (set back) a certain distance from the property boundaries.

Finding Out Who Is Subject to a Deed Covenant

Sometimes, even within the same neighborhood, not all owners are subject to the same deed restrictions. Someone who bought property before the restrictive covenants became part of the deeds, for example, is unaffected by them. And subdivisions have boundaries that may be visible only on paper. If you happen to live at the edge of the protected group, the people across the street or down the hill may not be under any restriction at all.

The easiest way to find out if the neighbor has the same restrictions in his deed that you do is to ask the subdivision homeowners association. It should have a list of all members of the protected property group. If you have an active association, it may also have a formal dispute resolution mechanism to help solve the problem (see "Help from Homeowners Associations," below).

But what if there is no association or no list of who is subject to the restrictions? Property deeds are part of the public record, and all deeds are on record at the county land records office, which is usually in the courthouse. You can go there and try to look up a neighbor's deed yourself. This may be possible if you have a helpful clerk who is not too busy to show you how to look up a deed.

Unfortunately, especially if you don't know the person's name, finding a deed can be time-consuming. If you have the address of the property, a clerk in the local tax assessor's office may help find the neighbor's name. Some post offices and public libraries provide cross-referenced name and address listings, which can give you the person's name if you have the address. You might need the assistance of an attorney or a paralegal trained in title searches.

Help From Homeowners Associations

Many homeowners associations in subdivisions and planned unit developments will assist when one member of the group violates the restrictions and creates problems for another. A committee or designated person may visit the one causing the problem and apply pressure to conform. Sanctions are often used, such as removing the privilege of using a swimming pool or other common area.

Some associations have the power to bring a lawsuit to enforce the restrictions in the deed. When this is the case and your neighbor violates the covenants, the association itself can sue and solve the problem for you. That's an expensive and time-consuming undertaking, however. The association may not want to sue except for serious violations of the rules.

If you and your neighbor can't work something out, and you believe there is a violation of your subdivision rules, contact the board of directors of your homeowners association. You may need to file a written complaint or appear at a meeting of the board.

Proceeding on Your Own

Some homeowners groups have no real power to pressure anyone and no will to sue. They may be sympathetic to your plight but, for any number of reasons, unwilling or unable to help you. And some subdivisions with deed restrictions have no active association at all. In either of these cases, you are on your own.

If the other neighbor is also under the tree height restrictions, it is time for a talk, even if you don't know the neighbor. Go over and ask the neighbor to please trim the trees to the limit allowed. Explain the problem with your view—try inviting him over to see his trees from your perspective. Most people just need to be reminded, and do not violate the restrictions intentionally.

If this particular neighbor is not like most folks, and she refuses your request, now you need to do some thinking. Even paying part of the trimming cost would be a lot cheaper than a lawsuit; you might want to make an offer to share the cost. If the neighbor is unsympathetic or drags her feet, put your request in writing. Some people respond better to a written request because they realize you are serious about the matter. Below is a sample letter.

1632 Lakeview Drive
Hilldale, CA 94567

May 15, 19__

Mr. Marvin Mott
1627 Lakeview Drive
Hilldale, CA 94567

Dear Mr. Mott:

As you know, I am the owner of a house several houses up the hill from yours. This spring your acacia trees have become so large that my view of the lake is obstructed. In our house deed restrictions, we are obligated to keep our trees trimmed to a height of twelve feet. Would you please have yours pruned so that my view will be restored?

Because I would benefit from the pruning, I am willing to share the cost of having this done. Please contact me so that we can work out a satisfactory arrangement. Thank you for your cooperation.

Sincerely yours,

Lillie Lewis

Give the owner time to respond before you follow up. If you run into a really stubborn neighbor, suggest sitting down with a trained, neutral mediator to work out a solution. (See Chapter 14, *Mediation.*)

Suppose that nothing you suggest works out. Or suppose your view is being blocked by a three-story addition going up in violation of the deeds. In either case, consult an attorney, who may be able to obtain prompt action with one stiff letter. If not, your only legal alternative is a lawsuit in regular (not small claims) court. You'll probably need to hire a lawyer to handle the lawsuit.

If you decide to take the neighbor to court, be aware that the enforcement of restrictive deed covenants can be a legal jungle. Covenants concerning trees and views are usually quite legal and enforceable.[8] But be prepared for a lengthy and expensive legal experience.

OTHER LAWS THAT MAY PROTECT VIEWS

If a neighbor is blocking your view or planning to, you might find help from local laws that do not directly address views—such as a law that restricts the height of fences or buildings or limits the square footage of a structure. In most places, local ordinances regulate trees, structures and fences, including trees that serve as fences.

If you do some research and determine the neighbor is in violation of a law, all that may be necessary is to talk to him or write him a letter. He could be unaware of the ordinance.

If you get no response, you can contact your local planning, zoning or building department, or the office of the city attorney; they should take it from there. The local government can cite a person for a violation, issue a fine and may even sue for conformity to the law.

For details on the laws on fences and trees, see Chapter 11, *Fences* and Chapter 6, *Boundary Trees.*

Here are some of the kinds of laws to look for:

Fence Height Limits

Local laws almost always limit artificial (constructed) fence heights. Commonly, they restrict fences in residential back yards to six feet and in front yards to three or four feet. They also restrict where you can build a fence—for instance, not too close to the street. Most of these types of regulations are found in the zoning laws.

But an artificial fence is not usually the culprit when a neighbor's view is blocked. The important application of fence laws in view cases usually occurs when the fence is a naturally growing one, such as a hedge. When bushes or trees are used as fences, height restrictions in fence laws can apply to them. Even if a tree owner claims that the trees are only for shade or greenery, if they are planted in a row and grow together to form a barrier, they are usually considered a fence and subject to the laws that govern fences. In these situations, a neighbor's view problem can be solved by the city when it enforces the fence ordinance.

A lawsuit in the town of Clyde Hill, Washington, provides a good example of how a local ordinance can be applied. The local law prohibited naturally grown fences above eight feet tall. A man who had thirteen Douglas fir trees along his border was found to be in violation of the ordinance and ordered to cut them, even though he claimed the trees were not a fence but only lovely landscaping.[9] We aren't told whether a view was involved, but can almost assume that it was; why else would someone want to cut back Douglas firs?

Remember that the violation occurred only because the trees were a fence, not because a neighbor's view was blocked. If your view is obstructed by a lone tree in someone's backyard, fence regulations won't apply.

A few states, such as Illinois, explicitly require natural growth to be cut back to a designated height when used as a division fence.[10] A state statute such as this one can be welcome relief to a person who has lost a view. Often the tree owner is unaware of the restriction, and pointing out the statute will result in prompt trimming. When only a state law is involved, you must sue the neighbor directly if you want to force compliance. To find out if your state has a law that specifically restricts natural fences, you may need to go to the law library. (See Chapter 13, *Legal Research*.)

For more on fence regulations, see Chapter 11, *Fences*.

UTILITY COMPANIES

Any time a tree is growing into wires or becoming a menace to them, the affected utility company will promptly cut them back when the situation is brought to its attention.

Laws That Regulate Trees

If your view is obstructed by a tree and the tree is not part of a fence, you may find help under local laws that regulate trees in general. Certain kinds of trees may be prohibited, for example, trees that cause allergies or tend to harm other plant growth. Height and location restrictions may apply—for instance, it may be too close to the street (especially an intersection) or electric wires or even an airport. If the tree looks sick or dangerous, specific laws could affect it, including nuisance laws. (See Chapter 5, *Unsound Limbs and Trees*.)

The city may remove such offending trees itself or require the property owner to do so. In the case of a dangerous tree, the city sometimes removes it and bills the owner.

Example: Roger notices one day that his neighbor's tree that blocks his view appears to be diseased and dying. He checks his local laws and discovers that there is not only an ordinance against objects on property that create a hazard, but that the city itself will remove a diseased tree under some circumstances. He simply reports the situation (in his town to the Department of Public Works) and looks up the next week to find the tree gone.

Zoning Laws

Just about all cities have local zoning regulations that control the size, location and uses of buildings. Zoning laws divide cities into different areas according to use, from single-family residential all the way to industrial. In a single-family area, height restrictions usually limit buildings to thirty or thirty-five feet. When multi-family units or commercial uses are allowed, the height limit goes up.

Another common restriction deals with "setbacks." The setback is the distance that must be left between the street and a structure or between the side and back of structures and the boundary lines.

A third important zoning regulation limits how much of a lot can be occupied by a structure. For instance, many suburban cities limit a dwelling to 40% to 60% of the property; no building is allowed over that portion.

These regulations can have a direct impact on property with a view. A next-door neighbor who suddenly throws up a 50-foot addition, blocking your view, may be violating the zoning laws. Sometimes a house is extended toward the boundary or street in violation of the setback rules. In other situations, someone may attempt to tack on a view-blocking addition that would be fine except for the fact that a city ordinance restricts structures to covering no more than 60% of a lot, and the offending neighbor is already at or near that limit.

Occasionally, an unusual law may help you—for instance, the three story colonial mansion going up in your view may be located in a district that limits house designs to southwestern ranch styles. Even in towns that require building permits before a structure goes up, some people ignore the laws or are unaware of them.

In almost every neighborhood there is at least one house that doesn't completely conform to current zoning laws. The builder may have ignored the law, and nobody complained. Or the house may have been built before the laws were passed. If the structure violates a restriction by just an inch or so, the builder may have substantially complied with the law and so have been left alone by zoning officials.

Sometimes a city allows what is called a "variance," an exemption from the zoning regulations for a particular property if there is a good reason. Be aware of this exception and always on the lookout for a "variance requested" sign on property that could affect your view. If the neighbors will be harmed by a variance, they can complain to the city; if enough of them so, it will probably be denied.

Using the Local Laws

When you have a view obstruction problem, you need to know exactly what your local laws say to see if something may help you. If your question is specific, such as a maximum fence height, try calling the city's planning or zoning department first. If you need to search a little to find a law that fits, the best thing to do is to make a trip to the public library or city hall to look at the ordinances. Be prepared to spend a little time; the indexing in some local ordinances is badly done.

You may have to sit down and read all of the ordinances under zoning, subdivisions, miscellaneous—practically the entire code. If you live in a small town or city, this can actually be fun. Most people never open the pages of their local ordinances. In many towns, you'll discover that almost anything causing someone to complain is against the law. If you want to check your state laws, you will probably need to go to a law library. (See Chapter 13, *Legal Research*.)

If you find a law that you think may help you, tell the neighbor about it. Give a copy of the law to the neighbor and then wait a reasonable time for a response. If you must complain to the city, you can usually find out from the city clerk's office where to complain and what the procedure is. In some towns, a phone call to the appropriate office will be enough. In others, you may have to go down to city hall and give someone the information or fill out a form.

Don't go in and simply tell a clerk that someone a block away from your house is obstructing or threatening to obstruct your view. Bring a copy of the law that is being violated with you and be sure you can document that a violation is taking place or imminently threatened. Have the address and be specific as to the details.

Ask which office will handle the matter, what the city will do and how long you must wait before you can expect action to be taken. If nothing happens within a week, call or go down there again. Especially in large cities, city offices can be terribly busy, understaffed and backlogged. Be persistent, so your situation will not end up at the bottom of the list.

VIEWS THAT ARE NOT LEGALLY PROTECTED

Now let's address the problems most of us face when a tree grows into our view. We own a house that isn't in a planned community, the neighbor's deed doesn't restrict tree height and there are no local zoning, tree or view laws to assist us. What can we do? The only avenue available may be diplomacy. To regain the view, you will have to convince your neighbor to cooperate.

The first step is to take a good look at the tree that is blocking the view. From the street you should be able to ascertain the property it's part of, the address, maybe even the name of the occupant on the mailbox.

You may gain a different perspective at the tree's own level. What is only a pain in the neck to you may be a highly valued asset to the owner. If it has a treehouse for the children or provides needed shelter to the property, you need to know this at the start. The owner may be resistant to you and extremely protective of the tree.

Next, review the material discussed in this chapter and consider whether the tree violates any local ordinances or

BREAKING THE LAW IS NEVER THE ANSWER

Never make the mistake one California fellow made and sneak a service in to cut the neighbor's trees. After proceeding to top 14 redwoods and one bay tree, he was sued by the owner and ordered to pay triple damages, based on the loss of the trees to the value of the property itself.[11] He was very lucky not to have been jailed and fined. If you even think of doing such a thing, first read about the penalties you'll face. (See Chapter 3, *When a Tree Is Injured or Destroyed*.)

interferes with utility easements. If it's on city property, too close to a street or soon to interfere with power or phone lines, you may have an obvious remedy.

If the tree is on a protected species list, find out what action the city will allow and what kind of permit is needed.

Answer these questions before you approach the owner:

- Does the tree affect the view of other neighbors? If it does, you could get them to approach the tree owner with you, and trimming costs could be divided among you.

- Which part of the tree is causing view problems for you—one limb, the top, one side of it?

- What is the least destructive action that could be taken to restore your view? Maybe the owner will agree to a limited and careful pruning.

- How much will the trimming cost? Be ready to pay for it. Remember that every day you wait and grumble is a day for the trees to grow and for the job to become more expensive. The loss of your personal enjoyment is probably worth more than the trimming cost, not to mention the devaluation of your property (which can be thousands of dollars).

Now, if you know the neighbor, go have a talk. Even if you don't know her, you may want to approach her in person. Be sure to put your money offer up front, so she won't think you are just criticizing her tree. Invite her over to see the situation from your property so she will understand the problem.

Give the neighbor a chance to voice any neighborhood concerns she has, even if they are unrelated to the tree. For example, if she is concerned about safety, noise, parking or anything else, perhaps you could do something to help. Your own offers to aid a neighbor could result in her cooperation with you.

If you would feel more comfortable keeping a distance, write a letter to the tree owner, instead. A sample letter is shown below.

---

                              46 Hilltop Drive
                              Oceanscape, CA 98876

                              June 15, 19___

Mr. Nathan Norris
44 Pine Lane
Oceanscape, CA 98876

Dear Mr. Norris:

   I am writing to offer to have your pine trees trimmed at my expense. The trees are obstructing my view, and because I would benefit from the pruning, I am willing to bear the cost. A skillful trimming would enhance the health and beauty of the trees and would restore my view.

   I suggest employing a professional service of your choice to perform the work at your convenience. The responsibility for clearing any debris will also be mine.

   If you are interested in pursuing this, I would be most appreciative. Please contact me at 555-4454 so that we may discuss arrangements. Thank you.

Sincerely yours,

Dennis Duke

Will it work? In some circumstances, it will. Given the chance, and approached properly, people are usually basically cooperative. They also like to be needed and to feel important. What do you have to lose?

If you run into a stone wall in your efforts, at least keep an eye on the house in case it changes hands. You may have lost your view for the time being, but be alert to the possibility of dealing with a new owner.

AVOIDING VIEW PROBLEMS

Before you part with your life savings to purchase the perfect view, you can take steps to find out if the view will be permanent. Ask if the property is protected by a view ordinance. If so, negotiate with the seller to be sure the view you buy is the one the seller is entitled to (see "View Ordinances," above).

Check with the seller or real estate agent to see if the property deed incorporates restrictions on your use of the property. If it does, ask to see a copy of the restrictions. Also find out about the homeowners association— whether it's active and enforces the restrictions.

You also need to know what the zoning is, not only for your own property, but for any property that might affect you. This means finding out where the zoning changes, and checking all property between you and the view. Can the neighbor down the hill add a second story addition? What's the height limit anywhere within the view? This kind of caution may sound a bit extreme, but it can pay off.

Example: Jack and Margaret, after saving for many years, purchase their dream house. It comes with a view of the ocean that adds $50,000 to the price. They know that their property is zoned single-family residential and think that the view is forever. Ten blocks away, however, the zoning allows ten-story condominium buildings. A few years later, up goes a five-building, ten-story complex, replacing their view with stone and glass. Jack and Margaret simply hadn't anticipated this problem, and they are out of luck. It happens all the time.

Before you buy, go to city hall or the planning department and look at the zoning map. See if you can get a copy of the zoning regulations; if not, proceed to the public library.

You need to go to the library anyway because you want to sit down and study other city laws as well. Look up all the topics in the checklist below.

Trees

- view laws
- protected and prohibited species

Structures (Zoning Laws)

- maximum heights
- setback rules
- percentage allowance—percentage of structure to lot
- style requirements
- permit requirements

Fences

- height limits
- setback rules
- natural fences (trees, shrubs)

If you find with pleasure that the zoning law prohibits people downhill from you from erecting a structure that will block your view, but there is no view ordinance, you can make one further effort to insure your view. Look very closely from the property to see just which trees might later become an obstruction to your view. Then go introduce yourself to the neighbor and explain your concerns. If the neighbor also has a view, he will probably understand your concern and admire your precautions. If you find an unfriendly and uncooperative neighbor, you stand warned.

Remember, even if the neighbors are reassuring and you feel quite comfortable, property changes hands. New owners may not be as receptive to your needs. A certain amount of risk may be unavoidable when investing in a view.

---

[1]*Lindsay v. First Nat. Bank of Asheville,* 115 N.C. 553, 20 S.E. 621 (1894).

[2]A right to solar access is becoming recognized in some states, such as California, when created in writing. (Cal. Civ. Code § 801.5.)

[3]Berkeley, Cal. Mun. Ord. 12.45.

[4]*Prah v. Maretti,* 108 Wis. 2d 223, 321 N.W.2d 182 (1982).

[5]Oakland, Cal. Mun. Ord. § 7-8.03.

[6]Berkeley, Cal. Mun. Ord., Chapter 12.45.040.

[7]*Ezer v. Fuchsloch,* 99 Cal. App. 3d 849, 160 Cal. Rptr. 486 (1979).

[8]13 A.L.R.4th 1346; *Mock v. Schulman,* 226 Cal. App. 2d 263, 38 Cal. Rptr. 39 (1964).

[9]*Clyde Hill v. Roisen,* 48 Wash. App. 769, 740 P.2d 378 (1987).

[10]Ill. Ann. Stat. ch. 54 § 3.

[11]*Roche v. Casissa,* 154 Cal. 2d 785, 316 P.2d 776 (1957).

Boundary Lines

Most of us don't know where our exact property boundaries are located, and many of us don't care. Unless we have the property surveyed, the only way we may be able to go outside and physically touch the limit of what is ours is when permanent markers are described in a deed, such as a tree or stone monument. And even when a permanent marker can be located, the boundary may not run in a straight line.

SETTLING UNCERTAIN BOUNDARY LINES

If you or your neighbor want to fence the property or build a structure close to the line, you need to know where the boundary line actually runs. If you can't figure it out from the property descriptions in your deed or subdivision map, or you and the neighbor think it is in different places, you have several choices.

Setting the Boundary With a Quitclaim Deed

To establish a clear boundary, adjoining property owners can decide where they want it to be and then make it so by signing deeds that describe the boundary agreed on. If you have a mortgage on the property, consult a local attorney for help in drawing up the deeds. Whoever holds the mortgage may need to be notified and permission obtained before you transfer even a tiny piece of the land. Some mortgage companies will not be concerned or want to be involved. But others put a clause in the mortgage that allows the company to demand full and immediate payment of the entire loan if the borrower transfers any interest whatsoever in the property.

Even if you have no mortgage, you might want to get an attorney to draw up the property descriptions in the deed, or just to look over your work if you draw up your own using *The Deeds Book* by Mary Randolph (Nolo Press). It may be worth spending the money for this small service to avoid any possibility of later confusion.

Each neighbor should sign a quitclaim deed, transferring to the other neighbor any right they have to the property that falls on the other side of the line they have agreed on. Once the deeds are recorded (put on file) in the county land records office (usually in the courthouse), there will never again be a question about the boundary. All future buyers will be able to find the deed and know what belongs to whom, when they buy the property.

Example: Janet and Rod, next-door neighbors, aren't sure where the boundary line is between their properties. Rod wants to enclose his yard with a fence, but doesn't want to pay for an expensive survey of the property to find the exact boundary. He and Janet agree that the fence will mark the boundary. Then they each draw up a quitclaim deed. Rod signs a deed giving any rights to the property on the other side of the fence to Janet, and she signs a comparable deed.

Sample Deed

Recording requested by

Rodney E. Rivera
245 Poplar Street
Sunset, CA 98876

  and when recorded mail
  this deed and tax statements to:

same as above

QUITCLAIM DEED

For a valuable consideration, receipt of which is hereby acknowledged,

Rodney E. Rivera
hereby quitclaim(s) to
Janet S. Johnson

the following real property in the City of _____Sunset_____,
County of _____Lake_____ California:

Any interest in Lot 4 of the Lake Park Tract, filed June 3, 1926, in Book 32 of Maps, at page 67, in the Office of the County Recorder of Lake County, California, and bounded on the north by a wooden fence, erected in April of 19__.

Date: _April 10, 19_   *Rodney E. Rivera*

State of California   )
County of ____Lake____   ) ss.

On ____April 10, 19____, ___Rodney E. Rivera___,
known to me or proved by satisfactory evidence to be the person(s) whose name(s) is/are subscribed above, personally acknowledged that he____ executed this deed.

Sarah Currington   [Notary Seal]
Signature of Notary

In the deed Rod signs, he describes and gives up any interest in Janet's property. Janet makes out a deed quitclaiming any interest in Rod's property. Each property is identified exactly as it is in the deed already on record, with the addition of the description of the fence. Then they both put the deeds on file (record them) at the county land records office.

If you have no mortgage on your property, setting a new boundary this way can be a very easy procedure. You can purchase quitclaim forms in some large office supply stores and do it yourself. However, because legal intricacies in property descriptions vary from state to state, it is always wisest to let a local real estate lawyer check the deed.

Setting Boundaries by Owners' Agreements

When a boundary line cannot be located because deeds or maps are ambiguous, the two adjoining neighbors may simply agree where the boundary line is. Once this agreement is made and certain conditions (discussed below) are met, the line is the permanent legal boundary. It is binding not only on those neighbors but also on later buyers.[1] The agreement does not change the ownership of land. Instead, it interprets ambiguous property descriptions in the deeds.

This approach has much to recommend it if both neighbors genuinely agree. It is easy, inexpensive and fixes a certain boundary line. Done properly, it will end confusion for the neighbors and for later buyers.

The purpose of this rule, according to one judge, is "to prevent strife and disputes concerning boundaries."[2] This may ring with truth for two neighbors who come to a solution, write it down and record it in the public land records. However, if the agreement isn't written down and recorded, it can wreak havoc when property changes hands or one of the neighbors dies.

Requirements for an Agreed Boundary

For neighbors to agree on a permanently binding boundary between their properties, four conditions must be met:

- There must be genuine uncertainty as to where the true boundary line runs on the ground

- Both landowners must agree on the new line

- The owners must then act as if the new boundary line really is the boundary (lawyers often call this "acting in reliance on the agreement")

- The agreed boundary must be identifiable on the ground.

Only after all these requirements are satisfied does the boundary the neighbors settled on become the legal line. Some courts can be extremely strict when looking to see if a boundary agreement meets these criteria. If one of the requirements is absent and the line is ever challenged in court, the agreement will be ruled to be void and the boundary line as uncertain as it ever was. We discuss each of these requirements below.

Original Uncertainty. For an agreed boundary line to become the fixed legal boundary, the two owners must not only agree, but agree because they really can't locate the line. This doesn't mean that the neighbors must call in a surveyor to try to find the boundary. It is enough if they cannot reasonably locate the line from their deed descriptions, from a previous survey recorded in the land records or from markers on the ground.

Usually, what happens is that someone wants to put up a fence, or maybe both neighbors want to put one up together. When they attempt to find the boundary, they discover that the property descriptions in their deeds conflict or perhaps make no sense at all. Not wanting hard feelings or lawsuits, they simply agree on a line convenient to both of them. Many are the neighbors who have done this and proceeded to live happily side by side for many years.

But if someone challenges the boundary line in court—perhaps the next buyer of one of the properties, who is unhappy with or confused by the agreed boundary—and the real boundary line could have easily been found, the general rule is that the owners' agreement doesn't count. A judge may make an exception to this requirement only if the owners had relied for many years on the agreement and great harm would result by not recognizing the agreed line.[3]

Example: A recent case from California illustrates the kind of legal microscope a court will often use when determining whether or not the requirement of uncertainty has been met. The new owner of a piece of property assumed that an 80- year-old fence was the boundary and proceeded to make major changes on the land. The next-door neighbor claimed that he was trespassing and sued him. Because the fence was so old, former owners from years before were brought in to testify as to whether or not it had been an agreed boundary. They gave conflicting stories; some had assumed the fence was the boundary, others had not. As it turned out, arguments about whether or not the fence was the agreed boundary made no difference whatsoever, because there were some old boundary markers on the property that could have been found by any of the owners if anyone had searched. In short, there was never real uncertainty. The new owner's mistake and his trespass on his neighbor's land cost him dearly: He was ordered to pay the neighbor $26,000.[4]

Agreement by the Owners: A neighbors' agreement about an uncertain boundary doesn't have to be in writing to be legal. But obviously, a written agreement avoids confusion and disputes later.

Sometimes, if a line has been treated as the boundary by both owners for many years, an initial agreement between them will be inferred by a court that is deciding on

MEDIATING AN AGREEMENT

If you and your neighbor can't seem to agree on where you think the boundary line should run, you may be able to get some help from a trained mediator. A mediator helps the people iron out difficulties and reach an agreement that is satisfactory to everybody involved. Mediation of disputes between neighbors is often free or very inexpensive. See Chapter 14 for more on this process.

the validity of an alleged boundary agreement. A court might make this inference when all of the other conditions of an agreed boundary have been met.

Acting in Reliance On a Boundary. Once adjoining landowners agree that a particular line marks an uncertain boundary, for that line to become the legal boundary they must then act as if it is the boundary. They can do this by simply going about their business, treating the line as the partition between their properties for whatever time period is required by state law. The time required ranges from five years to twenty years. If you need to know what your state's required time period is, you must find a state court opinion dealing with an agreed boundary in your state. (See Chapter 13, *Legal Research*.)

If, however, great harm would be caused were the agreed boundary not considered the legal one, the agreed boundary can become the legal one before the required time period has elapsed.[5] Courts will rule this way when one or both of the neighbors does a substantial act relying on the validity of the agreed line, such as building a house close to it.

Example: Two people purchase lots in a subdivision. The boundary line between their properties is unclear, both from the subdivision map and their deed descriptions. One wants to fence his lot, and they agree on a boundary. These two fellows are friendly neighbors; one even gives the other the lumber for the fence. A lovely split rail fence is built, along with a comfortable house. Both properties are then sold. The new owner of the fenced house comes home from shopping one day and discovers a crew tearing down his fence. The other owner has had a new survey done which shows the boundary line running squarely through the shopper's bedroom.

This actually happened in California, and the owner of the fence sued the other owner. When the lawsuit came before the court, the ruling was: The legal boundary line was the one agreed upon by the previous owners, even though the state had a five-year period for an agreed boundary to become fixed, and five years had not passed since the agreement. The court based its ruling on the fact that the housebuilder had relied on the agreed boundary to build a house. Making him tear the house down, the court decided, would be too severe and unfair. The man who tore down the fence was ordered to pay the neighbor not only the replacement value, but also $500 in extra damages for the malicious behavior he showed in ripping down his neighbor's fence.[6]

Identifying the Agreed Boundary: When two owners settle confusion by agreeing on a boundary line, the line should be physically obvious in some way. Often, a fence or a natural boundary marks the line. It could be a tree, road, creek, driveway, even the edge of a house. If not, something needs to be constructed, or stakes or some other markers put in the ground so that the owners can point to the line.

The reason to have a visible line is to alert a new buyer as to where the line is, to prevent trouble in the future. Anyone who purchases property is expected to make a visual inspection of the site. If someone else's driveway is two feet from the house he's buying, he is expected to notice it. This is the time to inquire about it and to call in a surveyor if necessary—not after buying the property and settling in.

Putting Boundary Agreements in Writing

An informal, unwritten boundary agreement can be a ticking time bomb, ready to go off when the property is sold. To avoid an explosion, if you make an agreement about a land boundary, put it in writing.

A sample agreement is shown below.

REAL PROPERTY BOUNDARY AGREEMENT BETWEEN

Alvin and Eloise Lewis and Warren Olsen.

Alvin and Eloise Lewis, owners of real property in the City of Sunset, County of Woodland, State of California, described as:

Lot 20, Subdivision Map of Lots 1, 2, 3, and 4, Ridge Park, Sunset, filed January 12, 1892, map book 11, page 32,

and

Warren Olsen, owner of real property in the City of Sunset, County of Woodland, State of California, described as:

Lot 19, Subdivision Map of Lots 1, 2, 3, and 4, Ridge Park, Sunset, filed January 12, 1892, map book 11, page 32, agree as follows:

1. Because of ambiguities in the property descriptions in our deeds and the subdivision maps, we are uncertain as to where the true boundary line between our properties is located.

2. The location of the split rail fence standing on this date between our properties is the true boundary line.

_____   _____
Alvin Lewis   Date

_____   _____
Warren Olsen   Date

_____   _____
Eloise Lewis   Date

NOTARIZATION

State of California   )
County of _____   )

On this _____ day of _____, in the year 19___ , before me, a Notary Public, State of California, duly commissioned and sworn, personally appeared _____ and _____, personally known to me (or proved to me on the basis of satisfactory evidence) to be the people whose names are subscribed to this instrument, and acknowledged that they executed it.

                          _____
                          Notary Public for
(Notary Seal)   the State of_____

                          My commission expires: _____,19___

If you and your neighbor make such a written agreement, use the exact property descriptions that are in your deeds. Be sure that all owners sign the agreement. Have it notarized and make copies to keep with your deeds.

Once you have a signed, notarized agreement, take it to the local property records office (often in the county courthouse) and ask the clerk to record it. When you record a document, it becomes part of a public record, so other people can find it. You will have to pay a small fee, probably just a few dollars per page of the document.

The clerk may be a little surprised at your request, because not a lot of boundary agreements are recorded. In a very few states—Kentucky is one—there is a procedure in the state statutes for setting an agreed boundary, putting the agreement in writing and recording it at the courthouse.[7]

If there is no standard procedure in your state, ask if you can put it on file with the land descriptions of both properties. In some states the clerk may be able to make a note in the margin of your deed that refers to the agreement. At least get it filed under both names on the agreement, so that it will be part of the public record.

Calling in a Surveyor

If you are willing to spend several hundred dollars or more to find out exactly where your boundary is, call a licensed surveyor. The surveyor will survey the entire property and give you a copy of the survey, showing the boundary lines of your property. He will also place official markers on the boundary lines, which will remain to mark the boundaries.

Be aware that you and the neighbor could be in for further conflict when the boundary is found. The line may run several feet away from what you expected—maybe even through one of the houses. When this happens, one neighbor may have to pay the other for property she was

DEALING WITH
THE SURVEYOR

When the surveyor comes out, do everybody a favor and stay out of the way. Find out what will be needed from you, such as a copy of your deed or any other records, and have everything ready. Then let the professionals do their job. You and the neighbor standing there explaining who built what and what belongs to whom is nothing but a waste of time and money.

occupying by mistake. This can get complicated, especially if the new survey conflicts with one in the past or the descriptions in the deeds, and you may need a lawyer.

In a new subdivision that still has markers from a city survey, the cost of a survey can run around $500. When streets have been renovated and the surveyor has to bring lines in from far away, the cost goes up accordingly. Be prepared to spend several hundred dollars to over a thousand dollars if you live in an area where no survey has been done for a long time, or the maps are unreliable and conflicting. Sometimes, the surveyor really can't know just what will be involved until the job begins. If you and your neighbor go in together on the cost, having both properties done at the same time by the same surveyor, you should be able to save some money.

If you are in the midst of a heated dispute with your neighbor and hire a surveyor on your own, the neighbor will probably have to allow the surveyor onto his property if necessary. It is against state law in many states to interfere with a surveyor or to refuse a right of entry. Always notify the neighbor that the surveyor is coming and what time, if practicable. This is required in California.[8] If the neighbor indicates that there will be trouble, have a lawyer write a letter outlining the law and asking for entry to the property for the survey. If necessary, the lawyer can get a court order to allow the survey.

Once you have a survey done, ask if the survey company will record it in the local public land records. If not, take a copy to the courthouse and ask that it be recorded; there will be a small fee.

Letting a Court Decide on the Boundary

When a boundary line is not clear and the neighbors can't agree, a few states have statutory procedures allowing one neighbor to ask a state court (regular court, not small claims court) to settle the line. This will probably involve a new court-ordered survey and will be expensive. In other states, you can hire a lawyer and file a suit to "quiet title" (decide who owns what). Again, the judge may order a survey done, and the whole thing will take a lot of time and money.

LAWS PROTECTING BOUNDARY MARKERS

Permanent boundary monuments or survey markers are protected by state law. A marker may be a naturally occurring landmark, such as a tree. Or, a surveyor may place iron stakes or small brass caps in the ground to officially mark the property line. In Massachusetts, anyone removing such a marker can be jailed for six months or fined $50 or both.[9] The penalty is stiffer in the District of Columbia, where the fine is up to $1,000 and the prison term can be a full year.[10] The law is similar and very serious in other states. Arkansas imposes a fine of at least $500, jail for at least thirty days, or both.[11]

WHEN A NEIGHBOR DOESN'T HONOR THE BOUNDARY

Most neighbors get along for years with no serious questions concerning their boundary lines. But one day you may look out your window to discover a frightening scene. There stands the next-door neighbor on what you think is your property, putting up a fence or taking yours down. Or perhaps he is sitting atop a backhoe, digging up your property for his new garage. What you have long assumed was the boundary line has been crossed.

If a neighbor starts to build on what you think is your property, do something immediately. If the neighbor's encroachment is minor, for instance a small fence in the wrong place, you may think you shouldn't worry. You are wrong. When you go to sell your house, the title company may refuse to issue insurance because the neighbor is on your land.

It is important to act promptly because if you don't, you could lose part of your property. When one person uses another's land, he can gain a legal right to do so and, in some circumstances gain title to the property. (See Chapter 10, *Using Another's Land: Trespass and Easements.*)

Also, if you don't get the construction stopped, even if you later sue for trespass and win, all you may be able to collect is a money award, not an order to remove the neighbor's addition. Judges do not like to order property destroyed. Only if the neighbor intentionally trespassed can you even hope for an order of removal of a substantial structure.

Any time a neighbor starts to build on what you think is your property, step over for a chat and find out what is going on. Most likely, a mistake has been made. There may be a conflicting description in the neighbor's deed or just a wrong assumption about the line. You may even discover that neither one of you is really sure where the boundary is. You may want to make your own agreement about a boundary or hire a surveyor to find the existing one. (See "Settling Uncertain Boundary Lines," above.)

If your neighbor is hostile and insists on proceeding, inform her that you will sue her if necessary to stop what he is doing. If you are already certain about the boundary and have proof, such as a survey, you can threaten to call the police and have him arrested for trespassing.

Perhaps a firm and threatening letter on legal stationery will at least stop the building. If a letter and a threatened lawsuit don't make the neighbor stop, waste no time in having a lawyer get a judge's order to temporarily stop the neighbor until a civil lawsuit for trespass (being on your property without authorization) can come before the judge.

If the neighbor is actually claiming part of your land, for example under a conflicting survey or because he has been using it (see Chapter 10), you'll need an attorney to file a lawsuit to have the neighbor or his property removed. Or the attorney can file a suit to "quiet title"—to let the court decide who owns what.

---

[1]For example, see *Needham v. Collamer*, 94 Cal. App. 2d 609, 211 P.2d 308 (1949).

[2]*Young v. Blakeman*, 153 Cal. 477, 95 P. 888 (1908).

[3]For example, see *Minson Co. v. Aviation Finance*, 38 Cal. App. 3d 489, 113 Cal. Rptr. 223 (1974). See also *Ernie v. Trinity Lutheran Church*, 51 Cal. 2d 702, 336 P.2d 525 (1959), where the property in dispute was a strip less than a foot wide.

[4]*Armitage v. Decker*, 90 C.D.O.S. 1770 (Cal. App. 1990).

[5]When one owner relies substantially on a boundary line and the other owner does not disagree, some courts will say that the other owner acquiesced to the boundary and is legally stopped from protesting otherwise. The end result is the same, no matter how it is described—the line becomes the legal boundary.

[6]*McCormick v. Appleton*, 225 Cal. App. 2d 591, 37 Cal. Rptr. 544 (1964).

A LITTLE COMMON SENSE

If you are having no trouble with your property and your neighbors, yet you feel inclined to go rushing out to determine your exact boundaries just to know where they are, please ask yourself a question. Have you been satisfied in the past with the amount of space that you occupy? If the answer is yes, then consider the time, money and hostility that might be involved if you pursue the subject.

When a problem exists on your border, keep the lines of communication open with the neighbor if possible. Learn the law and try to work out an agreement between yourselves. Boundary lines simply don't matter that much to us most of the time; relationships with our neighbors matter a great deal.

[7]Ken. Rev. Stat. 73.190. The procedure in Kentucky is quite elaborate and involves having a new survey done.

[8]Cal. Civ. Code § 846.5.

[9] Mass. Gen. Laws ch. 266 § 94.

[10] D.C. Code § 22-3109.

[11]Ark. Stat. Ann. § 5-38-214.

Using Another's Land: Trespass and Easements

Man, like a tree in the cleft of a rock, gradually shapes his roots to his surroundings, and when the roots have grown to a certain size, can't be displaced without cutting at his life.

—Justice Oliver Wendell Holmes

People have the right to keep unwanted intruders off their property. They do this all the time, sometimes with fences or with signs, sometimes just by asking trespassers to please stay away. In cases of serious, repeated annoyance or threatened harm, landowners can call the police. They will usually warn the person to stay away and, if necessary, make an arrest. Trespass is a minor criminal offense, and someone convicted of criminal trespass can be fined and jailed.

Another kind of trespass is more permanent: using another's property as an owner would use it. If someone drives across a neighbor's land every day, it is a trespass unless the owner has granted permission or the driver has a legal right, called an easement, to use that part of the neighbor's property (see "Easements," below.) The other neighbor who just put up a fence two feet over the boundary line is trespassing, as is the one whose garage has been in the wrong place on the neighbor's property for several years.

These trespassers can also be asked to leave or warned away. But there's a chance that any of them may in fact have a legal claim to the property.

TRESPASSERS WHO BECOME OWNERS

Many landowners are surprised to learn that under certain circumstances, a trespasser can come onto land, occupy it and gain legal ownership of it. The trespasser may acquire a few feet of property or whole acres in this way. If someone is using your property, even a small strip on the edge, you should be alert to the risk.

A trespasser may also gain a legal right to use part of someone else's property; this is called a prescriptive easement. (See "Easements," below.)

The legal doctrine that allows trespassers to become owners is called "adverse possession." Although the name sounds nasty (and the results can be), the trespasser is not necessarily an intentional evildoer—far from it. The trespasser may simply have made a mistake—relying on a faulty property description in a deed, for example. In rural areas, the person who moves in and occupies several acres may believe he owned it, having purchased it from a scoundrel who sold someone else part of the Brooklyn Bridge. Questions about ownership often wind up in court after an absent owner of rural property discovers that someone is living on his land or, when a piece of urban property is sold, a title insurance company refuses to issue insurance because the neighbor's garage is found to be standing squarely on the property. If the people involved can't work something out, the property owner may sue the trespasser, or the trespasser may bring a lawsuit to quiet title—a request for the court to settle who owns what. (For information on how next-door neighbors can work out boundary agreements themselves, see Chapter 9, *Boundaries.*)

Requirements for Obtaining Land by Adverse Possession

A trespasser is entitled to legal ownership of property if his occupation of the property is hostile, actual, open and notorious, exclusive and continuous for a period of years set by state statute. (We explain each of these terms below.) Some states, such as California, also require the trespasser to have paid the local property taxes on the land.[1] The time required, which varies from state to state, is usually twenty years. It can be as short as ten years when the trespasser pays the property taxes.

Hostile Claim

The word "hostile" does not mean that the trespasser barricades himself on the land with a shotgun. Most courts follow one of two legal definitions of hostile. One is called the "Maine rule" and requires that the person be aware that he is trespassing.[2] For example, a man in Nebraska, a state which follows this rule, gained ownership of the neighboring eight acres by using them for years. He knew the property was not his, and a court characterized his action as hostile.[3]

The other popular definition, the "Connecticut rule," defines hostile simply as occupation of the land.[4] The trespasser doesn't have to know that the land belongs to someone else. The Connecticut rule, kinder to the innocent trespasser, is followed by most states today.[5]

Example: Jesse isn't sure where his property line is, but he thinks an old fence marks the boundary. When he builds his new garage, he builds up to the fence line, which is actually ten feet over on his neighbor's property. Under the Connecticut rule, Jesse's intention doesn't matter, and his occupation is hostile even though he thinks he is on his own land.

A few states follow a third rule, which is directly opposite the Maine rule of requiring intentional trespass. The trespasser must be completely innocent and must have made a good faith mistake, such as relying on an invalid or incorrect deed. For example, in Iowa, which follows this good faith rule, a woman attempted to claim a strip of her neighbor's land by adverse possession. The court denied her claim because she knew it was not her property, even though she had treated the property as her own for thirty years.[6]

The chart below lists how each state has interpreted the requirement of hostile claim.

Hostile Claim Chart

Must intend to take the land	Must believe land is own
Arkansas	Georgia
Maine	Iowa
Michigan	Louisiana
Montana	
Missouri	
Nevada	
Texas	
Virginia	
Vermont	
Wyoming	

Possession alone has shown hostility in all other states.

Actual, Open and Notorious Possession

The trespasser must actually be in possession of the property and treat it as if he were an owner. This means there must be a physical presence on the land. It's not enough for someone just to make a claim, orally or in writing, of ownership.

The words "open and notorious" simply mean that it must be obvious to anyone, including an owner who investigates, that a trespasser is on the land. Actual (physical) possession is usually open and notorious. Someone out in the field harvesting crops is obvious, as is a person pruning the rose garden that she planted on a strip of the neighbor's back yard. Similarly, a neighbor who just put a fence up slightly on the next-door property is obvious. So is the one who just poured a concrete driveway two feet over the boundary line.

The point of this requirement is to let the owner know someone is occupying the land, so something can be done about it. An owner who allows someone to trespass for years without giving permission, complaining or taking action, the theory goes, loses the rights to the land.

Exclusive and Continuous Possession

The trespasser must possess the land exclusively and without interruption for the statutory time period. You can find how many years are required in your state from the chart below.

A trespasser can't give up the use of the property in such a way that he no longer acts as an owner, and then return to it and count the time that it was abandoned—that wouldn't be continuous possession for the whole time.

The person trespassing must be the only one occupying the property—he can't share possession with strangers or the owner. (By contrast, a trespasser can gain the right to use a certain part of another's property, a prescriptive easement, even if possession or use is shared with others. See "Easements," below.)

If one person uses the property for a while and leaves, and another shows up for a while, the times can't be combined—the possession hasn't been exclusive by one person.

If, however, the trespasser actually sells or gives the property to someone else, the recipient becomes the adverse possessor and the years that the first trespasser spent occupying the land count for the new one's claim. This is called "tacking." When one trespasser passes the land to the next, then that person's claim is tacked on to the previous one.

Example: Joe occupied part of someone else's land for ten years. He then sold his land (including the part that was not legally his) to Adam, who stayed for ten years. If his state's adverse possession statute requires twenty years of occupancy, Adam has met the twenty-year requirement through tacking. On the other hand, if Joe stopped trespassing before Adam bought the property and started his own trespassing, the ten years of Joe's trespass don't count for Adam.

Time Requirement Chart

A trespasser must occupy land for this long in order to claim ownership.

State	Years Required	State	Years Required
Alabama	20	Montana	5 (t)
Alaska	10	Nebraska	10
Arizona	10	Nevada	15 (t)
Arkansas	7		5 (t,d)
California	5 (t)	New Hampshire	20
Colorado	18	New Mexico	10 (t,d)
Connecticut	15	New Jersey	20
Delaware	20	New York	10
D. C.	15	North Carolina	20
Florida	7 (t,d)	North Dakota	20
Georgia	20		10 (t)
	7 (d)	Ohio	21
Hawaii	10	Oklahoma	15
Idaho	5 (t)	Oregon	10
Illinois	20	Pennsylvania	21
Indiana	10 (t)	Rhode Island	10
Iowa	10	South Carolina	10
Kansas	15	South Dakota	20
Kentucky	15		10 (t)
Louisiana	10 (d)	Tennessee	7
Maine	20	Texas	10
Maryland	20	Utah	7 (t)
Massachusetts	20	Vermont	15
Michigan	15	Virginia	15
Minnesota	15 (t)	Washington	10
Mississippi	10	West Virginia	10
Missouri	10	Wisconsin	20
		Wyoming	10

(d) You must have an ownership document (even if it is invalid).
(t) You must have paid the taxes on the property.

Payment of Property Taxes

Some states require the trespasser to have paid the taxes on the property for the statutory time period. If all the other requirements are met except the tax payment, a court will usually grant a prescriptive easement to use the property to the trespasser, instead of ownership through adverse possession. (See "Easements," below).

What Can the Owner Do?

A landowner who doesn't keep an eye on his property can lose it. Nobody should allow the boundaries to be redrawn by inattention and inaction—in a city, a loss of even twenty feet could be devastating to a property investment.

If you become seriously concerned that someone has a possible claim to your land, check the local property tax records to see if anyone has made tax payments for the property. Paying taxes always bolsters an adverse possession claim, even when it is not required for a successful claim.

There are several steps an owner can take to prevent a trespasser from gaining a legal claim to the ownership.

Post Signs and Block Entry

Some people put up "Posted" or "No Trespassing" signs to keep people off their properties. Signs can alert a trespasser that the land belongs to someone else, but are not protection against adverse possession unless state law requires the trespasser to believe that he is on his own land to make a claim (see "Hostile Claim," above). Signs are never a substitute for periodic inspection of the property. It is easy to imagine someone tacking up a few signs and returning 25 years later—or never, a new buyer returning instead. By that time, the signs are long gone and a neighbor may have shifted over onto the land.

Signs that don't tell trespassers to stay off, but instead grant permission to use the property may actually protect an owner from losing a property interest to the public as a whole (see "Easements," below).

Locked gates at entry points to the property when the land is enclosed, or across an access that is being used, will stop most trespassers. But you should routinely check to be sure someone is not ignoring them, or worse, removing them.

Give Written Permission

One effective way to thwart a possible claim is by giving permission to use your land. If Norma is out planting a garden in your backyard, treating it as her own land, step over and say "Hello, you are on my property by a few feet, but that's okay." You don't have to throw her off your property; simply claim it. Then put the permission in writing and obtain an acknowledgment from Norma. The chain has been broken. She can tend that garden for forty years and still never acquire a legal claim to your property if she has your permission.

An example of written permission is shown below.

AGREEMENT GRANTING PERMISSION TO USE PROPERTY

I, Frank Feldman, owner of the property located at 356 Hill Drive, Sunset, California, give my permission to Norma Neal to plant and tend a garden located on a five-foot strip of my property bordering the west side of the property line. I reserve the right to revoke this permission at any time.

_____   _____

Frank Feldman   date

I, Norma Neal, acknowledge that my use of this strip of land belonging to Frank Feldman is by permission only, and that the permission may be revoked at any time.

_____   _____

Norma Neal   date

This type of agreement can be used to grant permission for parking, using a shortcut across property or even growing crops. It not only can defeat adverse possession claims, but also a claim to an easement across your property (see "Easements," below). When you use such a written permission, be absolutely sure that the portion of your land being used is described in enough detail so that it is easily identifiable.

If your neighbor is upset or insulted by the idea of a written permission, show her this book. Explain that while you have no objection to her use of your land, you must protect your interest for later years.

If the neighbor refuses to acknowledge the permissive use, you are then on the alert of a possible claim that is adverse to your interest, and you should take steps to prevent further use of your property.

Offer to Rent the Property to the Trespasser

If someone wants to remain on your property, you can always offer to rent it to them. In fact, the presentation of a rental agreement can be very effective in getting some trespassers to immediately leave on their own.

Call the Police

If someone refuses to acknowledge a permission, and ignores your requests to stay off your property, you can call the police or notify the sheriff and have the person removed or arrested.

When the trespasser is a next-door neighbor, you may be understandably reluctant to bring in the police. But sometimes it is necessary to protect your property.

Hire a Lawyer

Any time it appears that a trespasser may be entertaining the idea of claiming your property under an adverse possession theory, see a lawyer. You may need to file a lawsuit to eject the trespasser from the land. Or you may want to ask a court to order a structure removed or a person to stay away. You must act before the trespasser has been on your land long enough, under your state's law, to make a successful adverse possession claim.

EASEMENTS

An easement is a legal right to use someone else's land for a particular purpose. For example, the municipal water company may have an easement to run water pipes under your property. Your name is on the deed (you're the title holder) and you still own the property, but the water company has the right to use a part of it, for its pipes. Easements are sometimes in writing and referred to in property deeds or title papers prepared by a title insurance company or attorney.

Easements are part and parcel of the land they affect. They don't change when the property changes hands. Subsequent owners are obliged to let whoever owns the easement use the property.

Whoever owns the property may not interfere with the purpose of a legal easement. If, for example, the electric company has wires strung across its right of way, you cannot take them down or block their path. A property owner who does interfere with an easement can be liable to the easement owner for any damage he causes.

For example, the city of New York was found liable for damage caused to privately owned water pipes which were on property located under the terms of an easement. The damage was caused by oak trees that the city had planted. When the pipes broke and the property owner sued, the court said the city should have known that roots from oak trees would cause damage, and held it liable.[7]

Utility Easements

Probably the most common kind of easement is the one that has been given in writing to a utility company or a city. Utility easements are sometimes described in a property deed or certificate of title as "those certain utility easements as set out and shown on the map and plat of record in such-and-such a book on page something-or-other."

The existence of these easements doesn't have much day-to-day effect. You can plant on the property, live on it, even build on it, as long as you don't interfere with the utility's use of the easement.

When an easement is underground—for instance, a water pipe easement (and increasingly, electric and phone line easements)— the land above it may be used. But again, you may not interfere with the purpose of the underground easement. An example of interference would be placing too much weight on the property if pipes are not built to withstand it. A man in Los Angeles, for instance, found himself having to spend an extra $32,000 when he erected a heavy building over a sewer. The building had to be designed so that the weight straddled the easement.[8]

Utility companies rarely bother property owners. If an occasional nightmare comes along, such as the property dug up for underground repair, the work is usually done with care. And if a utility company comes in and harms your property unnecessarily, you may be able to sue the company if it won't pay for the damages.

The existence of utility easements across your property (and your neighbor's) can sometimes even be an advantage. For example, when trees are encroaching on power lines or are diseased, the utility company or city is usually quite helpful, trimming and removing dangerous branches. (See Chapter 3).

If you want to know where these easements are located on your property, call the utility company. Or you can go to the county land records office or city hall and ask a clerk to show you a map of the easement locations. A survey of the property will also show the location of utility easements.

Other Written Easements

In addition to utility easements, property may be subject to another kind of written easement, an easement that an owner sells to someone else for use as a path or driveway or for sewer or solar access, for example. Private easements across another's property are not uncommon, but they are easily overlooked. If you see an easement mentioned in your deed or title certificate and assume it is a utility company easement, you could be wrong.

Especially in hillside communities, where the fall angle (degree or slant or fall) can be essential for water pipes, private sewer easements are often sold when the uphill house is being built, so the pipe from the house to the street can slant properly—sometimes right under your property.

WATCH OUT FOR PRIVATE EASEMENTS

The time to find out exactly what easements a property is subject to is before you buy. When some very good friends of ours bought a house, the title papers referred to what they thought were the usual utility easements. But years later, when the neighbor's sewer pipe backed up, it was discovered that the pipe causing the problem ran directly across our friends' property, about eight feet from their front door.

Our friends took their documents to the courthouse, where a clerk helped them look up their easements. There in the land records was a private easement, exactly where the pipe ran. The original owner (four owners back) had sold the easement to a previous owner of the neighboring house. None of the current owners had known of it.

The plumbers found, after digging up both yards and the driveway with a backhoe, that the neighbor's pipe was substandard and had been crushed by roots from a large tree belonging to our friends. Luckily, the neighbor's liability insurance paid for replacing the pipe, the yard and the driveway. If the pipe had not been substandard and our friends' tree had been the sole cause of the damage, they might have been liable for the whole mess because they had interfered with the easement.

If your title contains private easements, you should get copies of the actual easement documents. You need to know where the easements are and what uses they allow. If you are unaware of the terms of a private easement, you could unknowingly interfere with the easement rights and be liable for damage.

If a solar access easement has been sold to a neighbor, you may find that you are severely limited in what you can build or grow on your property, because you can't block sunlight from the neighbor's solar collectors.

Any private easement referred to in your property papers should have a reference number, such as a book and page number. Your county clerk can help you locate it in the public records and obtain a copy to keep with your deed.

Easements by Necessity

Even if it isn't written down, a legal easement usually exists if it's absolutely necessary to cross someone's land for a legitimate purpose. The law grants people a right of access to their homes, for example. So if the only access to a piece of land is by crossing through a neighbor's property, the law recognizes an easement allowing access over the neighbor's land. This is called an "easement by necessity." When land is subject to such an easement, the landowner may not interfere with the neighbor's legal right.

It's easy for a dispute to arise between neighbors when someone buys property without knowing about this kind of easement across it. For example, a new owner may discover that the neighbor is using his private drive for access to her own property. The new buyer puts up a locked gate and soon finds himself in court. If you find yourself in such a dispute, either as the neighbor with the private drive or the one who needs it, and you can't work out some sort of agreement between you, see a local property lawyer.

In fact, if you become embroiled in any escalating easement problem that appears to be headed for the courthouse, consult a local attorney who has experience with real estate problems. The doctrines of unwritten easements that are created by people's actions and certain circumstances can be very complicated. The laws vary slightly from state to state, and you may need more tailor-made advice than can be given in this book.

Easements Acquired by Use of Property

Someone can acquire an easement over another's land for a particular purpose if he uses the land hostilely, openly, and continuously for a set period of time. These terms are explained in "Requirements for Obtaining Land by Adverse Possession," above. The length of use required varies from state to state and is often the same—ten or twenty years—as that for adverse possession (acquiring ownership of land by occupying it). An easement acquired in this way is called a "prescriptive easement."

Comparing Prescriptive Easements and Adverse Possession

Depending on the circumstances and on state law, someone who uses another's property may eventually gain ownership of the property (by adverse possession) or gain the right to use part of the proprety for a particular purpose (prescriptive easement).

To gain ownership of someone else's land, a trespasser must occupy it hostilely, openly, exclusively and continuously for a certain period of time set by state law. Some states require that the trespasser also pay the property taxes on the land during the period.

The requirements are much the same for a prescriptive easement: For instance, if the trespasser abandons the use for several years and then goes back to it, the element of continuity is missing, and no easement will have been created. If a prescriptive easement is challenged in court, and one of the elements is missing, there is no easement.

But there are also important differences. First, payment of property taxes is never necessary for a successful prescriptive easement claim. In states that require the payment of property taxes to obtain ownership by a trespasser, courts will grant the trespasser a prescriptive easement, but not ownership, when all requirements have been met except paying the taxes.

Also, to acquire a prescriptive easement a trespasser does not need to be the only one using the land. A trespasser can gain the easement when others are also using the property—even the owner. It follows that more than one person can acquire a prescriptive easement in the same portion of land.

Courts sometimes appear more willing to grant a prescriptive easement than actual ownership (through adverse possession) to a trespasser. The results are far less drastic for the owner. The easement does not take away the ownership of the property; it only requires the owner to allow the particular use of the property by somebody else.

Establishing a Prescriptive Easement

Typically, a prescriptive easement is created when someone uses land for access, such as a driveway or beach path or shortcut. But many times, a neighbor has simply begun using a part of the adjoining property. He may have farmed it or even have built on it. After the time requirement is met, the trespasser gains a legal right to use the property.

When the trespassing is done by the public, a public right to use property can be created. It is often called an "implied dedication" instead of a prescriptive easement. A public dedication is often created if an owner allows the city or county to make improvements or maintain a portion of his land.[9] For example, the owner of beachfront property may let the county pave her private drive, which is used by many people for access to the beach. The public would then gain a right to use the drive.

When disputes over prescriptive easements find their way into court, judges vary on what kind of use of someone's property justifies creation of an easement. Some courts find that simply using a strip of land regularly for a shortcut is enough for a prescriptive easement. But some are very reluctant to grant rights on someone else's land and require the use to be substantial.

Example: In a lawsuit over a garage built partly on a neighbor's land in Indiana, a court gave the garage owner a prescriptive easement allowing him to use the three feet of garage on the neighbor's property. But it denied one for the grass and strip beside it, even though the trespasser had mowed it and treated it as his own for over forty years.[10] The building of a structure, in this case the garage, was a substantial enough use to create a prescriptive easement, but just mowing the strip of grass was not.

Blocking Acquisition of a Prescriptive Easement

Methods of removing intruders from property are discussed in "Trespassers Who Become Owners," above. But if you don't mind someone using part of your property, the simplest way to prevent a prescriptive easement is to grant the person permission to use the property.

Permission of the owner to use property cancels a trespasser's claim to a prescriptive easement. If your neighbor is parking his car on a small strip of your property and you give him permission to do so, he is no longer a trespasser, and he can't try to claim an easement by prescription. Giving permission to a current user also prevents neighbors who move in later from claiming they have inherited a prescriptive easement.

Sometimes, your permission can even be implied. For example, if you allow a neighbor to use your property because you are on friendly terms, your implied permission is called "neighborly accommodation." This implied consent based on a friendly relationship is only between you and that neighbor—not anyone else, including later owners.

For example, a new owner of property in Washington, D.C. went to court and tried to claim an easement across a neighbor's yard because the former owner had been allowed to cross the property. The court ruled that he had no right to use the property because the friendship between the previous owner and the neighbor created a limited implied permission.[11]

Depending on implied permission, or even oral permission, however, is not a wise idea for protection in the future. You could still end up in court having to let a judge interpret your intentions.

RESEARCHING PRESCRIPTIVE EASEMENTS

To find your state's law on prescriptive easements, look up "easements" in the index to your state statutes. To understand how the courts in your state have interpreted different requirements, you may also want to check court decisions in your state on prescriptive easements. (See Chapter 13, *Legal Research*.)

The safest way to protect your property interest when you do give someone permission is to put the terms in writing. The sample agreement ("Trespassers Who Become Owners," above) can be used for easements. If several neighbors use a strip of your property, you should draw up an permission agreement for each one to sign.

When the public is using a private strip, you can post signs granting permission. In some states, such as California, posting these signs at every entrance and at certain intervals protects the owner from claims of a prescriptive easement.[12]

Depending on posted signs alone for protection, however, is always risky. If possible, take a further step, putting your permission for the public in writing, taking it down to the courthouse and recording it (filing a copy) in the county land records. California has a statute providing for this procedure;[13] check at your local courthouse to see it's allowed in your area. Recording it makes the permission part of the public record and available for anyone to check.

---

[1]Cal. Civ. Proc. Code § 749.

[2]*Preble v. Maine Cent. R.R.*, 85 Me. 260, 27 A. 149 (1893).

[3]*Pettis v. Lozier*, 205 Neb. 802, 290 N.W.2d 215 (1980).

[4]*French v. Pierce*, 8 Conn. 439 (1831).

[5]Helmholz, *Adverse Possession and Subjective Intent*, 61 Wash. U.L.Q. 331, at 339 (1983).

[6]*Carpenter v. Ruperto*, 315 N.W.2d 782 (Iowa 1982).

[7]*Norwood v. City of New York*, 95 Misc. 2d 55, 406 N.Y.S.2d 256 (1978).

[8]*McCann v. City of Los Angeles*, 79 Cal. 3d 112, 144 Cal. Rptr. 696 (1978).

[9]For examples of the public gaining a right to use private property, see *Gion v. City of Santa Cruz*, 2 Cal. 3d 29, 84 Cal. Rptr. 162, 465 P.2d 50 (1970); *County of Los Angeles v. Berk*, 26 Cal. 3d 201, 161 Cal. Rptr. 742, 605 P.2d 381, *cert. denied*, 101 S. Ct. 111, 449 U.S. 836, 66 L. Ed. 2d 43 (1980); *Brumbaugh v. Imperial County*, 134 Cal. 3d 556, 184 Cal. Rptr. 11 (1982).

[10]*McCarty v. Sheets*, 423 N.E.2d 297 (Ind. 1981).

[11]*Chaconas v. Meyers*, 465 A.2d 379 (D.C. App. 1983).

[12]Cal. Civ. Code § 1008.

[13]Cal. Civ. Code § 813. The California statutes encourage owners of beach-front property to allow others access to the beach, without fear of claims of a prescriptive easement.

chapter 11

Fences

Good fences make good neighbors.

—Robert Frost

In the United States, no law requires us to place fences on or around our lands; the right to "let the land lie" is an old one. But most people do choose to enclose their properties for various reasons.

Look about you, wherever you live, at the neat wooden fence, the enduring stone wall, the practical chain link, the ornate wrought iron, the traditional white picket fence complete with climbing roses. They are often fascinating reflections of the personalities of the residents. In rural areas, one finds practical fences over farmland and imaginative, expressive ones along houses.

RURAL AREAS: FENCING LIVESTOCK IN OR OUT

Almost all states have fence statutes designed to protect livestock and also to protect people and property from the damage that livestock can do. These laws take two forms, called open range and closed range. States choose one pattern or the other, although some states also allow counties to make their own choices.

Open Range

In an open range area, animals are allowed to wander, and neighbors protect their properties by erecting fences to keep them out. Someone who doesn't put up a fence cannot, legally, blame a neighbor whose animals damage the unfenced property.

A landowner can protect himself from straying livestock by building a fence that meets construction standards set out in state or local laws. Then if the neighbor's cows, for example, break a farmer's fence and harm the crops, the farmer can sue the cattle's owner, if the farmer's fence was built according to proper standards. State fence laws often describe in detail what is required for such a "lawful fence." The regulations can get pretty exquisite, demanding certain types of wire, certain heights, even certain placement of posts.

Sometimes in open range areas, however, custom is more powerful than a state statute. It is not uncommon for a livestock owner to assume responsibility for damage done by his animals, regardless of the law.[1]

In the 19th century, most states chose open range. Some, including California, have shifted back to closed range, although a few California counties still have an open range system.[2]

Closed Range

In closed range areas, it is the responsibility of the animal owner to keep cattle or sheep enclosed or be liable for damage they do. In some states, if the fence is lawful—that is, it meets the requirements set out in the statute or local ordinance—normally the owner is protected from liability if the animals break out.

Missouri, for instance, a closed range state, sets out detailed descriptions of what is required to create a proper fence to hold animals.[3] Closed range statutes often refer to the lawful fences as "livestock tight."

In other closed range states, an animal's owner is liable for damage it causes, no matter what type of fencing he erects.

A livestock owner who has a lawful fence may, however, have to pay for damages if the fence is obviously inadequate for what it's being used for. An example would be an owner who acquires a large, raging bull with a penchant for breaking down and destroying everything in his path. If the owner realizes (or ought to realize) that a standard fence is not sufficient, she is expected to take reasonable steps to prevent damage to her neighbors.

URBAN FENCES

Most of us don't have the pleasure of country living, so state fence laws don't affect us directly. Exceptions are boundary fences—see "Property Line (Boundary) Fences," below—or spite fences erected to annoy the neighbors, which often regulated by state law (see Chapter 12). Urban fences, by contrast, are governed by local law and increasingly by rules of subdivisions or planned unit developments.

Local Laws

City and county fence ordinances in most urban and suburban areas can be amazingly strict and detailed. Most regulate height and location, and some also control the material used and even the appearance of a fence. Many cities require a building permit to construct a fence at all.

These fence regulations apply to all types of fences—any structure used as an enclosure or a barrier or a partition. Usually, they include hedges and trees.

In reality, however, local fence laws are usually loosely enforced, if at all. Cities are not in the business of sending around fence inspection teams, and most localities contain lots of fence violations that no one has complained

RESEARCHING FENCE LAWS

In any rural area, if you are concerned about liability for damage from livestock, you need to know exactly what your state or county fence law says. State laws are easy to find; look under "fences" in the index to the state statutes, which is available at a county law library (in or near the courthouse). You can also find the local ordinances on fences at one of these libraries or at the public library. (See Chapter 13 on *Legal Research*.)

about. As long as nobody else minds and no one complains, a nonconforming fence may stand forever.

Also, what may have started out perfectly legal may later exceed the law. For example, a nice little hedge fence may grow into a 15-foot natural wall. If both neighbors like it, nothing is ever said, and there it stands.

Before you complain about a neighbor's recently erected monstrosity (or one that is going up before your eyes), go to city hall or the public library and read your local fence ordinances carefully to see whether the neighbor is breaking the law. It's a wise idea to do the same thing if you are unsure of whether your own plans for a new fence comply with local law. Laws that affect fences may be found in the zoning ordinances, building codes and also under miscellaneous rules. (See Chapter 13 for more on looking up your local laws.)

If your neighbor's fence does not comply with the law and it creates a problem for you, tell the neighbor as soon as possible. She probably doesn't know what the law is and if the fence is still in the building stage, may be able to make modifications at a low cost.

If she suggests that you mind your own business, then you can alert the city. All it takes in most circumstances is a phone call to the appropriate office—usually the planning or zoning department or the city attorney's office. The neighbor who is in violation of an ordinance will be given a written notification of violation and asked to conform. If she doesn't, the city can fine the person and even sue her to force compliance (unless the fence is exempt from the law for one of the reasons discussed in "Exceptions to Local Laws," below).

A very slight violation will not usually be enough to trigger any help from the city or county authorities. When a fence doesn't quite comply with a local ordinance, the enforcement officials probably won't want to get involved. And if a neighbor or the city does sue, a court may look to see if there is "substantial compliance" with the ordinance. If part of a fence is a few inches too high, for ex-

THE IMPORTANCE OF COMPLAINING PROMPTLY

Enforcing fence laws is never a high priority for city governments. So if you want the city's help, complain as soon as you notice the violation when a disturbing fence is going up, or move into a new house next to an annoying violation. The city may enforce the law at any time, but if a complaining neighbor doesn't bother to speak up for a good long time, the situation will likely be on the bottom of the list of priorities.

And if you eventually bring a lawsuit, a judge will have little sympathy for someone who sat by and did nothing to protect his property while the offending fence was being built; you might even lose your case because of your delay.

ample, but most of it fits the ordinance, the builder can be said to have substantially complied with the law. Courts are not usually willing to order a whole fence removed because of an insignificant violation.

If you are bothered by a neighbor's fence that seriously violates a law and the city or town won't help you, you can sue the neighbor. If it's money you're after, you can sue in small claims court to compensate for your loss of enjoyment of your property caused by the offending fence. Unfortunately, the fence will stay up, although if it is a constant annoyance to you, you can sue more than once. (See Chapter 15 for more on small claims court.)

If you want the fence removed, you must sue in regular trial court where, unlike small claims court, a judge can issue an order (usually called an injunction) to accomplish this. Taking this route will probably require hiring a lawyer. And be aware that the judge will look for the least drastic remedy—such as removal of a small portion of the fence.

Below are some of the types of restrictions found in the local laws.

Maximum Heights

Almost all towns place height restrictions on fences. In residential areas, local rules commonly restrict artificial (constructed) backyard fences to a height of six feet. In front yards, the limit is often four feet. Maximums vary, but front height limits, especially, are usually low.

General fence height restrictions may apply to natural fences—fences of bushes or trees—whether or not they are specifically mentioned, if they meet the ordinance's general definition of fences. Whether trees and bushes are considered fences depends on the location of the trunks, the particular ordinance, and whether or not they are actually used as a fence. When natural fences are singled out in the laws, the height restrictions commonly range from five to eight feet.[4]

Example: A fellow in Washington state had thirteen Douglas fir trees on the border of his property. He called them "yard landscaping." His neighbor complained, probably because of a blocked view, and the town sued him to comply with its fence ordinance. The court called the trees a fence, which under the local town ordinance was restricted to eight feet. The particular regulation in this case contained the language "naturally grown or constructed," so it applied to the Douglas firs. The man had to cut them.[5]

Setback Requirements

Most local fence laws contain what is called a setback rule, requiring fences to be set back a certain distance from the street or sidewalk, sometimes with special rules for corner properties. This is to provide the city room to maintain its own property, and also to promote public safety. If the location of the fence poses a danger—creates a blind driveway or diminishes a view at an intersection, for example—it can not only interfere with the use of someone else's property, but also can be a hazard to the general public.

Prohibited Materials

As long as a fence is made of materials that pose no threat of harm to neighbors or those passing by, the materials used probably don't violate any law. Occasionally, however, a town planning board approves only certain types of new fences—such as board fences—in an attempt to create a harmonious architectural look. Subdivisions also often restrict the kinds of fences allowed (see "Subdivision Rules," below).

Some towns prohibit the use of certain materials—for example, electrically charged or barbed wire fences. And even without such a specific law, if a fence is made of unsound material or so poorly constructed that it is an eyesore or a danger, it may be prohibited by another law, such as a blighted property ordinance. (See "Appearance," below.)

There is a dreadful case from Texas which is an argument for the prohibition of barbed wire in a residential neighborhood. In this instance, using barbed wire, the developer of a subdivision fenced off the remaining unimproved land from the property already sold. The result was a barbed wire fence at the back of a yard occupied by a family with children.

After four children had been injured on separate occasions and the developer ignored the complaints, the homeowner ripped down the fence. The developer sued him for willful trespass and the removal of the fence. The court found itself having to award punitive damages to the developer because the barbed wire was a legal fence.[6] Punitive damages are an extra sum of money, sometimes quite high, that the wrongdoer must pay as punishment.

We probably all agree who the real wrongdoer was in this situation, but the homeowner was the one guilty of trespass and of destruction of someone else's property. Hopefully, this community now has an ordinance against dangerous fences.

Appearance

Unlike subdivision restrictions ("Subdivision Rules," below), local laws usually do not dictate what a fence must look like. There are rare exceptions, such as in the city of Albany, California, where an ordinance requires all new structures to have a "harmonious exterior color."[7] (The ordinance doesn't say what colors are harmonious.)

And a few laws allow only certain types of design. The community of Seaside, Florida has an extraordinary ordinance actually requiring a white picket fence on each property, and the same brand of paint can't be used twice on a single block.[8]

But in most places, owners are free to choose how their fences look. Occasionally, an eccentric owner puts up such an ugly fence that the neighbors hope it's against the law because of its appearance. A hideous fence could reflect an intent to annoy a neighbor, and if it's useless to the owner, it may be an illegal spite fence. (See Chapter 12.) But unless it is a true spite fence or violates a height restriction or some other law, if you are the unfortunate neighbor who has to look at a fence painted like a psychedelic leopard, you can probably do nothing about it. You may not impose your own aesthetic values on someone else. Conformity with the community must be balanced with a person's freedom to use her property in a reasonable manner.

Example: In a California case, one neighbor was unhappy when another erected a plain board fence. He sued, accusing the builder of trying to annoy him by building an ugly fence. The judge refused to set up any aesthetic standards for fences and suggested that such action without a particular ordinance would be a luxury and indulgence not within the government's power.[9] Judging from the language of the decision, if the fence had been painted bright purple, it probably would have made no difference.

The appearance of a fence does matter in one particular situation—when it is not maintained and becomes a real eyesore. Some local ordinances don't allow what they call "blighted property" that decreases the value of surrounding property. A deteriorated fence falls into this category.[10] A crumbling stone wall, a sagging chain link fence and a broken or graffiti-covered board fence may all be blighted property, depending on the particular ordinance.

A dilapidated fence can violate more than a blighted property law if it poses a risk of harm. There may be an ordinance prohibiting an owner from allowing a dangerous condition to exist on his property. If a fence has old rusty nails or sharp broken wires protruding into a neighbor's yard or public sidewalk, it may pose harm to others. And a fence can be dangerous when it is a retaining wall—its becoming unsound meaning that the property it holds back is about to slide into the neighbor's driveway.

Exceptions to Local Laws

There are a few situations in which a fence that appears to violate a local ordinance is perfectly legal.

Fences Built With Permits for Variances

Someone who needs to build a fence that violates a fence law—for instance, to screen a house from a noisy or unsightly neighboring use, such as a busy highway or a gas station—can apply to the city for a one-time exception to the fence law. The exception is called a variance. The ordinances explain how to apply for a variance, what kind of notice must be given to neighbors, when a hearing will be held and who makes the final determination.

Once a variance application is made, a sign is usually posted on the property to alert the neighbors that a variance has been requested. In some towns, the request is also published in the local newspaper. After a certain period of time, the city holds a hearing on the request. A neighbor who wishes to object can do so at the hearing. If the city decides that the variance is justified, it will grant it. Unless the variance is limited to a specific time period, it's permanent. So someone who moves in later can't complain about a fence that was already built with a variance.

Example: Stephanie runs a day care center in her home. The house is located near a busy street, and she fears for the children who can easily scale her legal three-foot front fence. She applies to the city for a variance, a permit to allow a five-foot fence. The sign is posted, nobody objects, and the city planning commission grants the variance. Stephanie builds her five-foot fence, legally.

POINTERS TO FOLLOW
WHEN SEEKING A VARIANCE

▲ Be reasonable about your needs.

▲ Talk to the neighbors before you do anything else, to explain your problem and get them on your side. If you don't have support lined up before a notice is posted in your yard, someone may fear any change at all and try to organize objection.

▲ Work with the city zoning department staff so they understand the situation and are likely to recommend in your favor.

Fences Built Before the Law Was Passed

If a fence that is in violation of an ordinance existed before the law was passed, the city will probably allow it to remain. However, when the time comes to replace it, normally the new fence must conform to current regulations. If it doesn't, the city can step in and enforce the law, or a neighbor can sue for conformity.

This issue can arise when trees are used as a fence and are replaced with an artificial fence. For example, when one fellow in New York tried to replace a twelve-foot natural fence with a six-foot board fence, he learned only after he had erected the fence that the local height limit was four feet. A neighbor sued, and the court ordered him to lower it.[11]

Subdivision Rules

House deeds in planned unit developments and subdivisions often restrict the owners' freedom to erect fences, dictating the materials to be used, maintenance and maximum heights. This is done to assure uniformity and adherence to design standards in the subdivision. People who buy property in the subdivision obligate themselves to abide by these restrictions.

If the restrictions are simple and very few in number, they may be in the deed itself—for instance, if the only restriction is that the property is to be used for a single family dwelling only. However, when they are elaborate—and most are—the deed refers to a separate document usually called the Covenants, Conditions and Restrictions (CC&Rs). Fence regulations are usually found in these CC&Rs.

If one member of the group does not follow the rules, either a homeowners association or an affected neighbor can sue to enforce the terms of the deed. Before the association brings a lawsuit, it usually tries a number of less drastic tactics to get the owner to come around. For example, it may revoke the recalcitrant owner's right to use common areas such as swimming pools or tennis courts.

Example: Rhonda buys a house in a planned subdivision. Her deed tells her that the use of her property is subject to the terms of the CC&Rs. In the CC&Rs are these restrictions: "nor shall any backyard fence exceed six feet in height nor any fence in front of a house exceed four feet." Rhonda apparently thinks that nobody will care when she builds an eight-foot fence around her house to "ensure my privacy." The homeowners association notifies her in writing that she is violating her deed restrictions. When she doesn't respond to repeated warnings, the association sues her for an order to remove four feet of the fence in front and two feet in back. If there were no association with enforcement powers, other homeowners, who are bound by the terms of the CC&Rs, could sue her directly for the same order.

PROPERTY LINE (BOUNDARY) FENCES

A boundary fence is a fence that is located on the line between two properties and is used by both owners. It may also be called a division fence or a partition fence. A fence on a boundary line is subject to all the state and local laws that control fence height, materials and so on. In addition, almost every state has a myriad of other laws specifically addressing boundary fences.

Who Owns What

Unless the property owners agree otherwise, fences on a boundary line are owned by both owners when both are using the fence. Neither may remove it without the other's permission. When the property is sold, the new owner purchases the mutual ownership of the fence.

Co-ownership Under the Law

Normally, the key to who owns a boundary fence, according to the law, is normally who uses the fence. A fence on the boundary, built and used by only one owner, belongs to the builder. It does not become a real boundary fence unless the neighbor actually uses it as his own fence.

The concept of fence "use" is a unique semantic jungle. Suffice it to say that a common sense guess as to what the term means may well be wrong. Here is how "use" is legally interpreted in different states:

- A few states interpret use as occupancy. For example, Pennsylvania refers to using the land up to the fence[12]—such as planting crops or putting in a yard.

- Other states, such as Tennessee, Utah and Wisconsin, use the term "join" for use—hooking up another fence to the boundary fence.

- Most states interpret use more narrowly—a fence is used by a landowner only when the landowner's property is enclosed. When a neighbor chooses to let the land lie, he is not using the fence.[13]

- And some states do not define use at all.

Example: If Amy has neighbor's fences on two sides of her property which tend to keep her children in her yard, but she has nothing across the other two sides, under the enclosure rule followed by most states, she is not using the neighbor's fences and they are not boundary fences. If she fences the front and the back, and her property is then enclosed, the side fences become boundary fences.

A person who encloses property by using part of a neighbor's fence probably owes the neighbor some money. See "Exceptions to Local Laws," below.

If you need to know whether or not a fence is a boundary fence, you should look up your state's fence law. There are not only variations among the states on what constitutes use of a fence, but also ambiguities in other terms. If a statute refers only to "partition fences," and not boundary fences or division fences by name, it may be talking about a plain division fence, or it could mean a different legal animal—a fence erected as a result of a court order dividing one property into several parcels.

Appendix 3 lists the state boundary fence laws. You can look up the law at your local county law library. If the statutes themselves are unclear, you can try to find some judges' decisions on fence cases in your state. (See Chapter 13, *Legal Research*.)

In states that have no boundary fence statutes, local law may define boundary fences and create the joint ownership in the same ways that the statutes do. A few states exempt municipal areas from the state statute anyway and allow towns to regulate boundary fences as they choose. If there are local laws, they will probably be in the town's building code. You can check with city hall or at the public library for your specific ordinance. The local ordinances will likely contain lots of fence regulations that apply to all fences, including boundary fences. However, special rules for these particular fences will refer by name to them as either boundary, partition or division fences.[14] (See Chapter 13, *Legal Research*, on how to find local ordinances.)

Regulations in the house deeds in subdivisions and planned unit developments may also address boundary fences specifically. These can be more explicit than the statutes, for instance, apportioning the building costs between owners. If you live in one of these restricted areas, check your Covenants, Conditions and Restrictions (CC&Rs).

Fences on Agreed Boundary Lines

Neighbors are often unsure of exactly where the boundary between their properties is, and surveys are expensive. Fortunately, you don't need to locate the precise boundary line to have a jointly owned boundary fence.

If the deed, map or plat of your property is confusing, and you are unable to determine the property line, you and your neighbor can simply agree that a fence—one you build or an existing one—marks the boundary. This is called an "agreed boundary." Certain requirements must be met: the line must be uncertain, both neighbors must agree that the fence is the line, and then both neighbors must treat the fence as the property boundary for a period of time. Once these requirements are fulfilled, the fence becomes the legal boundary line on the ground.

If you want to make such an agreement, it should be in writing and put on file (recorded) in the county land records office in case there is later any question about the boundary. (A sample agreement is in Chapter 9, *Boundary Lines*.)

Even without an explicit agreement, when two neighbors treat a fence as a boundary fence for a long period of time—for example, if both contribute to its maintenance for many years—it can become the legal boundary. (See Chapter 9, *Boundary Lines*, for a full discussion of Agreed Boundaries.)

A fence on an agreed boundary is subject to all the laws that affect any boundary fence. So when one of the properties is sold, the fence remains the boundary, and the new landowner buys mutual ownership of it along with the property.

You and your neighbor can also agree to co-own and maintain a fence that is not on the boundary line. (See "Sharing a Fence That Is Not on the Boundary," below.)

Fence Ownership Agreements Among Landowners

If neighbors don't want to share ownership of a boundary fence equally, as the law apportions it, they are free to make their own arrangements. For example, two property owners could agree that a boundary fence is to be the responsibility of only one of them, or that its ownership is to be shared unequally.

In reality, whoever puts a fence up usually considers it his fence, takes care of it and doesn't want his neighbors meddling in his business. When purchasing property, it can be quite difficult to figure out who is responsible for what. In some areas it is customary for the builder to have the unfinished side, the side with the stakes, facing his property. In other areas, the smooth side faces in. Ask a real estate agent or the neighbors what the custom is in your area and if there are any long-standing assumptions of which fence belongs to whom. Tradition and custom may be so strong that the law on the subject never comes up. If you try to rock the boat, you can find yourself an outcast in your own neighborhood.

Although it's unusual, neighbors can sometimes sign formal ownership agreements on boundary fences. In a few states—Vermont, for example—the statutes provide a procedure for placing written fence ownership agreements on public record (recording them). Once this is done, the agreement is not only binding on both owners, but also on anyone who later buys the property.[15]

Most states don't have such a recording procedure, and any agreement you make is just between you and your neighbor. When your neighbor's property is sold, you will need an agreement with the new owner, or the statutes will dictate ownership of the fence between you and the new neighbor.

Example: Jenny and Elmer are next-door neighbors who both plan to enclose their properties with fences. Jenny wants to simply unroll some chicken-wire and hold it up with a few posts. Elmer has grandiose plans to build a decorative wooden fence around his yard and wishes to maintain ownership of it. He also prefers that Jenny use this fence on her side and cringes at the thought of chicken-wire along his borders. Jenny and Elmer simply agree that the portion of wooden fence between their yards is Elmer's, even though Jenny uses it as a part of her enclosure. But the agreement is only between them. If one of them sells the property, the new owner will need a new agreement or they could assume, under state law, joint ownership of the elaborate wooden fence.

Paying a Neighbor for the Fence

If someone erects a fence on a boundary line, the fence remains that person's unless, or until, the neighbor uses the fence—which in most states means until the neighbor actually encloses her property. (See "Who Owns What," above.)

If someone encloses his property, using an already existing fence on any side, most state fence laws require that he pay the other owner for the value of the fence. In other words, he must actually buy a share of the fence. Then he becomes a co-owner of the boundary fence. California describes this as a refund to the other owner of a just proportion of the value of the fence at that time.[16] Many states set the required payment at one half of the value of the existing fence to the other landowner.

Some boundary fence statutes appear to be intended only for farmers and ranchers. New York, for example, does not require landowners to pay anything to a neighbor for a boundary fence if the person enclosing has kept no livestock on the property for five years.[17] Minnesota provides town boards with the authority to exempt property when the land is less than twenty acres.[18]

In an urban setting, although the purposes of the statutes, such as retaining livestock, may not be applicable, the principle is the same. Many of us simply do not consider it fair to use someone else's property without compensation. In a suburb where back yards are neatly separated by fences, when a new neighbor encloses a yard using the fences already there, if the statutes are followed, the new neighbor buys in.

Example: Claudia buys property that is unenclosed but bordered on either side with back yard fences erected by her neighbors. She builds a fence across the back and from her house to the sides, joining the other two. Her back yard is now enclosed, and she must compensate the neighbors who have given her the benefit of the fences already there. According to the most state statutes, unless there is a different agreement, Claudia owes one half of the value of each of the portions of side fences she used to the respective neighbors.

The state laws requiring a neighbor to pay for an existing fence are actually almost never enforced in urban areas because of tradition, implied agreements and because most people are probably unaware of them. But the statutes are there if someone wants to enforce them. In rural areas, where miles of fencing may be involved, they are enforced more often.

If someone encloses his property by using a neighbor's fence, the statutes provide that the neighbor can demand a just proportion of the current value of the fence. The request for money must be a reasonable request. A fence owner should not expect to be paid a full half for an elaborate fence that the neighbor didn't choose. Sometimes the kind of fence that the owner can demand contribution for is set by statute—for example, wire fencing for rural land. Most likely, if a request is refused and the fence owner sues the neighbor for the money, the owner will receive a proportion of the value of the kind of fence most often used in the area.

Responsibility for Maintenance

Perhaps the most important aspect of boundary fences is that, unless agreed otherwise, both owners are mutually responsible for keeping a boundary fence in good repair.

State and Local Laws

State boundary fence statutes and most local ordinances place joint responsibility for maintenance on the owners of boundary fences, unless the owners work out their own agreement. For example, the Oklahoma statute says that adjoining owners are to equally maintain a boundary fence between them.[19] The requirements are pretty much the same across the country when there is a statute. If the fence needs fixing, the cost comes out of both pockets.

Some states impose special maintenance requirements on natural boundary fences—that is, those made of trees or hedges. For instance, Illinois requires division hedges to be trimmed seven years after planting to four feet, and after that every two years to five feet.[20] Both owners are responsible for the trimming. Iowa demands that they be trimmed twice a year to a height of five feet unless a different agreement is made in writing between the neighbors and recorded (put on file) at the county land records office (usually at the courthouse).[21]

WHEN THERE IS NO STATUTE OR LOCAL ORDINANCE

In the few states that do not address fences in their laws, if there is also no local law on the subject, one neighbor can still ask the other to chip in for repair to a fence on the boundary that they both use. If the neighbor wants to pursue the matter all the way into a court, he could make two arguments to support mutual maintenance responsibilities. One is simply that the laws are so similar in all of the other states that they should be followed everywhere—a "law of the land" argument.

But secondly, and probably more important, is this: If two people use and benefit from the same fence, located on a property boundary, they should both be responsible for it. Unless they agree otherwise, the common use creates a mutual ownership. This is the logic behind the statutes—when you benefit from a fence, and it's on the boundary, you pay.

In states with no statutes, there may be some published court opinions on boundary fence responsibility. You can check in a law library for one that might help you understand your state's law. (See Chapter 13, *Legal Research*.)

Owners' Agreements

Even when two neighbors own a boundary fence together, one owner may want to be responsible for the fence's care. The neighbors may discuss this arrangement, or it may simply happen without anything ever being said. Especially if only one owner built the fences, he may really consider it her fence and not want the neighbor bothering it. Also, sometimes fences are used unequally; for instance, if a neighbor is using only a few feet of an extensive fence, the other may never expect payment for repair. And if one owner has children or a dog, she simply may be more interested in maintenance than the other.

These agreements are only between the current neighbors. Unless they are made part of the public land records (possible in a very few states), when a new owner comes in, the old agreement is no longer in force.

Disputes Over Maintenance

Disputes usually occur when one neighbor thinks the fence needs repair or preventative maintenance, such as painting, and the other doesn't. A good general rule to follow is that the fence should be kept in such a condition that it enhances the value of both properties. If its appearance takes away from the property values, it needs repair. Following this rule will keep requests reasonable and objective.

If one owner refuses to cooperate in reasonable maintenance of a boundary fence, the other can fix the fence and demand reimbursement of the other's share. If the neighbor won't pay up, the neighbor who has fixed it can sue the other in small claims court under the state boundary fence statute. (See Chapter 15, *Small Claims Court.*)

A few states have harsh penalties for refusing to chip in for maintenance after a reasonable request is made by the other owner. Connecticut, for example, allows one neighbor to go ahead and repair, and then sue the other owner for double the cost.[22]

Negotiating With the Neighbor

If you are faced with a recalcitrant neighbor, first try to work something out. The other owner may not really have noticed how bad the situation has become. If simply pointing out the problem doesn't work, write a letter like the one below.

```
                        4501 Cypress Road
                        Springdale, CA 92345

                        Aug. 15, 19__

Dear Alice,

   As I mentioned to you last week, the
boundary fence between our properties is in
terrible need of repair. Four of the main
posts appear to be completely rotten at the
bottom and several boards are broken.
According to the state law which I have en-
closed, we are mutually responsible for the
maintenance of this fence.

   I have obtained the enclosed estimate of
$300 for having the necessary work done. Your
share is $150. Please contact me so that we
may proceed.

Sincerely yours,


Nelson
```

If Nelson's request is ignored or refused, he should get out his camera and take some pictures of the fence that clearly show the state of disrepair. It would also be a good idea to get at least two estimates for the cost of the work, to be certain that the charge is reasonable. If Alice is determined to avoid her responsibility, Nelson can now fix the fence and demand her share of the cost. Afterwards, he should write another letter like the one below.

Dear Alice,

   I have had the necessary repair work done on our boundary fence. Enclosed is the bill for $300. Please send your share of this amount, $150, to me promptly, or I will have to take the matter to small claims court.

Sincerely yours,

Nelson

What Nelson has just written is called a demand letter. If he gets no response, he can sue Alice in small claims court for the money and show this letter—along with all the written documents and pictures—to the judge.

Using Mediation

Before going to court, it's usually a good idea to seek help first from a mediator, an impartial third person who will help you and your neighbor arrive at your own solution. This is far less expensive than court, not only in money terms, but also in emotional drain. Neighbors can often work out an agreement in mediation that both solves the current situation and heads off future trouble.

(See Chapter 14 on how to use mediation.) If you and your neighbor don't work something out, with or without a mediator, you will find strangers telling you what you can and cannot do with your own property. Remember, the purpose of a fence is to prevent problems between neighbors, not create them.

Going to Local Authorities

Most boundary fence laws contain detailed methods of enforcement. Many statutes across the country—from Vermont to Indiana to Wisconsin—provide for "fence viewers" to come out and inspect the property and make recommendations as to who owes what. These viewers are usually ordinary citizens appointed by a constable, sheriff or other local official. The decision of the viewers is binding on the neighbors, although it can be appealed to a court.

Many people have never heard of fence viewers. Before you file a lawsuit against your neighbor, check with your local sheriff, constable or at city hall to see if you can use this method in your area.

If you go to the office in charge of the fence viewers and make a complaint, the fence viewers will not only consider whether the fence needs repair at all, but whether the amount sought by the neighbor is reasonable. If the viewers decide in favor of the one complaining, the uncooperative neighbor can be ordered to contribute his fair share of the cost of the maintenance. If he doesn't pay, he may risk a fine.

Example: The wooden boundary fence between Leslie's and Tony's houses has been sagging for a couple of years. Tony has propped up a few boards with stakes and considers the fence okay. Leslie wants to replace the sagging boards but Tony refuses to help. Leslie learns that her state statute has a fence viewer procedure, so she goes to city hall and fills out a complaint about the fence. The viewers come out, inspect the property and issue a decision that the boards are rotten—that Tony and Leslie are to split the cost of replacing them. Tony can either pay up or risk being sued by Leslie—he may even have to pay an extra penalty. Even if he wants to go to the trouble of appealing to a judge, he will not likely win because the objective decision of the viewers is a very strong argument in Leslie's favor.

DISPUTES OVER BOUNDARIES

If you or your neighbor is putting up a fence, pay close attention to boundary lines. Don't make the mistake of putting up a fence on what you think is the boundary if it could be on the neighbor's property. She can sue you for trespass, and ask for money damages and removal of the fence. You might not even get to keep the fence materials. This is true even if you thought you were on your own land.[23]

If your neighbor starts to erect a fence on what you think is your property, do not stand by without objection. As soon as he starts to build, ask him to please stop until you can reach an agreement or have a survey done. A talk with the neighbor or a letter may be all that is necessary, especially if a mistake is involved. However, these circumstances are serious; be ready to hire an attorney if you are ignored. If the fence is entirely on your property, you have the right to tear it down or take the neighbor to court to have it removed. If you do nothing, you could be giving away part of your property or the right to use it after a certain amount of time. (See the sections on Adverse possession and prescriptive easements in Chapter 10.)

Of course, don't go tearing down your neighbor's new fence unless you are absolutely certain of the true boundary and have already asked the neighbor to take it down. When the neighbors really disagree, the cost of a survey may be well worth it.

An example of this kind of fence dispute in Oregon shows what can happen. Call it "the case of the yo-yo fence." It would be amusing were it not for the time and expense involved.

Two neighbors disagreed on the location of the boundary line. One proceeded to go ahead and put up a fence where he believed he was within his legal rights. He erected the fence in the daytime, and his neighbor took it down at night. The builder tried again and the same thing happened. This up-and-down scenario was completed six times before the neighbors went to court. The behavior of these neighbors is all the more amazing because this was no backyard dispute; forty acres of land were involved, lots and lots of fencing.

The court found that the fence builder was within his rights and was on his own property. Every inch of fence that he erected was entirely proper, and his neighbor had no right whatsoever to take it down. The neighbor was found guilty of willful trespass and had to pay punitive damages (a form of punishment) for the continuous destruction he had accomplished under the cover of darkness.[24]

SHARING A FENCE THAT IS NOT ON THE BOUNDARY

If you want to use a fence slightly over on another's property, or if your neighbor wishes to share yours, be careful unless you want to make the fence the legal boundary. Write down your agreement, setting out your intentions in detail. Include the expenses and duties of each of you, and clearly state that use of the fence and land is by permission of the owner only and that the agreement conveys no right of land ownership. You might want to check with a local land use lawyer to be sure that your agreement covers everything that is necessary.

This type of agreement only binds the signers, not future purchasers. Should you later sell the house, you can show the agreement to the prospective buyer (or his title insurance company), who may be confused when he compares the description of the property with the location of the fence.

Having your intentions clearly in writing is important for another reason. This fence is not a real boundary fence. Unlike a real division fence for which a new owner is responsible for a share of the maintenance and prohibited from removing the fence without permission of the other owner, future neighbors won't have the rights or responsibilities of co-ownership.

Changing boundaries: Of course, you or your neighbor can always sell a small strip of land up to the fence to the other. This must be in writing and recorded because it does change the boundary line and conveys the ownership of land. (See Chapter 9, *Boundary Lines.*)

---

[1]Custom is one of the topics of a fascinating study of ranchers in Shasta County, California described in Ellickson, *Of Coase and Cattle*, 38 Stan. Law Rev. 623 (1986). I recommend it not only to those interested in rural fence laws, but to anyone who seeks to understand behavior between neighbors. It is available at larger law libraries.

[2]Cal. Agric. Code § 17.124.

[3]Mo. Stat. Ann. § 272.220 and following.

[4]For example, see *People v. Berlin*, 62 Misc. 2d 272, 307 N.Y.S.2d 96 (1970) (limit only six feet).

[5]*Clyde Hill v. Rotsen*, 48 Wash. App. 769, 740 P.2d 378 (1987).

[6]*Gardner v. Kerly*, 613 S.W.2d 795 (Tex. Civ. App. 1981).

[7]Albany, California Mun. Code § 20-10.

[8]Seaside, Florida Urban Code. The residents of Seaside favored this ordinance because the fences not only enhance the appearance of this resort town, but also create an attractive privacy shield between the houses and the tourist foot traffic. The different paint brand requirement spreads the purchase of paint among suppliers. In addition, the Seaside Code requires a front porch on each house, further contributing to an overall design.

[9]*Haehlen v. Wilson*, 11 Cal. App. 2d 437, 54 P.2d 62 (1936). This case, a spite fence case, was more complicated than just a question of the fence being ugly. However, appearance was an element of the neighbor's complaint and the court was forced to discuss it.

[10]Fences are specifically mentioned in the blighted property laws of some cities, for example, Oakland, California Mun. Ord., § 15-1.01.

[11]*Bornscheuer v. Corbett*, 175 N.Y.S.2d 913 (1958).

[12]29 Pa. Con. Stat. 42.

[13]Cal. Civ. Code § 841.

[14]For example, Article 4502 of the New Orleans Building Code requires both owners to pay for construction and maintenance when the fence is a boundary fence. Providence, Rhode Island limits the height of partition fences between properties to four and a half feet, while other fences can be as high as six feet. Code of Ordinances of the City of Providence, Secs. 5-46 and 5-54.

[15]Vt. Stat. Ann. 3812. Also see N.D. Cent. Code Ann. 47-26-02; R.I. Gen. Laws 34-10-14; Wis. Stat. Ann. 90.05.

[16]See Cal. Civ. Code § 841(2), requiring payment when the neighbor encloses.

[17]N.Y. Con. Laws, TOWN § 300.

[18]Minn. Stat. Ann. § 344.011. This Minnesota solution was adopted in 1982, yet in the same year Indiana passed a law requiring mutual responsibility on landowners in general. Ind. Code Ann. 32-10-9-3. Louisiana directly compels contribution and responsibility within cities, La. Civ. Code art. 686; see *Hughes v. Brignac*, 72 So. 2d 22 (La. 1954), enforcing this statute.

[19]60 Okla. Stat. Ann 70.

[20]Ill. Stat. Ann. Ch. 54 § 3.

[21]Ia. Code Ann. 113.2

[22]Conn. Gen. Stat. Ann. 47-51.

[23]The rights of neighbors in this situation is discussed in a treatise called the *Restatement (Second) of Torts* § 164 (1977).

[24]*Lemon v. Maddox*, 216 Or. 539, 340 P.2d 977 (1959).

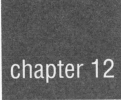

chapter 12

Spite Fences

When next-door neighbors can't stand the sight of each other, or when small disagreements fester into open warfare, people no longer want to be neighbors. Because moving away is usually impractical, they sometimes choose the next best thing. They build a high fence near the edge of their property, a fence that serves to put the neighbor out of sight and out of mind and, at the same time, has the added advantage of annoying and perhaps inconveniencing the neighbor. Such fences are aptly called "spite fences."

A fence builder who builds a fence to get back at a neighbor can easily go too far. The fence may be illegal under laws and regulations that limit fence height. And even if it isn't, if the fence meets the legal definition of a spite fence, the affected neighbor can sue the builder, have the fence removed or lowered, and receive money to compensate for his trouble.

GENERAL RESTRICTIONS ON FENCE HEIGHT

State and local laws regulate fences in general—their height, type, even their appearance. In addition, many subdivisions and planned communities have their own rules on fences. These laws and restrictions will take care of most fence complaints.

The most useful ones, to someone annoyed by a neighbor's fence, are local ordinances that restrict fence height and sometimes dictate fence appearance within the city limits. For instance, if a neighbor's offending fence is unlawful under a local ordinance because it's too tall, you may get all the help you need from the city itself. Call the local zoning or planning office and ask what the rules say about fences. Or go to the public library and read your city's fence ordinances (See Chapter 13, *Legal Research*.)

Once you're clear on the law, tell the neighbor about the it; delivering a copy is even better. If that doesn't produce results, notify the office of the city, county or township attorney, depending on which ordinance is involved. An official will then warn the violator and demand conformity to the ordinance. If she doesn't conform, she can be fined, and the city or county may even take the person to court.

Many subdivisions and planned unit developments have even stricter regulations on fences height and materials. These regulations are usually found in a document referred to in each property owner's deed called the Covenants, Conditions and Restrictions (CC&Rs). If someone violates a fence rule in the CC&Rs, just pointing out the violation to the person may be all that is necessary. When a neighbor complains, the homeowners' association often takes action. It may begin by revoking privileges to use common areas, such as swimming pools. Some associations have the power to sue to enforce conformity to the regulations. One neighbor who is subject to the restrictions can also sue another directly to enforce the rules.

For more details on fence laws and regulations, see Chapter 11, *Fences*.

If a neighbor's fence isn't violating a local law or subdivision regulation, it may still be illegal under spite fence laws. For the most part, these laws trace their historical roots to a time when towns had not yet adopted local fence regulations. Even though spite fence law has been largely superseded in many communities by local or subdivision fence regulations, in some situations the legal concept of the spite fence is still relevant. The rest of the chapter discusses these laws.

WHAT IS A SPITE FENCE?

A spite fence is a fence that is erected to annoy or harm someone, and serves no reasonable purpose to the owner. Natural fences—trees and hedges—are not spite fences because they always serve some purpose to the owner.

If you are harmed or annoyed by a spite fence, you may be able to get relief under a state or local spite fence law, or if none exists, from a court under the common law theory of "private nuisance." If a court agrees with you that the fence is a spite fence, a court can order its removal. It can also order the neighbor to pay you money to compensate you for the interference with the use and enjoyment of your property. If your neighbor is in the process of building a spite fence, you can obtain a court order halting the work.

Spite Fence Laws

Several states have adopted laws defining spite fences. These laws create a presumption that a useless fence over a certain height, built to annoy a neighbor, is a nuisance to the neighbor. Under these laws, the neighbor has the right to sue the builder of such a fence on the ground that the fence is legally a nuisance.

Not all states have statutes on spite fences. To see if your state has a statute, check the chart below.

Spite Fence Statutes

In these states, a fence over the designated height, built to annoy the adjoining neighbor, and with no reasonable use to the owner is a private nuisance:

California	Cal. Civ. Code 841.4 (10 feet)
Maine	17 Me. Rev. Stat. 2801 (6 feet)
Massachusetts	Mass. Gen. Laws Ann. 49.21 (6 feet)
Michigan	Mich. Comp. Laws Ann. 561.02 (any height)
Minnesota	Minn. Stat. Ann. 561.02 (any height)
New Hampshire	N.H. Rev. Stat. Ann. 476.1 (5 feet)
New York	Con. Laws N.Y. Ann. R.P.A.P.L. 843 (10 feet)
Rhode Island	R.I. Gen. Laws 34-10-20 (6 feet)
Vermont	Vt. Stat. Ann. 3817 (any height)
Wisconsin	Wis. Stat. Ann. 844.10 (6 feet)

The definitions of spite fences in state statutes tend to be very similar. The differences are usually just the height that is allowed. California law, for example, states that a fence exceeding ten feet, built maliciously for the purpose of annoying an owner or occupant of adjoining property, is a private nuisance. Wisconsin and Massachusetts set the height at six feet. New Hampshire places the restriction at five feet.

A few states set no height limit and include all structures, not just fences. The Minnesota spite fence law says that a fence or any other structure, maliciously erected or maintained for purposes of annoying owners or occupants of adjoining property, is a private nuisance.

Spite fence laws can be very effective when a neighbor builds over the height limit. The neighbor may lower the fence as soon as he's told about the law or realizes he could be sued.

Even if your neighbor builds a spite fence that is under the height limit of your state spite fence law, you may still be able to sue the neighbor. Your options are discussed in the next section.

If No Spite Fence Law or Other Fence Law Applies

If a neighbor's offending fence doesn't violate any state statute, local fence law or subdivision restriction, you can still sue the owner under the common law (written decisions in court cases). The legal theory is that the fence is a nuisance—an unreasonable interference with another's enjoyment of her property. Malicious creation and maintenance of a useless fence that harms a neighbor is considered an unreasonable use of property and a nuisance in every state.

You also may be able to successfully sue under the nuisance theory if your neighbor's fence doesn't quite fit the definition of a spite fence in your state's statute—for instance, if it's shorter than the limit in the statute. However, it's usually harder to convince a judge that a fence is a spite fence if a statute exists and the fence doesn't meet the description.

Under the common law, for a fence to be a spite fence and a legal nuisance to the neighbor, three conditions must exist:

- The fence builder's motive was malicious

- The fence serves no reasonable purpose

- The neighbor's use and enjoyment of property are harmed by the fence.

How to prove each of these elements if you sue is discussed in "Going to Court," below.

NEGOTIATING WITH THE NEIGHBOR

It's really never too late to negotiate or mediate a solution with the neighbor, even when such a thing seems impossible. By the time a neighbor dispute reaches a spite fence stage, there is probably little or no communication. However, the real threat of a lawsuit may give even the most stubborn of neighbors second thoughts. The one building the spite fence may have no idea that it violates the law. It can't hurt to approach the neighbor to try to stay out of court.

Also consider mediation to resolve the problem. Mediation is a process in which a third party helps you work out your own solution. In a spite fence case, mediation may be a much more effective tool than an expensive and time-consuming lawsuit, not only to get rid of the fence, but to improve relations between neighbors.

Mediation may be especially appropriate in a spite fence case because the builder of the fence is almost certainly angry too. More is probably involved here than ten feet of wooden planks; there may likely to be a history of misunderstandings on both sides. If mediation is successful, you could gain an enormous amount of satisfaction from reaching your own solutions, saving everybody involved a lot of money and helping to prevent future trouble. (Chapter 14 discusses the process of mediation at length.)

GOING TO COURT

When all attempts at communication fail, you may choose to have your day in court and ask a judge for relief from a spite fence.

But before you go jumping into the legal system, do use a little common sense. How bad is the fence compared to a court battle? Are you really harmed, or just angry at your neighbor?

If you're determined to get the fence removed, no matter what it takes, be aware that pursuing your goal could cost a small fortune if the neighbor is willing to fight.

Example: One Rhode Island man sued his neighbor, claiming his property had gone down $8,000 in value because of the neighbor's fence. The state spite fence law set a height limit of six feet, as did a local ordinance addressing regular fences. This particular fence was six feet tall, but one picket of the fence was seven-eighths of an inch above six feet. The case went all the way to the Supreme Court of Rhode Island. That court ruled that the offending picket had to be cut by seven-eighths of an inch.[1] How much time was spent? How much money did the attorneys charge? The winner of this case has the dubious distinction of a Supreme Court order forcing the other to trim one picket.

What the Court Can Do

A court can order the builder of a spite fence to stop construction, lower the fence, remove it or pay the neighbor for the damage the fence has caused.

Depending on how much money you want to sue for, you may need to hire a lawyer and bring your lawsuit in regular trial court, not small claims court. And if you want the court to order the fence lowered or removed, small claims court is definitely out. Most small claims court

CAN TENANTS SUE?

What if you're a tenant, not an owner, bothered by a neighbor's spite fence? The language of most spite fence laws uses the word "occupant" as the one who can be harmed, so tenants should be able to sue under these statutes. Similarly, in the absence of a statute, most courts will likely find that a tenant has the right ("standing" in legalese) to challenge a spite fence. Such court decisions are rare, but over a century ago, a court in Massachusetts stated that under its statute, either a tenant or an owner could bring a lawsuit.[2]

judges do not have authority to order someone to take down a fence.

Halting the Work

Instead of wringing your hands while you watch a spite fence going up, you can try to stop the construction. Always remember to check subdivision regulations and local fence laws as well as spite fence laws. When a local ordinance is being violated, some city attorney offices might be willing to help by issuing a citation and a fine.

Once the fence is obviously above the height limit in any law, you can get an emergency order from a judge requiring the neighbor to stop building, at least until the judge makes a formal ruling on the legality of the fence. You will have to go to regular court (not small claims) and probably hire a lawyer. That may be worth the money—once a fence is up, a judge may be reluctant to order the owner to destroy it.

Getting the Fence Removed

You can ask a court to order the removal of a neighbor's spite fence, but be aware that a judge will not lightly order someone to remove or destroy property. The judge will look for the least drastic remedy—for example, ordering the top four feet of a 12-foot fence removed, instead of having the owner tear down the whole thing. If a fence has been placed right next to a house to block the windows, the judge would likely order it lowered below the windows. Or, there could be a court order to reduce a high fence to the height that is customary in the community.

To get a judge who has the authority to order the fence to come down or be lowered, you will have to use regular (not small claims) court.

Making the Fence Owner Compensate the Neighbor

Most neighbors upset by a spite fence don't particularly want money—they want the fence, or at least part of it, removed. But a court can order the fence owner to compensate the neighbor, if the neighbor can prove she's been harmed. Even if your primary goal is to get your neighbor to tear down a monstrous spite fence, the threat of having to pay a substantial sum can be a powerful impetus for getting a spiteful neighbor to take the fence down or at least to lower it.

One situation in which compensation is definitely appropriate is when a spite fence makes life so uncomfortable that the injured neighbor throws up his hands and moves out. He may no longer care whether the fence remains, but he can still sue for the harm it caused him.

Example: A neighbor dispute from the hills of Los Angeles wound up in court after one family had literally run another off their property, having made life so miserable that they sold their house. Among the activities of the spiteful neighbors were hurling insults, "accidentally" flinging paint on the other house and placing their garbage can under the other's dining room window. Oh yes, they also built a spite fence. The relocated neighbor sued the spite fence's owner, demanding money for his aggravation. The fence was under the height specified in the California spite fence statute, but the court declared the fence a spite fence under the common law. The judge ruled that it had been built with no reasonable purpose to the owner and solely to annoy the neighbor—an unreasonable use of property and a private nuisance. The judge awarded damages for the whole mess, and scolded the guilty neighbors for "delight in their display of malice and hatred for fellow man."[3]

If you sue for money alone, you can avoid lawyers and sue in small claims court if the amount is within the limit of your state's small claims law. Most states allow claims of $2,000 to $5,000.

If you win your lawsuit but the fence owner does not remedy the situation, the fence is what is called a continuing nuisance, because its presence continues to harm you. You can sue again and again. (Chapter 15 explains how to use small claims court and lists each state's small claims court limit.)

What You Must Prove

When you take your neighbor to court for building a spite fence, you must prove that according to the law, the fence meets the definition of a spite fence.

If you sue based on your state's spite fence statute, the fence must be:

- over the height limit set out in the statute
- built to annoy the neighbor (maliciously built)
- serving no reasonable purpose for the owner.

The statutes declare that such a fence is a legal nuisance and harm to the neighbor is presumed. If you want money from the neighbor, you must also show that you are harmed by the fence, what your harm is, and how much money it would take to compensate you for it.

If you sue based on the common law, the fence must be:

- built to annoy the neighbor (maliciously built)
- serving no reasonable purpose for the owner
- harming the neighbor.

These ingredients cannot easily be separated. For instance, a high useless fence suggests malice on the builder's part. On the other hand, a high fence truly necessary for some reason is not a spite fence, even when the neighbors can't stand each other or the fence does create harm.

Let's look at these elements one at a time.

Motive of the Fence Builder

To be a spite fence, a structure must be "maliciously" erected or maintained. There are several ways for a court to make a determination of the fence builder's motive.

Appearance of the Fence. The appearance itself of a fence may be evidence of the builder's malicious intent. Often a spite fence looks like a monstrosity, its ugliness being part of the attempt to annoy the neighbor.

There are no laws that control, from an aesthetic point of view, what a person can do with his property. That would interfere with the constitutionally guaranteed freedom of expression. But when a simple photograph of the property would produce shock and outrage in an objective observer, the fence itself is probably ample evidence of the builder's malice.

A TYPICAL SPITE FENCE

Close your eyes for a moment and picture a spite fence in your mind. Have it pictured? No matter what you have designed in your imagination, it probably is not nearly as awful as what some neighbors have actually done to each other.

In one spite fence case, the court actually included a picture of the fence with its written decision—most unusual for stuffy law books. If you are ever in your local law library, ask the librarian to help you find volume 273 of the Northwest Reporter. Look on page 660. I will try to describe the picture.

There are two houses side by side, separated by about 30 feet. One house was apparently built very close to the boundary line. The fence erected by the other neighbor appears to be about six inches from this house. It is made of rough boards and is taller than the top of the windows. There is no room to walk between the fence and the house, no room for light and air. Any view from the windows is one of only the rough boards. If these houses were along the Atlantic coast, one would assume the owners were preparing for a major hurricane, boarding up against the expected fury of the storm.

But these houses are in a South Dakota town. The only fury involved was that of the neighbors. The fence itself clearly shows malice. This is a typical spite fence.[4]

The Neighbors' Conduct. Sometimes, a court looks at the neighbors' relationship—fight between them the night before. When there is hostility between the neighbors, or an obvious attempt at some kind of revenge, the words and actions of the fence builder may reflect a malicious motive.

Example: Two Washington state neighbors, a man and a woman, had a disagreement. The man ended his argument with the promise "Never mind, I will fix you." Soon the fence went up, over eight feet high, made of unplaned wood and standing above the top of the woman's windows. It effectively boarded up the side of her house. After her tenant on that side promptly moved out because she couldn't see in the dark, the neighbor sued, asking that the fence be declared a spite fence.

The judge asked the fence builder what the fence's use was. He claimed that he needed it to keep out children and chickens. On cross-examination, he admitted that he could do this with a five-foot fence. The judge found that "malevolence" was his dominant motive and ordered the fence reduced to five feet.[5]

Sometimes the appearance of the fence and the circumstances between the neighbors together contribute to a strong presumption of the builder's malicious motive.

Example: For many years, a family enjoyed a panoramic view of the ocean on one side and the mountains on the other. "Upstart newcomers," in their words, bought the lot next door and built a two-story house. The house, perfectly legal under local law, completely blocks the ocean view, and the other family was furious. In retaliation, the first family erected a huge fence to block the new family's view of the mountains. This fence is the exact dimensions of the two-story house: 30 feet high and 100 feet long. Taken together, the fence itself and the situation of the neighbors unmistakably add up to a spite fence.

Usefulness of the Fence

When a fence is challenged in court and it appears to the court that it was erected to annoy the next-door neighbor, it will be ruled a spite fence unless the owner can show that he needs it for another reasonable purpose. But once a court finds malice, if the neighbor is truly harmed by the fence, the court will look extremely closely at the use claimed by the builder. After all, most people are content with fences from three to six feet high around their yards. The owner must show that the unusually high fence is useful.

Here are some of the most common justifications for an extra-high fence:

Privacy: Privacy in one's own yard is an uncommon treat. Many of us want to enjoy early morning coffee in a bathrobe. Others may wish to indulge in a midday hot tub respite or swim in a pool with some privacy. Many of us would simply like to sit outside with a good trashy novel without a neighbor being able to comment on our taste in literature. We just don't like being watched at home.

In today's crowded cities and increasingly tiny properties, outdoor privacy is difficult. Putting up a fence is a reasonable way to get it. Sometimes, a lot slopes steeply, and obtaining privacy means a six-foot fence on one end and a ten-foot one on the other. Or an even higher fence may be desirable if a prying neighbor glues himself to a second-story window every time he hears the lid come off the hot tub.

But if a neighbor is harmed by the fence and complains, the desire for privacy will have to be balanced against the relief for the neighbor, and privacy may not be a sufficient reasonable purpose to prevent the fence from being ruled a nuisance.

Fencing in Children or Animals: This is probably the most common reasonable use found throughout the country for a proper fence. In the absence of height ordinances or subdivision restrictions, when it comes to height, common sense and community norms together decide what's reasonable, given what needs to be fenced in or out.

One court has found nine feet to be excessive for the keeping of horses.[6] All courts would surely find that a seven-foot fence is higher than reasonably needed to keep a Pomeranian. Similarly, an eight-foot fence to contain an active two-year-old would be considered unnecessary by most people. This would be true even if the parent argued that he was looking a few years ahead. However, on the theory that two-year-olds grow, a six-foot fence might not be.

Stopping Trespassers: Fences offer protection from intruders. Stopping unwanted people from entering your property is a legitimate use of a tall fence.

Example: A California neighbor in a city with no backyard fence height ordinance, who was annoyed by a six-and-a-half-foot fence, sued the builder for erecting a spite fence. At trial, the owner showed that people had climbed over a smaller fence, using the property as a short cut. The judge agreed that this was a good reason to build a big fence and ruled that it wasn't a spite fence.[7]

Supporting Flowers and Vines: Roses in full bloom trained up and along a fence are a lovely sight. However, if the fence is unnecessarily high and bothering the neighbor, this use will not be sufficient to keep the fence from being a spite fence and a nuisance.

One owner, actually wishing to block an unsightly house from his view, erected a ten-foot fence and claimed it was necessary for gardening. He said he intended to grow decorative greenery on it, to use it as a trellis. The court said no. Training vines, as a reasonable activity, did not require a ten-foot fence.[8]

Enclosing Swimming Pools: Enclosing a swimming pool with a fence is not only reasonable but responsible and may be required by law. Maintaining privacy and preventing accidents are both valid purposes for a fence around a pool, if the height of the fence is reasonable.

The presence of a pool, however, doesn't justify any fence the owner decides to build. Consider this creative attempt at a little spite and its result. One neighbor erected what was evidently a lovely wooden fence to enclose his swimming pool, dogs and shrubbery. It was six feet and four inches tall as it ran along the property. But as the fence approached the next door neighbor's house, it rose to a height of nine feet and three inches, blocked the house effectively, and then dropped back down to six feet four inches.

The next-door neighbor sued, and the judge ruled that the extra feet alongside the neighbor were a spite fence and ordered them cut off.[9]

Harm to the Neighbor

If someone who wants to annoy a neighbor builds a fence that has no reasonable use, the neighbor must prove one more thing to win a lawsuit under the common law: harm from the fence. If a neighbor is suing under a spite fence statute and asking for money damages, the harm is presumed, but it must be translated into a money amount.

In a spite fence case, the neighbor's harm is the interference with his enjoyment of property caused by the fence. The harm is often couched in terms of a loss of light, air and view. Normally, there is no legal right to light, air or view. (See Chapter 8, *Obstruction of Views*.) But in many states, a neighbor may sue the owner of a spite fence for a loss of light, air and view.

The neighbor can show other harm as well, such as loss of rental income and annoyance. (See "How Much to Sue For," below.)

How Much to Sue For

In figuring how much to ask the court to award you, don't be too conservative. If you go to court and present a reasonable amount of what you really think your loss is and explain how you arrived at that figure, the judge will respect you for it. It is a welcome relief for the judge to have someone come in who has made a real effort to set an honest amount on a loss.

Here are some things to consider when you're trying to put a dollar figure on the harm the fence has caused you.

Deprivation of Light and Air

No one would build a house without windows. We like to be able to look outside. We welcome fresh air to breathe and to eliminate stale or even noxious household

LIGHT, AIR AND VIEW

Most of us have seen (or lived in) a house or apartment building that is extremely close to another structure. The effect can be a window that opens to reveal nothing but a blank wall. In that situation, we may complain that we have no view, or very little light and air. However, we can't do anything about it legally because the building next door serves a useful purpose, such as housing, office space, even storage. A spite fence is quite different, hurting us in the same way, but of no real value to the owner. (For more on obstruction of view, see Chapter 8.)

fumes. Many of us prefer sunlight to artificial light. A high fence can seriously diminish the enjoyment of our living quarters.

The loss varies greatly according to circumstances, and calculation is not easy. Let's try a little common sense. If your monthly housing cost (mortgage, insurance and taxes, or rent) is $900 a month, that is roughly $30 a day. If you have lost light, air and view for one whole side of the house, $10 a day would seem reasonable as damage.

What about damage to the yard? Flowers, trees, gardens and grass also need light, air and often direct sun to survive. If your prized vegetable garden is dead, you have both an increase in your grocery bill and a loss of enjoyment of gardening. Surely, a total amount like $300 would be reasonable for that loss. Did you lose beautiful flowers and the lawn itself on that side? How about $500?

Utility Bills

If your utility bills have gone up because of the neighbor's fence, ask the court for an award to cover your out-of-pocket expense. Be prepared to document the increase.

Loss of Rental Income

You should be able to show the court if the fence made the property unrentable or if, as is more likely, it lowered its rental value. Either way, you can ask for the amount you are out as a result of the spite fence.

Diminished Value of the Whole Property

The property value loss is the difference between the value of your property with the spite fence next door and without it. Even if you aren't intending to sell the house anytime soon, you are entitled to this amount if the fence stays up.

A spite fence serves notice to others that there is a neighbor problem, something that can in itself lower the value of the property. If the fence is hideous, its aesthetic impact can contribute further to diminishing market value of the property. If the fence blocks a spectacular view, it has undoubtedly taken thousands off the market value of your house.

Normally you couldn't sue a neighbor for ugliness that lowers your property value. However, if an unlawful act by the neighbor (creating a spite fence) caused a lowering of property value, asking for compensation is worth a try. A good real estate appraiser (see your phone book for listings) can help you estimate diminished property value.

Annoyance

Some judges say that they do not consider the neighbor's hurt feelings and embarrassment when evaluating harm in spite fence cases, yet some grant money for annoyance.

Example: In a case in Kentucky, an eight-foot solid wall was built one inch over on the neighbor's property, and the neighbor sued both for trespass and a spite fence. Once the lawsuit was filed, the owner took down the wall, but the neighbor still went to court. The jury awarded the neighbor one cent for trespass and $1,999.99 for annoyance.[10]

Probably the best you can do is to understand that it's possible, although tricky, to be compensated for your fence-building neighbor's figurative slap in the face. This seems reasonable; probably the most important effect of a spite fence is psychological. Think for a moment about how prisons use windowless cells as a form of punishment. Suddenly being blocked, shut off by a fence in our faces, can make us feel like we are in jail in our own houses.

To put a dollar amount on your irritation and annoyance, try this approach: When you get up each morning and look out at the despised spite fence, what do you think? Do you say "By golly, I'd give $100 to have that thing out of my face?" Feel that way every day? That's $100 a day. You may not get it, but don't short-change yourself. Just because these amounts are subjective does not mean you can't convince a court they are real.

Other Out-of-Pocket Expenses

Include anything else that has cost you money as a result of the fence. If it has made you physically ill, list your medical bills. Every situation is different, so keep your own accurate account of all out-of-pocket expenses and ask to be compensated for them.

---

[1] *Piccirilli v. Groccia,* 114 R.I. 36, 327 A.2d 834 (1974). The neighbor in this case also tried to object to the fence under another local law limiting the height of boundary fences to four and a half feet, but the fence turned out to be an inch from the boundary and didn't come under the boundary fence regulation.

[2] *Smith v. Morse,* 19 N.E. 393 (Mass. 1889).

[3] *Griffin v. Northridge,* 67 Cal. 2d 69, 153 P.2d 800 (1944).

[4] *Racich v. Mastrovich,* 65 S.D. 321, 273 N.W. 660 (1937).

[5] *Karasek v. Peier,* 22 Wash. 419, 61 P. 33 (1900).

[6] *Whitlock v. Uhle,* 53 A. 891 (Conn. 1903).

[7] *Haehlen v. Wilson,* 11 Cal. 2d 437, 54 P.2d 62 (1936).

[8] *Bar Due v. Cox,* 47 Cal. 713, 190 P. 1056 (1920). Also, for a discussion on trellises as a reasonable use, see *Rideout v. Knox,* 148 Mass. 368, 19 N.E. 390 (1889).

[9] *Rapuano v. Ames,* 21 Conn. Supp. 110, 145 A.2d 384 (1958).

[10] *Humphrey v. Mansbach,* 265 Ky. 675, 97 S.W.2d 439 (1936). This case was sent back for a new trial because the court considered the amount awarded for annoyance too high under the circumstances.

Legal Research

When you are involved in a neighbor dispute, you need to know what the law is on the subject. No deep mysterious powers are required. You simply need the few simple skills necessary to find the relevant local ordinances, state statutes and, occasionally, judicial decisions that speak to your particular problem. Whether you are preparing for a neighborly meeting, hoping to use mediation, heading for small claims court or about to hire a lawyer, you will almost surely benefit from doing some basic research on your own.

LOCAL LAWS

As noted throughout this book, much of the law affecting neighbor relations is local, passed by a city council (or board of selectmen) or a county (parish) board of supervisors. Local laws often cover topics such as the following:

- animals
- blighted property
- building codes
- fence appearance
- fence height
- fence location
- garbage
- noise
- protected trees
- sick trees
- trash
- view obstruction
- weeds
- zoning

You can often get some answers to local law questions simply by phoning the appropriate government office—for instance, a zoning or planning office will answer questions about fence height restrictions or building permits. However, it also pays to read the law yourself. Certainly, when it comes time to deal with the neighbor, you will want a copy of the law in your hand. Some city offices will send you a copy of a particular law if you know exactly what you want.

If you're on your own, you can find the whole set of local laws, called ordinances at city halls, county courthouses and public libraries. Or check the county law library, which is usually located in or near the courthouse. Simply go in and ask the clerk or librarian where the ordinances are. The whole set is sometimes called the municipal or county code.

Once you have the ordinances in hand, look for your topic in the index. Be prepared to look under several different terms. Some indexes are not as helpful as they should be. For instance, if you have a dangerous tree problem, you may not find anything under "danger" or "tree." Keep looking. Try "sick trees," "hazardous conditions," "nuisance" or even "miscellaneous."

Often, local ordinances are kept in a big looseleaf binder, and the pages get jumbled from people taking parts out and copying them. Be aware of this in case you find something in the index and can't find the page. You may have to do some searching.

If the index doesn't get you anywhere, read the table of contents and see if you can find your particular problem. If you are looking for building height restrictions or fence regulations, and there is no entry under height or fence, check under zoning laws. Don't stop your search until you have read all ordinances that might possibly be relevant.

For example, if your downhill neighbor plans a large addition to his house that will block your view, you probably won't find anything in the ordinances to help you under "view." Look instead at the building code and the zoning restrictions. You'll obviously want to check any building height ordinances. But you'll also want to read road setback rules and any ordinance that limits the ratio of building area to that of the total lot. If you find an ordinance limiting a building to 55% of a lot, and your neighbor's proposed addition will exceed the legal limit, you can stop the project.

But don't stop reading. Go on and see if other restrictions apply. Some ordinances call for design review and approval by a city commission. If such an ordinance exists, you may be able to appeal to the planning authority on the basis that your neighbor's planned addition is so large that it upsets the scale of the neighborhood.

In sum, take your time and keep reading. You may end up reading quite a lot of laws, but you may also find yourself quite entertained, and you could run across something that may help you in a different situation. In some cities, you really will find that almost anything bothering a neighbor violates a local ordinance.

If you can't find what you are looking for, ask the librarian or clerk to help you. Even if you find exactly what you want, check with the librarian to make sure you've got an up-to-date version of the law. The new updates for local laws may be in an different place, like the front or back of the book, or even a different volume. Ask the librarian when the library received its most recent update. Public libraries are sometimes out of date. If you're not sure whether or not you have the most recent ordinance, call the city or county clerk's office and ask when the law was last amended.

Occasionally, the language of an ordinance is confusing. If you find one on your topic that is a little unclear, try calling the relevant office and ask exactly how they interpret the law.

If you want to see whether or not any of your state's courts have issued written opinions interpreting a particular ordinance, you can use a set of books called

"Shepard's Citations." Shepard's is available in a law libraries. For instructions on how to use it, refer to one of the legal research books listed in "Other Resources," below.

STATE STATUTES

Some situations that affect neighbors are regulated by state laws, passed by the legislature. These subjects include:

- adverse possession
- boundary fences
- damage to trees
- disorderly conduct
- easements
- nuisance
- spite fences
- trespass

You can find your state statutes in the county law library and probably in a large public library. Many publicly funded law school libraries, which will also have the state statutes, allow people to use their facilities. Use a law library if possible, especially if your question is complicated, because law librarians can be wonderful in sharing their research skills and directing you to the books you need.

Finding a Statute

State statutes (also called the state code) come in two forms: brief, containing only the laws themselves, and annotated. The annotated version also includes small summaries of cases and other helpful resources following the text of each law.

Ask the librarian to show you to the annotated version of your state statutes. What you will find looks like a set of encyclopedias and has a separate index.

Sit down with the index for a few moments and become comfortable with it. If you look under fences, for example, the index will probably list several numbers to find. These are not page numbers but the actual numbers of the state laws that have to do with fences. Each statute is numbered, and in most states, they are arranged in numerical order.

Example: In Maine, under "fences," you would find a reference to 30.3452. This means Title 30, Section 3452. The titles are arranged in numerical order and then the sections within them.

In Utah, under "fences," you would find just Section 4-26-5. Several states number their laws only with section numbers. The sections are printed in numerical order and easy to find.

Often, the numbers are on the outside of the particular volume you are looking for, on the spine of the book. The book may say "Title 30," or it could say "Section 3-1-1 to Section 4-20-17," depending on which system the state uses.

A few of the larger states, such as California, New York and Texas, break their codes down by subject matter. For instance, California has a Civil Code, a Health and Safety Code and so on. If you are looking for fences in California, the index refers you to C.C. 841; this means Civil Code, section 841. The index has a table explaining abbreviations in the front of the volume. If you have any trouble, ask a librarian for help.

Also check to see if there is a paper supplement in the back of a hardback index volume. The supplement will contain any additional laws passed since the hardback index volume was printed. When the index itself is in paperback, look on the shelf beside it for any smaller sup-plemental paper index volumes.

Once you see how the index works, and it is usually pretty straightforward, make a list of terms to look up in the index for the subject you need. Ask the librarian for a legal thesaurus, which will suggest more terms for the subject, probably including some legal terms that you may not be aware of. Also, look in the statute index under "words and phrases." This section can point you in the right direction. Take the time to look under all the terms you can think of that might possibly apply to your situation; if you don't, you may miss a crucial statute.

If someone has cut down your tree, look under trees. Not there? Try timber or trespass—anything you can think of. For next-door neighbor problems, always check under adjoining landowners.

TOPIC: DAMAGE TO A TREE	
Index term	**Statute Number**
trees	
timber	
adjoining landowners	
vandalism	
trespass	
negligence	

We wish we could tell you that finding a particular state statute is easy. Sometimes it is. But sometimes, depending on the subject and the particular state, it can take quite a bit of time and patience. A few states have pretty bad in-dexes.

Reading a Statute

When you find a statute on your subject, read it carefully. The language of the statute may be unnecessarily complicated. Try to keep your cool and remember that the laws are written by lawyers, many of whom seem unable to write in plain English. (How wonderful it would be if other states could learn from North Dakota. That state has not only a good index, but the laws are clearly written in a style that puts other state statutes to shame.)

Next, always check the back of the book for a paper supplement that has been slipped into a pocket in the inside back cover. This is called the "pocket part." It contains any changes in the law that have been made since the hardback volume was printed. Just look for the number of the law in the pocket part. If nothing is there under that number, it means there has been no change. If you find a change, it replaces the law printed in the hardbound volume. If there is nothing but the word "repealed" after the number of the law, the law printed in the hardbound volume is no longer in effect.

Also, look at the notes following the laws in both the main volume and the pocket part. You may find a reference to a court decision in a case that is very similar to yours. ("Court Decisions," below, discusses how to find the entire text of these written decisions.) You could also find a reference to another statute that you want to read, or even to an article written about the subject.

Below is an example of a state statute (Figure 1). This state law on spite fences is from the annotated laws of Massachusetts. Note the references beneath the law to other sources, especially the court opinions that interpret different questions that have come up in the state regarding the law on spite fences.

SPITE FENCES

§ 21. Definition; remedy of injured occupant

A fence or other structure in the nature of a fence which unnecessarily exceeds six feet in height and is maliciously erected or maintained for the purpose of annoying the owners or occupants of adjoining property shall be deemed a private nuisance. Any such owner or occupant injured in the comfort or enjoyment of his estate thereby may have an action of tort for damages under chapter two hundred and forty-three.

Historical Note

St.1887 c. 348.   R.L.1902 c. 33 § 19.

Library References

Nuisance ⊂⇒3(12).
C.J.S. Nuisance § 39.

Comment. Damnum absque injuria, see M.P.S. vol. 14, Simpson, § 1373.

Notes of Decisions

Constitutionality 1
Distance from boundary line 3
Motive in erecting fence 2
Persons liable 4
Subsequent proceedings 5
Validity 1

1. Validity

St.1887, c. 348, declaring fences unnecessarily exceeding six feet in height for annoyance of adjoining owner to be private nuisances, applies to existing structures subsequently maintained as well as those afterward erected and is consti-

tutional. Rideout v. Knox (1889) 19 N. E. 390, 148 Mass. 368, 2 L.R.A. 81, 12 Am.St.Rep. 560; Smith v. Morse (1889) 19 N.E. 393, 148 Mass. 407.

2. Motive in erecting fence

Under St.1887. c. 348, purpose of annoyance must be dominant motive for erecting and maintaining fence. Rideout v. Knox (1889) 19 N.E. 390, 148 Mass. 368, 2 L.R.A. 81, 12 Am.St.Rep. 560.

3. Distance from boundary line

Where defendant maliciously erected fence unnecessarily more than 6 feet

5A M.G.L.A.—29   449

Figure 1

BOOKS LISTING AND EXPLAINING COURT OPINIONS

Most of the law concerning neighbor relations is addressed either by local ordinance or state statute. But a few problems are up to the courts to decide. And some state legislatures have not passed laws on questions that are covered by state law in other states.

Even when you find a certain law that looks like it will help you, you may wonder how courts have actually interpreted some issues.

In most states, courts have addressed the subjects of:

- boundary lines

- boundary trees

- encroaching trees

- hazardous trees

- negligent behavior

- nuisances

- other next-door neighbor questions (adjoining landowners)

You must use a law library for research into case law. County law libraries, especially in larger cities, as well as public law school libraries, will have the books you need. Even if your county seat is located an hour or so away, it may well be worth the trip to read what is available.

Before you go, call ahead to learn the library hours; you need to give yourself several hours to do this kind of reading. You don't want to make a trip and land on the doorstep just as the library closes.

Help in finding and understanding court cases on such topics is available from several sources.

Legal Encyclopedias

When you can't find a specific law on your problem, ask the librarian to point you to the legal encyclopedias. Some states have their own; if yours doesn't, use a national one, such as *American Jurisprudence* (almost always called *Am. Jur.* for short). Like regular encyclopedias, these books are arranged alphabetically by topic. They discuss how courts have ruled in actual court cases.

Some of them have more than one series; you want the most recent. For instance, the current series of *Am. Jur.* is *Am. Jur. 2d*. The encyclopedias also have updated pocket parts in the back of the hardback volumes.

Figure 2 shows a page from *Am. Jur. 2d,* discussing uncertain boundary lines—in this example, neighbors setting a boundary by building a fence. You can see the small summaries of court decisions that follow each issue that is raised.

---

12 Am Jur 2d   BOUNDARIES   § 88

mutual acquiescence and recognition by the adjoiners is essential to practical location, provided that there is, at the time of the location, a disputed, indefinite, or uncertain boundary line between the adjoining owners.[11] A practical location of a boundary line has been said to be simply an actual designation on the ground, by the parties, of the monuments and bounds called for by the conveyances,[12] and it has also been said that when a disputed or uncertain boundary line is fixed by practical location it is binding, not by way of transfer of title, but by way of estoppel.[13]

§ 88. Erection of fence.

Where there is doubt and uncertainty as to the location of the true boundary line[14] between adjoining landowners, they may agree that a fence may be the division line between their lands.[15] To constitute the fence the boundary line it is not necessary that the agreement be express; it may be inferred from or implied by the conduct of the parties, especially where the fence is acquiesced to as the boundary line for the period of the statute of limitations.[16] It has

11. Drury v Pekar, supra, quoting Kincaid v Peterson, 135 Or 619, 297 P 833.

The practical location of a boundary line can be established in any one of three ways: (1) the location relied upon must have been acquiesced in for a sufficient length of time to bar a right of entry under the statute of limitations; (2) the line must have been expressly agreed upon between the parties claiming the land on both sides thereof and afterward acquiesced in; or, (3) the parties whose rights are to be barred must have silently looked on, with knowledge of the true line, while the other party encroached upon it or subjected himself to expense in regard to the line which he would not have done had the line been in dispute. Fishman v Nielson, 237 Minn 1, 53 NW2d 553.

12. Wells v Jackson Iron Mfg. Co. 47 NH 235.

Boundary lines may be determined by physical indications of the lines on the ground accepted by the parties over a period of time. Failone v Gochee, 9 App Div 2d 569, 189 NYS2d 363, app den 9 App Div 2d 699, 191 NYS2d 560.

The actual location of a deed may be satisfactorily established, not only by the natural objects found on the ground, but by the fact that all the parties who knew the facts and were interested in the land located the deed in a certain way. Kenmont Coal Co. v Combs, 243 Ky 328, 48 SW2d 9 (holding that location of deed by grantor and his grantee, subsequently acquiesced in for more than 30 years, could not be disputed).

13. Adams v Warner, 209 App Div 394, 204 NYS 613, quoted with approval in Drury v Pekar, 224 Or 37, 355 P2d 598.

14. Uncertainty of or dispute as to the location of the true boundary line is essential in order that a fence built on a line agreed as the boundary line may operate to preclude the parties from later claiming a different boundary line. Vowinckel v N. Clark & Sons,

217 Cal 258, 18 P2d 58; Pederson v Reynolds, 31 Cal App 2d 18, 87 P2d 51; Blank v Ambs, 260 Mich 589, 245 NW 525; Talbot v Smith, 56 Or 117, 107 P 480, 108 P 125. Annotation: 170 ALR 1146.

But it is not necessary that there should be an actual dispute between the parties regarding the true division line; it is sufficient if it appears that they were uncertain as to the true line and therefore agreed to a designated and certain boundary upon which they constructed a fence and occupied and cultivated or improved their respective portions to that division fence for more than the statutory period. Martin v Lopes (Cal App) 164 P2d 321, superseded 28 Cal 2d 618, 170 P2d 881.

When the real boundary line between contiguous landowners is known to them, neither of them may acquire title by acquiescence beyond such line by merely building a fence upon the other's property and cultivating and claiming the land to that point, since title to land by acquiescence is founded on an agreement when an uncertainty exists as to the true line. Martin v Lopes, supra.

15. An oral agreement fixing an uncertain and disputed dividing line of lands, and execution thereof by the building of a fence thereon, is not in violation of the statute of frauds, since the parties do not thereby undertake to acquire and pass title to real estate, but merely fix the location of the boundary of the land that they already own, the purpose being to identify their several holdings and make certain that which they regard as uncertain. Holbrooks v Wright, 187 Ky 732, 220 SW2d 524.

Generally as to oral agreements fixing boundary lines, see §§ 78 et seq., supra.

16. Hannah v Pogue, 23 Cal 2d 849, 147 P2d 572; Roberts v Brae, 5 Cal 2d 356, 54 P2d 698; Kandlick v Hudek, 365 Ill 292, 6 NE2d 196.

Annotation: 170 ALR 1145.

Figure 2

On the page from *Am. Jur. 2d*, you will see a reference at the bottom to *A.L.R.*, a set of volumes whose full name is *American Law Reports*. This is another excellent national compilation of court decisions, books and articles published concerning all areas of the law. *A.L.R.* also comes in several series—the 4th is current—and has updated pocket parts in the back. *A.L.R.* has separate index volumes that list the topics in alphabetical order.

HOW LONG DO YOU THINK THE WESTONS WILL KEEP THIS SOUTHWEST THEME?

Books on Particular Subjects

Books on particular topics can be most helpful for gaining an overall perspective on the subject, and also for getting more citations to court cases in your area.

- For property questions, a huge series of volumes called *Powell on Property* covers topics like boundaries, easements and adverse possession in detail.

- For questions on nuisance (such as encroaching tree branches) and negligence (such as allowing a dangerous tree to fall) see *Prosser and Keeton on Torts* (a single volume).

- For information on problems between next-door neighbors, look at a recent book called *A Practical Guide to Disputes Between Adjoining Landowners —Easements,* by James H. Backman and David A. Thomas. This large, loose-leaf volume covers many subjects of concern to next-door neighbors, is updated periodically, and lists court cases for most states.

Because all of these books are written for lawyers, they are predictably full of frustrating legal jargon. However, if you approach them with a little patience, you can learn a lot about a particular subject. The Prosser book, especially, is quite readable and punctuated with Professor Prosser's fine sense of humor.

Digests

In Figure 1, showing the spite fence statute, under the library references you'll notice a small symbol of a key that says "Nuisance 3(12)." Every topic in the law has its own "key number," which is listed in state and regional digests published by West Publishing Company. Each digest has an index by subject which tells you that subject's key number.

Once you find the key number in the index for the topic you want, you can look in the digest under the number for that topic and find citations to any court cases in your state that talk about that issue.

The digests can be the most helpful tool of all in finding exactly what you are looking for, because the issues in every published court opinion are broken down into these key numbers for the whole country. For example, if you look in any state digest under the key number "Nuisance 3(12)" (referred to in the Massachusetts spite fence statute above), all spite fence cases for that state should be listed.

COURT DECISIONS

When there are no state statutes or local ordinances to help you, you have to rely on what's called the "common law"—court decisions in a particular state that govern what the law is. When the highest court in a state (usually the state Supreme Court) decides an issue, that decision binds other courts in that state to that law until the decision is later changed by the same highest court. Although judges are sometimes influenced by decisions in other states, each state has its own common law. The court decisions are published and available for anyone to read.

When you are depending on case law, you need to read the actual court opinions to completely understand the law that affects your problem. And sometimes, you may also want to look up and read a case referred to in the annotations to a statute, a legal encyclopedia or this book to learn the court's interpretation of a law.

Once you have a reference (called a citation) to a court decision, it is time to read the court opinion itself. Never depend on what a reference book tells you an opinion says. The people doing the research for these books are only human, and occasionally summaries are very misleading.

Example: In the written opinion of a case in Washington, D.C. called *Sterling v. Weinstein*, 78 Wash. Law Rep. 942,

75 A.2d 144 (1950), the judge talked at length about the fact that some states allow a neighbor to sue and win when tree branches next door grow across the boundary and damage the neighbor's property. However, in this case, the court ruled for the tree owner, and the judge told the neighbor who had brought the lawsuit that he should have cut the damaging branches himself. This is still the law in the District of Columbia. Unfortunately, somebody doing some research must have confused the part when the judge talked about the other states with how the court actually ruled. Now, references in some books indicate that a neighbor can recover money for tree damage in Washington, D.C., because of this case. This is dead wrong. It is easy (and horrifying) to imagine somebody in that area reading only the reference book and then going into court asking a judge for money. The person will wish he had never gone to court, because he didn't bother to read the case.

Tracking down exactly what you need does take a little work, but there is no reason why you can't do it yourself if you are so inclined. Let's take an example.

Suppose you are worried about a neighbor's dying tree and wonder who pays for what if it falls. In a legal encyclopedia, you look under "adjoining landowners." The book tells you that the tree owner may have to pay for the damage and then cites *Israel v. Carolina Bar-B-Que,Inc.*, 292 S.C. 282, 356 S.E.2d 123 (1987). Here's how to decode the citation.

The case name: Israel versus Carolina Bar-B-Que (who sued whom).

Books it is printed in: *South Carolina Reporter*, Volume 292, page 282, and *Southeastern Reporter, 2nd Series*, Volume 356, page 123.

The date: 1987, tells you when the court ruled on the case.

The second book listed in the citation, *Southeastern Reporter, 2nd Series*, contains cases from several states in the region and is called a regional reporter. Abbreviations for particular reporters are listed in the front of the volumes of reporters and also in some encyclopedias. Opinions from all states (except two) and the District of Columbia are published in the regional reporters. New York and California use only state reporters for most of their states' court opinions.

Regional reporters are available in most law libraries, although the state ones may not be. The regional reporter is usually the easiest one to find and use. In the example, once you have volume 356 of the *Southeastern Reporter, 2nd Series* and look on page 123, there's the case.

Let's take another example, this time from New York. The reference book you are using says that a neighbor was not able to collect money for damage caused by a healthy tree next door, and cites *Turner v. Coppola*, 102 Misc. 2d 1043, 424 N.Y.S.2d 864 (1980).

New York and California reporters are usually available in law libraries across the country, just like the regional reporters. For this case, you take the last citation, volume 424 of the *New York State Reporter, 2nd Series*, look on page 864, and find the court opinion.

Figure 3 shows a copy of this page. You'll see a summary of the history of the case first, including what this court ruled. Then there's a sentence about each issue in the case and the West key number for that issue (see "Digests," above). The full judge's opinion follows this kind of introduction in all published cases.

864   424 NEW YORK SUPPLEMENT, 2d SERIES

"8. The instruction and supervision given * * * were so negligently given as to result in the * * * injuries sustained."

No other factual averment was made by plaintiff which in any way indicates a basis for his conclusion of negligence (*Koppers Co. v. Empire Bituminous Products, Inc.*, 35 A.D.2d 906, 316 N.Y.S.2d 858); and, such is not satisfied by a mere repetition of the complaint without factual evidence upon which to impose liability upon the movant (*Golding v. Weissman*, 35 A.D.2d 941, 316 N.Y.S.2d 522).

Defendant, Senior's motion is granted.

102 Misc.2d 1043
Barbara G. TURNER, Plaintiff,

v.

Caroline COPPOLA, Richard Petersen, Minna Petersen and Freda Amster, Defendants.

Supreme Court, Special Term, Nassau County, Part I.

Feb. 13, 1980.

Plaintiff, who alleged that branches on defendants' trees encroached on plaintiff's property, caused cosmetic damage to her garage and prevented her lawn from receiving adequate sunlight and that twigs, branches and buds from the trees constantly fell on her property, brought action for omnibus relief. On defendants' motion to dismiss complaint for failure to state cause of action, the Supreme Court, Nassau County, Special Term, B. Thomas Pantano, J., held that: (1) the trees were not a "nuisance per se," in such a sense as to sustain an action for relief; (2) complaint did not state cause of action for relief from private nuisance; (3) plaintiff did not have a cause of action in trespass; (4) plaintiff did not

have a cause of action in negligence; but (5) plaintiff could protect herself by self-help consisting of a reasonable cutting of branches to extent that they invaded her property.

Motion to dismiss complaint granted.

1. Nuisance ⟊1
Essence of a "private nuisance" is interference with the use and enjoyment of land amounting to an injury in relation to a right of ownership in that land.
> See publication Words and Phrases for other judicial constructions and definitions.

2. Nuisance ⟊3(1)
In light of fact that defendants' trees, whose branches allegedly encroached on plaintiff's property and from which twigs, branches and buds were alleged to have constantly fallen onto such property, were not poisonous or noxious in their nature, the trees were not a "nuisance per se," in such a sense as to sustain an action for relief.
> See publication Words and Phrases for other judicial constructions and definitions.

3. Nuisance ⟊42
Right to recover damages from overhanging branches depends on presence of actual injury to plaintiff or plaintiff's property.

4. Nuisance ⟊48
Complaint, in which it was alleged that branches on defendants' trees encroached on plaintiff's property, caused cosmetic damage to her garage and prevented her lawn from receiving adequate sunlight and that trees, branches and buds from the trees constantly fell on plaintiff's property, did not state cause of action for relief from private nuisance. RPAPL § 871.

5. Nuisance ⟊3(1)
    Trespass ⟊10
If an invasion of plaintiff's interest in exclusive possession of his land also deprives him of use and enjoyment of the land, trespass and nuisance would jointly arise, so long as the interference causes

Figure 3

CLUES TO A JUDGE'S REAL OPINION

Reading the case opinions yourself can teach you more than just how a court ruled on an issue. For instance, if you are researching cases on trees and you find the word "beauty" in the written court decision, or the words "shelter and shade," be on the alert. When a tree is damaged, the judge is likely to grant a substantial monetary judgment for the owner.

On the other hand, if the owner is the one being sued, for instance because the neighbor is bothered by the tree, there is likely to be little recovery. The reason? The judge likes trees. Because the standards for setting damages in cases like tree injury cases can be broad to the point of vagueness, the attitude towards trees of the judge who hears any particular case is likely to greatly influence the result.

You can also predict the outcome of a case when the language shows that the judge is angry. Sometimes a judge becomes outraged at neighbors cluttering up the court with silly quarrels, or at one neighbor for acting like a real chump. When the judge is angry, look out. Whoever has incurred the wrath will probably be most unhappy with the court's decision.

OTHER RESOURCES

In the rare situation where you would be going to court alone over a neighbor problem and relying only on a court decision, you need to be sure that the law is still good, that the court has not changed its position. Sometimes a case that is a hundred years old is still the law in a state. But many cases are later overruled or reversed, and are no longer good law. The law can change from one day to the next.

You can check to see if a case opinion is still good law by using an update service called Shepard's. This task is fairly complicated, and explaining it is beyond the scope of this book. But there is no reason you can't learn how to do it. For detailed instructions in updating cases and guides for doing more extensive research by yourself, we recommend using one of the resources listed below.

Because lots of folks, especially law students and paralegals, want to know about legal research, there are a lot of legal research books available. Some of them are heavyweights; others are short and sweet.

All of these books, or at least most of them, should be in almost every large law library. Many will be in your public library.

- *Legal Research: How To Find and Understand the Law,* by Elias (Nolo Press)
  In a nontechnical but detailed way, this book covers all the basic research legal materials and is designed for the average person. One of the best features is the first four chapters, which help you decide what words and concepts might guide you in framing a particular research question.

- *Legal Research Made Easy: A Roadmap through the Law Library Maze,* by Berring (Legal Star/Nolo Press).
  This entertaining two-and-a-half-hour videotape gives a six-step strategy for legal research and explains all the legal research tools you'll come across in a law library.

- *Legal Research in a Nutshell,* by Cohen (West Publishing Co.)
  This book is more technical but still can help the nonspecialist. It discusses, in detail, the types of books used in the legal research process. This book is a classic that should be in almost every law library. It is a paperback and is usually inexpensive, at least as law books go. Unfortunately it is now a bit out of date.

- *How To Find the Law* (9th Ed.), by Cohen, Berring and Olson, (West Publishing Co.)

- *Fundamentals of Legal Research,* by Jacobstein and Mersky (Foundation Press)

If you want an even more detailed approach to the subject, these are two text books are written for law students. Both come complete with lots of illustrations and detail.

Each has a paperback abridgement that contains selected chapters from the larger book. *How To Find the Law* becomes *Finding the Law* when it shrinks to paperback size, and *Fundamentals of Legal Research* transforms into *Legal Research Illustrated.* Each of these paperback editions is used in law schools, paralegal schools and some colleges. You will find them in most big law libraries. The problem with these books is that they can overwhelm you with detail, and their style is stiff and pompous. They are great places to go if you just need one or two specific pieces of information.

- *The Legal Research Manual: A Game Plan for Legal Research and Analysis,* by Wren and Wren (A-R Editions)

  This paperback textbook, which should be in all major law libraries, uses a nontechnical approach, but it is written with law students in mind. It concentrates on the way law books are used, not on the description of the law books themselves.

- *The Process of Legal Research: Successful Strategies,* by Kunz (Little-Brown)

  This paperback is a cross between the traditional and new methods of writing about legal research. An interesting feature of the book is that librarians work through model problems.

- *Legal Research and Writing: Some Starting Points,* by Statsky (West Publishing Co.)

This volume contains photographs of the books that are discussed along with simple descriptions of how to use them. It is very straightforward and easy to use.

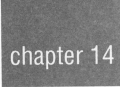

chapter 14

Mediation

One of the most troublesome aspects of neighbor disputes is that they can fester for years. One neighbor becomes angry, the other retaliates, the first neighbor adds fuel to the fire and the dispute escalates. Sadly, it is not uncommon to find neighbor quarrels that have gone on for years where the people can't even agree on how it started. If one neighbor actually sues another, the lawsuit drains not only money and time, but usually ends any possibility of salvaging a friendly relationship. Then the neighbors continue to live side by side, sometimes not speaking ever again, more often finding something else to fight about.

Happily, there is a way out of this problem—it's called mediation, and in one form or another it's probably available in your community. Today, many judges commonly order disputing neighbors into mandatory mediation after they get to court. Far better for the neighbors to arrange it early on by themselves, and to avoid ever darkening the doors of the courthouse.

WHAT IS MEDIATION?

Mediation is a process in which the people involved in a dispute sit down and find their own solution with the help of a mediator. A mediator is a person who is neutral to the dispute and has training in techniques to get people talking.

Mediators are not necessarily lawyers; in fact, many are not. Some undergo hours of intensive training in mediating disputes. Many are volunteers, which helps enormously in keeping costs down. Often a mediation service provides disputing neighbors with a panel of several skilled people to hear and guide them.

The job of the mediator is to help keep the neighbors focused and reasonably civil, to allow the presentation of each person's side and to suggest compromise. The mediator has no power to impose a solution or order any action. If the neighbors reach an agreement, the mediator helps to put it in writing, so everyone can remember exactly what was agreed.

The amazing thing about neighbor dispute mediation is how well it works. Unlike a court of law, each neighbor comes in not to win at any cost, but to simply be heard and to work at a solution. The fact that no judge or arbitrator can impose a decision greatly reduces the need to posture and shade the truth. The mediator's expertise helps, but usually most neighbors are tired of the quarreling and really would prefer peace in the neighborhood.

Another great feature of mediation is that unlike a court proceeding, where only matters relevant to the dispute can be considered, anything can be discussed in a mediation session. Often, the result is that hidden problems, not even mentioned at first but at the heart of the dispute, emerge. For example, a dispute over a tree may really have its roots in a perceived slur about one neighbor's race, religion or taste in motorcycles.

HOW TO FIND A MEDIATOR

If you live in an urban area, you will probably have little trouble finding a mediator. The small claims clerk at the courthouse, the county law librarian or the police may have a list of free community mediation services. For example, in San Francisco, an organization called Community Boards provides free mediation services on a neighborhood by neighborhood basis. In some east coast cities, the Society of Friends has provided mediation services for many years. And in other areas, state or city funds support local mediation (dispute resolution) centers.

In any planned unit development or subdivision, the homeowners association may offer mediation services to its members. If there is no neighborhood or community mediation service where you live, contact your local or state bar association. The American Bar Association has thrust its support behind mediation in the past few years. Many attorneys volunteer as mediators through their local bar associations.

Private mediators are listed in the yellow pages of the phone book. Some lawyers may also mention mediation services in their telephone book listings under "attorneys." If you choose a mediator at random like this, find out first what their training is and how much they charge. Some may be as high as $75 or $100 an hour, but if they are good, the cost can still be far less than a lawsuit.

In areas that do not yet have organized mediation services, a troubled neighbor can still arrange for mediation of a dispute. All it takes is someone who is respected by both parties, who can remain neutral and who is willing to help. A respected member of the neighborhood or of the clergy, a retired cop—you can probably think of someone who would be willing to help you and a neighbor work out a problem.

HOW MEDIATION WORKS

When they choose mediation, the disputing neighbors simply decide that they are willing to try to work something out themselves. They make no obligation beyond agreeing to sit down together in the same room with the mediator. Often the mediator has her own set of procedures. For example, sometimes a mediator wants to meet alone with each disputant before the mediation session.

At the mediation session, the neighbors may feel comfortable attending alone or may bring someone with them. Typically, each neighbor has a turn to explain his side, with the mediator sometimes asking questions. It is the mediator's job to try to keep the neighbors from interrupting each other and guide them toward a dialogue. In some instances, a mediator also explains relevant laws, but the neighbors don't have to follow the solution the law sets out; they are free to make their own agreement. If an agreement is reached, the mediator helps puts it into writing.

Let's take an example:

Mary and John have been next-door neighbors for years. In the last year John has begun to complain bitterly about the debris in his yard from Mary's oak tree. Mary does nothing. John gives veiled threats about cutting down the tree. One day they have harsh words over the tree, and Mary warns him to leave her property alone.

John doesn't say anything more but turns up the volume on his TV when he watches late night movies. And he moves his TV closer to a window on Mary's side of the house, which he leaves open a few inches. When Mary complains, John just smiles and does nothing.

A few weeks later, while watering her yard, Mary just happens to place the sprinkler too close to the property line, wets down John's tools, and soaks his cactus garden. John says nothing but begins parking his car right at the edge of Mary's drive so it's hard for her to turn into her driveway and even harder to see traffic when she pulls out. (Does this sound familiar to anyone?)

Mary and John no longer complain; they no longer speak. One night when the TV keeps Mary awake, she calls the police, claiming John is in violation of the local noise ordinance.

A cruiser pulls up, and the war goes up a notch. The police talk to both of them (with all of the neighbors watching, of course). Fortunately, a perceptive officer senses that there is more going on than one loud television set. He hands them both the name and address of a free local mediation project with offices at the local courthouse. Although it's a voluntary program, the officer gets both Mary and John to somewhat reluctantly agree to try it.

Mary and John are interviewed separately by the mediator. He takes notes in each session and prepares a tentative summary of the complaints. A date is scheduled for them to meet together. John, who lives alone, attends alone. Mary, upset over a confrontation with John, takes along her son, Bill, for support. Here is what happens:

Mediator: Thank you for coming. We will do this in an orderly fashion, with one complaint at a time. Mary, please begin by telling us what is happening. John, please do not interrupt; you will have plenty of time for your own story.

Mary: I don't really know why I am here. The only problem is that John here has suddenly begun turning up the volume on his TV at all hours and I can't get any sleep. I just want him to turn it down, or off.

Mediator: You told me earlier that John is also blocking your driveway and threatening your tree.

Mary: That too. I don't know what has happened. We used to get along, but then he started acting like a real jerk.

John: Jerk? Who's a jerk? You're the one who ruined my tools.

Mediator: Slow down. Let's start by keeping language as civil as possible. It's fine to be mad, but calling each other names won't help. Also, John, let Mary tell her story first in as much detail as she wants. Then it will be your turn.

Mary: I don't mind dealing with the tools. I was just watering my yard. There must have been a surge of pressure. I'm not the kind of person to deliberately harm someone else's things. (pause) I didn't mean to ruin any tools. John has just made me so angry.

Mediator: Mary, I have written down three complaints that you have about John: his loud television set, his blocking your driveway, and his threatening your tree. Would you like to add anything?

Mary: No. That's about it, and that's enough.

Mediator: John, you have the floor.

John: I never was going to hurt her precious tree, even though it drives me crazy. Living downwind from that thing with all the leaves it sheds is a nightmare. But the real problem here is Mary. She ruined $200 worth of my tools and destroyed my garden. I should be taking her to court.

Mediator: What about the loud television?

John: It's my house, and I can watch TV anytime I please. Besides, noise doesn't seem to bother her when she's throwing those loud parties.

Mary: Parties? What parties? (This is the first time she has heard this and she is surprised. She thinks back for a moment. The only party she had this year was her annual Christmas open house. It didn't seem loud, even though it did go a bit late. And John knew he wouldn't be invited this year, after he had been so nasty.)

Mediator: Just a minute, Mary. John, let's talk about the tree, the oak in Mary's back yard. You say it is driving you crazy?

John: I've never seen so much debris in my life. I dread the fall when I'll have to spend all of my time raking up the leaves.

Mediator: How long have you two been next-door neighbors?

Mary and John: For ten years.

Mediator: During the past years, have you had any trouble before?

Mary: No. (pause) In fact, John has been a good neighbor in the past. I don't understand what is wrong. He used to like my tree; he even raked the leaves in my yard sometimes when he raked his. Now all he does is complain. I won't allow my tree to be harmed. And John, I have never had loud parties.

John: There just seemed to be so many more leaves last year. I can't rake as well after my back surgery. I can't do much of anything anymore. (He thinks maybe he should have told Mary about his back, and maybe asked her son, Bill, to do the raking. He realizes that he does still like the tree.)

Mary: Surgery, what surgery? When did you have surgery? Why didn't you tell me? I'm your next-door neighbor.

At this point the anger over the television and the tools is subsiding. Both Mary and John are beginning to see the trap they have made for themselves with their quarrels. They both are beginning to want out of the hostilities.

The mediator suggests that they make an agreement between them covering the issues that have caused their disputes. With the mediator's help, they draft one in writing, so they will have it for future reference.

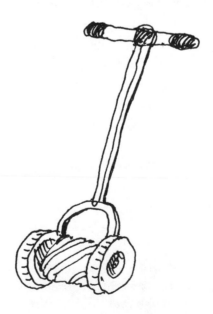

AGREEMENT

Mary Malone and John Jasper, in an effort to settle their differences and live peaceably, make the following agreement:

- The entire oak tree in Mary's back yard is to be trimmed and thinned every three years, cost to be borne by Mary.

- Any branches of the oak tree over John's property may be cut at his expense at any time, if he chooses.

- There will be no loud television playing that disturbs the other. If John watches TV after 11 p.m., he will use earphones or move the TV from the wall on Mary's side of the house.

- At least a three foot clearance will be left between John's car and Mary's driveway.

- Watering of lawns will be done with care and attention to each other's property.

- Any parties will be held at a reasonable time and without excessive noise.

In the case of any future dispute, Mary and John agree to talk to each other, with or without a mediator, to try to solve the problem amicably.

_____   _____
Mary Malone   Date

_____   _____
John Jasper   Date

And yes, Bill started raking the leaves and John was invited to the next Christmas party. Corny? Not really. This is not nearly as emotional as some neighbor disputes. The real problem is usually lack of or missed communication.

Of course there are times when mediation doesn't work. Sometimes, one neighbor just flatly refuses to participate in the process. Other times, the neighbors storm out, unable to agree, and head straight to court. There are also situations when it appears that only one neighbor is completely at fault and there is no room for compromise. Even when this seems to be the case, the mediator can be on the alert for hidden problems. They can pop out just as they did with John and Mary, letting the settlement process begin.

chapter 15

Small Claims Court

When all lines of communication between neighbors are severed and a legal dispute remains, consider using small claims court. You can do this yourself, without a lawyer, and avoid the expense and delay of regular court.

WHAT IS SMALL CLAIMS COURT?

Small claims court is a local court where you can go to sue a person who has caused you damage. In a few areas of the country this court is called by other names such as "justice" court or "pro se" court. Wherever you live, one of these courts should be available to you.

The hallmark of small claims court is that it's cheap and easy to file a case, and court procedures have been simplified to the point that attorneys are not necessary and in some states not even allowed. The hearing before the judge, magistrate or commissioner (sometimes a volunteer lawyer) usually happens quickly and the decision is made on the spot or in a few days.

The amount you can sue for is limited, usually to $2,000 to $5,000. The chart below lists the limits for every state. These limits increase regularly, so double check the amount with the court clerk if you decide to use this court.

You may well want to use small claims court even if your losses are higher than the amount you can sue for, because of the attorney fees and the enormous amount of time required to use regular court. For example, if you have an $6,000 claim and a lawyer will take a third of what you win as a fee, you could use a small claims court with a limit of $3,000 and still come out ahead, once the delay and expenses are figured in.

Small Claims Court Limits

Most states raise their small claims limits frequently. If you plan to sue in small claims court, ask the court clerk for up-to-the-minute information on the court's claims limit and procedures.

State	Amount	State	Amount
Alabama	$1,000	Montana	$2,500
Alaska	$5,000	Nebraska	$1,500
Arizona	$1,000	Nevada	$2,500
Arkansas	$3,000	New Hampshire	$2,500
California	$5,000	New Jersey	$1,000
Colorado	$2,000	New Mexico	$5,000
Connecticut	$2,000	New York	$2,000
Delaware	$2,500	North Carolina	$2,000
District of Columbia	$2,000	North Dakota	$2,000
Florida	$2,500	Ohio	$1,000
Georgia	$5,000	Oklahoma	$2,500
Hawaii	$2,500	Oregon	$2,500
Idaho	$2,000	Pennsylvania	$5,000
Illinois	$2,500	Puerto Rico	$500
Indiana	$3,000	Rhode Island	$1,500
Iowa	$2,000	South Carolina	$2,500
Kansas	$1,000	South Dakota	$2,000
Kentucky	$1,500	Tennessee	$10,000[†]
Louisiana	$2,000	Texas	$2,500
Maine	$1,400	Utah	$1,000
Maryland	$2,500	Vermont	$2,000
Massachusetts	$1,500	Virginia	$1,000
Michigan	$1,500	Washington	$2,000
Minnesota	$3,500	West Virginia	$3,000
Mississippi	$1,000	Wisconsin	$2,000
Missouri	$1,500	Wyoming	$2,000

[†]$15,000 if county population over 700,000.

Most small claims courts can award only money. If you want a judge to order your neighbor to do something, such as remove a fence or stop an obnoxious noise, you will probably have to use regular court. But keep in mind that a lawsuit asking for money can get a neighbor's attention, even though the court can't directly order the neighbor to solve the problem. And if you are suing for a nuisance—for instance, a noise problem—you can sue more than once. As long as the neighbor doesn't correct the problem, you can sue again and again.

PREPARING FOR SMALL CLAIMS COURT

You must know the law before you go in front of a small claims court judge. If you are using a state statute or a local ordinance, have a copy of it available to hand to the judge. If you are relying on a court opinion, you must be certain that a more recent court decision or statute hasn't changed the law. (Read Chapter 13, *Legal Research*.)

Ask the small claims court clerk about any special procedure that you need to follow before you file, such as writing a demand letter for the money to the person you are suing. Some courts require proof that this has been done before you can file a lawsuit. In some states, small claims courts have free advisors who will give you information and help you prepare for court.

Go down and watch a few small claims court cases before your case is scheduled, so you will be more comfortable and know what to expect.

For help preparing and presenting a suit in small claims court, read *Everybody's Guide to Small Claims Court,* by Ralph Warner (Nolo Press).

HOW SMALL CLAIMS COURT WORKS

Let's take an example of a simple neighbor dispute and follow it through the small claims court process.

In his back yard, Steve has a spreading black walnut tree of which he is very proud. Ralph, who lives next door, does nothing but gripe about the tree: too many leaves, too much shade and the tree kills his flowers. One day Steve comes home and discovers that the tree has been cut down. Sally, his neighbor across the street, tells him that she saw Ralph doing the cutting and assumed he had permission. Steve takes photos of the damage and notifies the police and his insurance company. The insurance company informs him that his policy doesn't cover damage to trees. Steve calls a local nursery and learns that they can put in a good sized but smaller tree of a different kind for $900. He learns to his disappointment that he can't have another black walnut tree because a local ordinance has declared them harmful and prohibits planting new ones. The cost of removing the old stump will be an extra $200. He obtains a written estimate from the nursery.

The next step for Steve is a trip to the law library, where he looks up his state statutes on trees. He finds that under his state law, a person who willfully cuts down another's tree is liable to the owner for triple the amount of damages. He makes copies of the statute and writes this letter to Ralph:

Dear Ralph,

   Last Thursday, October 2, 19__, you deliberately and without permission cut down my black walnut tree. Instead of trying to resolve any problems you had with the tree in other ways, you waited until I was not at home, deliberately trespassed on my property and destroyed the tree.

   I am enclosing the state law concerning your action and an estimate of my repair and the replacement cost of a smaller tree. I will never be able to have another black walnut tree. ·

   As you can see, my actual damage is $1100. The law says that you owe me triple this amount or $3300. I demand that you pay this amount to me immediately or I will pursue legal action.

Yours truly,

Steve Simpson

Ralph does not reply. Steve knows from doing research that because the tree can't really be replaced, he could use regular court and base his losses instead on the diminished value of his entire property. (See Chapter 1.) This would put his damages as high as $5,000 or $6,000. But he also knows that a lawyer may charge a third of the money award as a fee and that the case could take about two years.

In Steve's state, the small claims court limit is $3,000. What he really wants is a good-sized new tree and he wants it now. He considers the lawyer's fees and the time it would take to use regular court. He decides to do it himself, use small claims court and ask for the limit—$3,000. He proceeds to the small claims clerk, fills out the papers and pays a small filing fee. A hearing is scheduled within three weeks.

Steve sits down and writes out:

- what happened
- what the law is
- how much money he should be paid and why.

He gathers the few documents he will want to use: the police report, the pictures, the estimate, a copy of the statute and a copy of his letter to Ralph. He calls Sally and gets her to agree to go to court with him and testify. He makes a few notes on a card so he won't forget anything.

That week, Steve goes down to the small claims court for a few hours and watches some actual cases, learning what to expect and how to proceed. Now he's ready.

SMALL CLAIMS COURT POINTERS

- Be organized
- Know the law
- Be brief
- Be polite
- Be comfortable. Go down to court a few days before your hearing and watch the proceedings so you will know what happens.

The Hearing

Clerk: The next case is Steven Shapiro vs. Ralph Rogers. Please step forward.

Judge: Good morning. Mr. Shapiro, will you please begin?

Steve: Your Honor, on October 2, my neighbor Mr. Rogers cut down my black walnut tree in my back yard. He did this deliberately and without my permission. Here is a picture of the tree that he cut (hands the judge the picture). I asked Mr. Rogers to pay me for the damage he caused and he did not respond (hands the judge a copy of the letter, which the judge reads).

Judge: Go on, Mr. Shapiro.

Steve: Here is the estimate from a nursery for $1100 for removing the stump and replacing the tree with a smaller tree of a different kind (hands the judge the estimate).

I am asking for $3,000 because our state statute provides for me to receive triple the amount of my damages (hands the statute to the judge).

Judge: Mr. Shapiro, how do you know Mr. Rogers was the one who cut down the tree?

Steve: Your honor, this is Sally Smith, who saw what happened.

Judge: Ms. Smith?

Sally: Your honor, I saw Mr. Rogers cut down Mr. Shapiro's black walnut tree, the one in the picture.

Judge: Thank you. Mr. Rogers, what do you have to say about this?

Ralph: Your honor, the tree was an absolute nuisance. The leaves and sticks were all over my yard and the tree poisoned my flowers. Black walnut trees are so harmful that they have been outlawed in this town (hands a copy of the local ordinance to the judge). I complained several times to Mr. Shapiro and he did nothing about it. The tree was an illegal tree and I was within my rights.

Judge: Well, Mr. Rogers, this local ordinance prohibits planting any new black walnut trees. This tree was legal when it was planted so the fact that black walnuts can't be planted now isn't relevant. Under the laws of this state, any limbs that were hanging over your own property and bothering you were a nuisance and you had the right to cut them back to the property line. But you did not have a right to go over and cut down the tree. Did you cut it down?

John: Yes I did, and I didn't think I was doing anything wrong by taking the law into my own hands. At least the thing is gone and I can enjoy one autumn without all those leaves and grow my flowers.

Judge: Thank you. You will get my decision in a few days by mail.

The decision was for Ralph to pay Steve $3,000.

Some of you are thinking that Steve should have had Ralph arrested and thrown into jail. In some states this would have indeed been an option. If you think a neighbor has committed a crime, you can notify the police. They will decide if the neighbor can be charged.

State Statutes on Injury to Trees

HOW MUCH AN OWNER CAN SUE FOR

The following list shows how much someone whose tree has been damaged can sue the person responsible for. (See Chapter 3, *When a Tree Is Injured or Destroyed.*)

Actual loss

Georgia	Ga. Code Ann. 5 1-12-50

Double damages

Mississippi	Miss. Code Ann. 95-5-10
Pennsylvania	18 Pa. Con. Stat. 1107
Rhode Island	R.I. Gen. Laws 34-20-1 (sometimes triple)
Wisconsin	Wis. Stat. Ann. 26.09

Triple damages

Alaska	Alaska Stat. Ann. 09.45.730
Arkansas	Ark. Code Ann. 18-60-102
California	Cal. Civ. Code 3346
Connecticut	Conn. Gen Stat. Ann. 52-560
Delaware	Del. Code Ann. 25-1401
Idaho	Idaho Code Ann. 6-202
Illinois	Ill. Stat. Ann. Ch. 96 1/2 § 9402

Iowa	Ia. Code Ann. 658.4
Louisiana	La. Civ. Code 3:4278.1
Maine	14 Me. Rev. Stat. Ann. 7552
Maryland	Md. Code Ann. N.R. 5-409
Minnesota	Minn. Stat. Ann. 561.04
Missouri	Mo. Stat. Ann. 537.340
Montana	Mont. Code Ann. 70-16-108
Nebraska	Rev. Stat. Neb. 25-2130
Nevada	Nev. Rev. Stat. 40.160
New York	Con. Laws N.Y. Ann. R.P.A.P.L. 861
North Dakota	N.D. Cent. Code Ann. 32-03-30
Ohio	Ohio Rev. Code Ann. 901.51
Oklahoma	23 Okla. Stat. Ann. 572
Oregon	Ore. Rev. Stat. 105.810
South Dakota	S.D. Comp. Laws Ann. 21-3-10
Utah	Utah Code Ann. 78-38-3
Vermont	13 Vt. Stat. Ann. 3606
Washington	Rev. Code Wash. Ann. 64.12.030
West Virginia	W.Va. Code Ann. 61-3-48a

Five times the amount of damages

New Hampshire	N. H. Rev. Stat. Ann. 539.1

Punitive damages

Kentucky	Ken. Rev. Stat. 364.130

FINES OR JAIL SENTENCES FOR DAMAGING A TREE

Alabama	Ala. Code Ann. 35-14-1
California	Ca. Pen. Code § 384a
Delaware	Del. Code Ann. 7-3301
District of Columbia	D.C. Code Ann. 22-3108
Idaho	Idaho Code Ann. 18-7021
Massachusetts	Mass. Gen. Laws Ann. Ch. 266 §§ 113, 114
Michigan	Mich. Comp. Laws Ann. 750.382
New Jersey	N.J. Stat. Ann. 2C.18-5
New Mexico	N.M. Stat. Ann. 68-2-22,23
North Carolina	N.C. Gen Stat. 14-128
Ohio	Ohio Rev. Code Ann. 901.99
Oklahoma	21 Okla. Stat. Ann. 1768
Oregon	Ore. Rev. Stat. 527.260
Rhode Island	R.I. Gen. Laws 11-44-2
South Carolina	Code of Laws S.C. 16-11-520
Virginia	Code of Va. 18.2-140
Wisconsin	Wis. Stat. Ann. §§ 814.04, 26.05

The following states have no directly applicable statutes; however, the owner should be able to sue for actual damages and trespass.

Arizona
Colorado
Florida (has a law but no penalty)
Indiana
Kansas
Tennessee
Texas
Wyoming

appendix 2

State Statutes on Private Nuisance

COMMON LAW DEFINITION

The following states have statutes that follow the common law definition of private nuisance. Typically, they define nuisance something like this: "Anything which is injurious to health, indecent or offensive to the senses, or an obstruction to the free use of property, so as to interfere with the comfortable enjoyment of life or property."

Alabama	Ala. Code Ann. 6-5-120 (slightly different language)
California	Cal Civ. Code § 3479
Georgia	Ga. Code Ann. 41-1-1 (slightly different language)
Idaho	Idaho Code Ann. 52-111
Indiana	Ann. Ind. Code 34-1-52-1
Iowa	Ia. Code Ann. 657.1
Minnesota	Minn. Stat. Ann. 561.01
Montana	Mont. Code Ann. 27-30-101
Nevada	Nev. Rev. Stat. 40.140
Utah	Utah Code Ann. 78-38-1
Washington	Rev. Code Wash. Ann. 7.48.010

CONDUCT OR CONDITION MUST BE UNLAWFUL OR UNREASONABLE

In these other states, conduct must be unlawful or unreasonable to be a nuisance.

New Jersey	N.J. Stat. Ann. 2C:33-12 (limiting public nuisance)
New Mexico	N.M. Stat. Ann. 30-8-1 (limiting public nuisance)
North Dakota	N.D. Cent. Code Ann. 42-01-01
Oklahoma	50 Okla. Stat. Ann. 1
South Dakota	S.D. Comp. Laws Ann. 21-10-1

The states not listed above have no statute, but use common law definition of nuisance.

appendix 3

Boundary Fence Statutes

These states have statutes providing for joint expense and maintenance of division fences.

Alabama	Ala. Code Ann. 35-7-3
Arkansas	Ark. Code Ann. 2-39-105
California	Cal. Civ. Code 841
Connecticut	Con. Gen. Stat. Ann. 47-49
Delaware	Del. Code Ann. 25-1304
Idaho	Idaho Code Ann. 35-103,104,105
Illinois	Ill. Stat. Ann. 54-3,4
Indiana	Ann. Ind. Code 32-10-9-3
Iowa	Ia. Code Ann. 113.1
Kansas	Kan. Stat. Ann. 29-301
Kentucky	Ken. Rev. Stat 256.04+
Louisiana	La. Civ. Code 685
Maine	30 Me. Rev. Stat. 3452
Massachusetts	Mass. Gen. Laws Ann. Ch.49 §§ 4,13
Michigan	Mich. Comp. Laws Ann. 43.1+
Minnesota	Minn. Stat. Ann. 344.02 (Town board may exempt.)
Mississippi	Miss. Code Ann. 89-13-11
Missouri	Mo. Stat. Ann. 272.060
Montana	Mont. Code Ann. 70-16-205
Nebraska	Rev. Stat. Neb. 34-102.
New Hampshire	N.H. Rev. Stat. Ann. 473.1
New Jersey	N.J. Stat. Ann. 4:20-7. (for pasturage or animals)
New York	Con. Laws N.Y. TOWN 300

North Dakota	N.D. Cent. Code Ann. 47-26-05
Ohio	Ohio Rev. Code Ann. 971.02 (unless agreement; lots within municipal areas exempt)
Oklahoma	60 Okla. Stat. Ann. 70
Oregon	Ore. Rev. Stat. 96.020
Pennsylvania	29 Pa. Con. Stat. 11
Rhode Island	R.I. Gen. Laws 34-10-10,14 (unless agreement)
South Dakota	S.D. Comp. Laws Ann. 43-23-1-1/2 (unless agreement or no livestock for five years; also local option)
Tennessee	Tenn. Code Ann. 44-8-202
Utah	Utah Code Ann. 4-26-5
Vermont	Vt. Stat. Ann. 3802
Virginia	Code of Va. 55-317
Washington	Rev. Code Wash. Ann. 16.60.020
West Virginia	W. Va. Code 19-17-6 (livestock)
Wisconsin	Wis. Stat. Ann. 90.03+

Cora Miner Jordan earned her undergraduate degree at Millsaps College and her law degree at the University of Mississippi.

After living in ten cities in seven different states over the last twenty-five years, Cora has found, as she says, "Neighbors are similar everywhere, with common needs, problems and hopes. The best way to recognize the concerns of any neighbor is to take a good look in the mirror."

index

ESTATE PLANNING & PROBATE

Plan Your Estate With a Living Trust

This book covers every significant aspect of estate planning and gives detailed specific, instructions for preparing a living trust to avoid probate. *Plan Your Estate* includes all the tear-out forms and step-by-step instructions to let you prepare an estate plan designed for your special needs.
$19.95/NEST

Nolo's Simple Will Book

It's easy to write a legally valid will using this book. The instructions and forms enable people to draft a will for all needs, including naming a personal guardian for minor children, leaving property to minor children or young adults and updating a will when necessary. Good in all states except Louisiana.
$17.95/SWIL

The Power of Attorney Book

Who will take care of your affairs if you can't? With this book you can appoint someone to carry out your wishes and stipulate exactly what kind of care you want or don't want. Includes Durable Power of Attorney and Living Will Forms.
$19.95/POA

How to Probate an Estate

If you find yourself responsible for winding up the legal and financial affairs of a deceased family member or friend, you can often save costly attorneys' fees by handling the probate process yourself. This book shows you the procedures to transfer assets that don't require probate.
$29.95/PAE

The Conservatorship Book

The Conservatorship Book will help you determine when and what kind of conservatorship is necessary when a family member becomes incapacitated. The book comes with complete instructions and all the forms necessary to file a conservatorship.
$24.95/CON

GOING TO COURT

Everybody's Guide to Small Claims Court

These books will help you decide if you should sue in small claims court, show you how to file and serve papers, tell you what to bring to court and how to collect a judgment.
National $14.95/NSCC
California $14.95/ CSCC

Dog Law

Dog Law is a practical guide to the laws that affect dog owners and their neighbors. You'll find answers to common questions on such topics as biting, barking, veterinarians and more.
$12.95/DOG

Fight Your Ticket

This book shows you how to fight an unfair traffic ticket—when you're stopped, at arraignment, at trial and on appeal.
$17.95/FYT

The Criminal Records Book

This book shows you step-by-step how to seal criminal records, dismiss convictions, destroy marijuana records and reduce felony convictions.
$19.95/CRIM

Collect Your Court Judgment

This book contains step-by-step instructions and all the forms you need to collect a court judgment from the debtor's bank accounts, wages, business receipts, real estate or other assets.
$24.95/JUDG

How to Change Your Name

This book explains how to change your name legally and provides all the necessary court forms with detailed instructions on how to fill them out.
$19.95/NAME

BUSINESS

How to Write a Business Plan

If you're thinking of starting a business or raising money to expand an existing one, this book will show you how to write the business plan and loan package necessary to finance your business and make it work.
$17.95/SBS

Marketing Without Advertising

This book outlines practical steps for building and expanding a small business without spending a lot of money on advertising.
$14.00/MWA

The Partnership Book

This book shows you step-by-step how to write a solid partnership agreement that meets your needs. It covers initial contributions to the business, wages, profit-sharing, buy-outs, death or retirement of a partner and disputes.
$24.95/PART

How to Form Your Own Nonprofit Corporation

This book explains the legal formalities involved and provides detailed information on the differences in the law among 50 states. It also contains forms for the Articles, Bylaws and Minutes you need, along with complete instructions for obtaining federal 501(c)(3) tax exemptions and qualifying for public charity status.
$24.95/NNP

The California Nonprofit Corporation Handbook

This book shows you step-by-step how to form and operate a nonprofit corporation in California. It includes the latest corporate and tax law changes, and the forms for the Articles, Bylaws and Minutes.
$29.95/NON

How to Form Your Own Corporation

These books contain the forms, instructions and tax information you need to incorporate a small business yourself and save hundreds of dollars in lawyers' fees.
California $29.95/CCOR
New York $24.95/NYCO
Florida $24.95/FLCO

The California Professional Corporation Handbook

Health care professionals, lawyers, accountants and members of certain other professions must fulfill special requirements when forming a corporation in California. This book contains up-to-date tax information plus all the forms and instructions necessary to form a California professional corporation.
$34.95/PROF

The Independent Paralegal's Handbook

The Independent Paralegal's Handbook provides legal and business guidelines for those who want to take routine legal work out of the law office and offer it for a reasonable fee in an independent business.
$19.95/ PARA

Getting Started as an Independent Paralegal

Approximately three hours in all, these tapes are a carefully edited version of a seminar given by Nolo Press founder Ralph Warner. They are designed to be used with *The Independent Paralegal's Handbook.*
$24.95/GSIP

PATENT, COPYRIGHT & TRADEMARK

Patent It Yourself

From the patent search to the actual application, this book covers everything from use and licensing, successful marketing and how to deal with infringement.
$29.95/PAT

The Inventor's Notebook

This book helps you document the process of successful independent inventing by providing forms, instructions, references to relevant areas of patent law, a bibliography of legal and non-legal aids and more.
$19.95/INOT

How to Copyright Software

This book tells you how to register your copyright for maximum protection and discusses who owns a copyright on software developed by more than one person.
$39.95/COPY

LEGAL REFORM

Legal Breakdown: 40 Ways to Fix Our Legal System

Legal Breakdown presents 40 common sense proposals to make our legal system fairer, faster, cheaper and more accessible. It explains such things as why we should abolish probate, take divorce out of court, treat jurors better and give them more power, and make a host of other fundamental changes.
$8.95/LEG

FAMILY MATTERS

The Living Together Kit

The Living Together Kit is a detailed guide designed to help the increasing number of unmarried couples living together understand the laws that affect them. Sample agreements and instructions included.
$17.95/LTK

A Legal Guide for Lesbian and Gay Couples

Laws designed to regulate and protect unmarried couples don't apply to lesbian and gay couples. This book shows you step-by-step how to write a living-together contract, plan for medical emergencies, and plan your estates. Includes forms, sample agreements and lists of organizations, and AIDS organizations.
$17.95/LG

The Guardianship Book

The Guardianship Book provides step-by-step instructions and the forms needed to obtain a legal guardianship without a lawyer.
$19.95/GB

How to Do Your Own Divorce

These books contain all the forms and instructions you need to do your divorce without a lawyer.
California $18.95/CDIV
Texas $14.95/TDIV

How to Adopt Your Stepchild in California

This book provides sample forms and step-by-step instructions for completing a simple uncontested adoption by a stepparent.
$19.95/ADOP

California Marriage & Divorce Law

This book explains community property, pre-nuptial contracts, foreign marriages, buying a house, getting a divorce, dividing property, and more.
$17.95/MARR

MONEY MATTERS

Barbara Kaufman's Consumer Action Guide

This practical handbook is filled with information on hundreds of consumer topics. Barbara Kaufman, the Bay Area's award-winning host and producer of KCBS Radio's *Call for Action*, provides addresses and phone numbers of where to complain when things go wrong, and providing resources if more help is necessary.
$14.95/CAG

How to File for Bankruptcy

Trying to decide whether or not filing for bankruptcy makes sense? *How to File for Bankruptcy* contains an overview of the process and all the forms plus step-by-step instructions on the procedures to follow.
$24.95/HFB

Money Troubles: Legal Strategies to Cope With Your Debts

Are you behind on your credit card bills or loan payments? This practical, straightforward book is for anyone who needs help understanding and dealing with the complex and often scary topic of debts.
$16.95/MT

Simple Contracts for Personal Use

This book contains clearly written legal form contracts to buy and sell property, borrow and lend money, store and lend personal property, release others from personal liability, or pay a contractor to do home repairs.
$16.95/CONT

OLDER AMERICANS

Elder Care: Choosing & Financing Long-Term Care

This book will guide you in choosing and paying for long-term care, alerting you to practical concerns and explaining laws that may affect your decisions.
$16.95/ELD

Social Security, Medicare & Pensions

This book contains invaluable guidance through the current maze of rights and benefits for those 55 and over, including Medicare, Medicaid and Social Security retirement and disability benefits and age discrimination protections.
$15.95/SOA

LANDLORDS & TENANTS

The Landlord's Law Book: Rights & Responsibilities

This book contains information on deposits, leases and rental agreements, inspections (tenant's privacy rights), habitability (rent withholding), ending a tenancy, liability and rent control.
$29.95/LBRT

The Landlord's Law Book: Evictions

Updated for 1991, this book will show you step-by-step how to go to court and get an eviction for a tenant who won't pay rent—and won't leave. Contains all the tear-out forms and necessary instructions.
$29.95/LBEV

Tenant's Rights

This book explains the best way to handle your relationship both your landlord and your legal rights when you find yourself in disagreement. A special section on rent control cities is included.
$15.95/CTEN

HOMEOWNERS

How to Buy a House in California

This book shows you how to find a house, work with a real estate agent, make an offer and negotiate intelligently. Includes information on all types of mortgages as well as private financing options.
$18.95/BHC

For Sale By Owner

For Sale By Owner provides essential information about pricing your house, marketing it, writing a contract and going through escrow.
$24.95/FSBO

The Deeds Book

If you own real estate, you'll need to sign a new deed when you transfer the property or put it in trust as part of your estate planning. This book shows you how
$15.95/DEED

Homestead Your House

This book shows you how to file a Declaration of Homestead and includes complete instructions and tear-out forms.
$9.95/HOME

RESEARCH & REFERENCE

Legal Research

A valuable tool on its own or as a companion to just about every other Nolo book. This book gives easy-to-use, step-by-step instructions on how to find legal information.
$14.95/LRES

Family Law Dictionary

Finally, a legal dictionary that's written in plain English, not "legalese"! *The Family Law Dictionary* is designed to help the nonlawyer who has a question or problem involving family law—marriage, divorce, adoption or living together.
$13.95/FLD

Patent, Copyright & Trademark: The Intellectual Property Law Dictionary

This book explains the terms associated with trade secrets, copyrights, trademarks, patents and contracts.
$19.95/IPLD

Legal Research Made Easy: A Roadmap Through the Law Library Maze

2-1/2 hr. videotape and 40-page manual

If you're a law student, paralegal or librarian—or just want to look up the law for yourself—this video is for you. University of California law professor Bob Berring explains how to use all the basic legal research tools in your local law library.
$89.95/LRME

■

SOFTWARE

WillMaker

This easy-to-use software program lets you prepare and update a legal will—safely, privately and without the expense of a lawyer. Step-by-step in a question-and-answer format, *WillMaker* builds a will around your answers. *WillMaker* comes with a 200-page legal manual which provides the legal background necessary to make sound choices. Good in all states except Louisiana.
IBM PC
(3-1/2 & 5-1/4 disks included)
$69.95/WI4
MACINTOSH $69.95/WM4

California Incorporator

Answer the questions on the screen and this software program will print out the 35-40 pages of documents you need to make your California corporation legal. Comes with a 200-page manual which explains the incorporation process.
IBM PC
(3-1/2 & 5-1/4 disks included)
$129.00/INCI

For the Record

For the Record program provides a single place to keep a complete inventory of all your important legal, financial, personal and family records. It can compute your net worth and also create inventories of all insured property to protect your assets in the event of fire or theft. Includes a 200-page manual filled with practical and legal advice.
IBM PC
(3-1/2 & 5-1/4 disks included)
$59.95/FRI2
MACINTOSH $59.95/FRM2

The California Nonprofit Corporation Handbook

This book/software package shows you step-by-step how to form and operate a nonprofit corporation in California. Included on disk are the forms for the Articles, Bylaws and Minutes.
IBM PC 5-1/4 $69.95/NPI
IBM PC 3-1/2 $69.95/NP3I
MACINTOSH $69.95/NPM

How to Form Your Own New York Corporation & How to Form Your Own Texas Corporation

These book/software packages contain the instructions and tax information and forms you need to incorporate a small business and save hundreds of dollars in lawyers' fees. All organizational forms are on disk. Both come with a 250-page manual.
New York 1st Edition
IBM PC 5-1/4 $69.95/NYCI
IBM PC 3-1/2 $69.95/NYC3I
MACINTOSH $69.95/NYCM
Texas 1st Edition
IBM PC 5-1/4 $69.95/TCI
IBM PC 3-1/2 $69.95/TC3I
MACINTOSH $69.95/TCM

new!

Simple Contracts for Personal Use

2nd National Edition
by Attorney Stephen Elias &
Marcia Stewart
$16.95

All the forms you'll need, included.

This new edition of *Simple Contracts for Personal Use* provides clearly written legal form contracts to buy and sell property, borrow and lend money, store and lend personal property release others from personal liability, or pay a contractor to do home repairs. It also includes agreements to arrange child care—in or out of your home.

Order **Simple Contracts for Personal Use** today!

Call our-toll free telephone lines and charge your order
1-800-992-6656 (continental US);
1-800-640-6656 (CA)
or use the order form in the back of this book

■ VISIT OUR STORE

If you live in the Bay Area, be sure to visit the Nolo Press Bookstore on the corner of 9th &

Parker Streets in West Berkeley. You'll find our complete line of books and software—new and "damaged"—all at a discount. We also have t-shirts, posters and a selection of business and legal self-help books from other publishers.

■ HOURS

Monday to Friday	10 a.m. to 5 p.m.
Thursdays	Until 6 p.m
Saturdays	10 a.m. to 4:30 p.m.
Sundays	10 a.m. to 3 p.m.

950 Parker Street / Berkeley, CA 94710

■ ORDER FORM

Name

Address (UPS to street address, Priority Mail to P.O. boxes)

Catalog Code	Quantity	Item	Unit price	Total
		Subtotal		
		Sales tax (California residents only)		
		Shipping & handling		
		2nd day UPS		
		TOTAL		
		PRICES SUBJECT TO CHANGE		

SALES TAX
California residents add your local tax:
6%, 6-1/2% or 7%

SHIPPING & HANDLING
$4.00   1 item
$5.00   2-3 items
+$.50   each additional item
Allow 2-3 weeks for delivery

IN A HURRY?
UPS 2nd day delivery is available:
Add $5.00 (contiguous states)
or
$8.00 (Alaska & Hawaii)
to your regular shipping and handling charges

**FOR FASTER SERVICE, USE YOUR CREDIT CARD
AND OUR TOLL-FREE NUMBERS:**
Monday-Friday, 7 a.m. to 5 p.m. Pacific Time
US   1 (800) 992-6656
CA   (outside 415 area code)   1 (800) 640-6656
          (inside 415 area code)   549-1976
General Information   1 (415) 549-1976
Fax us your order   1 (415) 548-5902

METHOD OF PAYMENT
☐ Check enclosed
☐ VISA   ☐ Mastercard   ☐ Discover Card   ☐ Am Ex

Account #   Expiration Date

Signature

Phone

NL

Keep Up To Date With the Nolo News

Nolo Press publishes a complete line of self-help law books and software programs—they are affordable, they explain (in plain English) what the law says, and they show readers how to handle many routine tasks without a lawyer.

Nolo also publishes a quarterly newspaper, the *Nolo News*. It contains an update section to keep readers up-to-date on law changes that affect our books, and explores legal issues of interest to non-lawyers. In addition, the *Nolo News* contains book reviews, an ever-popular lawyer joke column, and a complete catalog of Nolo products.

Send in the registration card below and receive a FREE two-year subscription to the *Nolo News* (normally $12). Your subscription will begin with the first issue published after we receive your card. (This offer available to U.S. residents only.)

REGISTRATION CARD

Neighbor Law

Fill out and return this postage-paid card for a FREE two-year subscription to the *Nolo News*.

If you're already a subscriber, we will extend your subscription for two more years.

Please print clearly, or type.

YOUR **NAME**

STREET ADDRESS

STREET ADDRESS

CITY, **STATE & ZIP**

Because we respect your privacy and hate all the junk mail we get in our mailboxes too, we pledge never to sell, rent or give your name and address to any other organization.

YOUR **COMMENTS**

N O L O